T0178811

RIGHTEOUS REBELS

RIGHTEOUS REBELS

AIDS HEALTHCARE FOUNDATION'S CRUSADE TO CHANGE THE WORLD

PATRICK RANGE MCDONALD

RARE BIRD
LOS ANGELES, CALIF.

THIS IS A GENUINE RARE BIRD BOOK

Rare Bird Books
6044 North Figueroa Street
Los Angeles, CA 90042
rarebirdbooks.com

Set in Minion Pro
Printed in the United States

10 9 8 7 6 5 4 3 2 1

Library of Congress Cataloging-in-Publication Data available upon request.

For AHF employees and clients…for my parents, Beanie and Pat McDonald…and for anyone who wants to change the world for the better.

Contents

PART THREE
A Year of Fighting for What's Right Continues

AHF Timeline
1986–2021

1986: Los Angeles activists establish Stop the AIDS Quarantine Committee to defeat California's Proposition 64, a statewide ballot measure that would create "concentration camps" for people living with HIV and AIDS. The quarantine committee is instrumental in defeating the initiative.

1986: Soon after the Proposition 64 victory, Stop the AIDS Quarantine Committee members create Los Angeles AIDS Hospice Committee. The new advocacy group holds a major public hearing on the AIDS crisis in Los Angeles County, which examines the failures of local government to help people living with HIV/AIDS. The event plays a key role in strengthening the AIDS movement in LA.

1987: LA AIDS Hospice Committee members establish AIDS Hospice Foundation, which starts with only one full-time employee and a $50,000 budget. The organization advocates for hospice care for terminally ill AIDS patients in LA County.

1988: AHF opens Chris Brownlie Hospice near Dodger Stadium to serve terminally ill AIDS patients. Nearly 1,200 people die at the facility between 1988 and 1996.

1989: AHF cofounder Chris Brownlie passes away from AIDS.

1990: AIDS Hospice Foundation changes name to AIDS Healthcare Foundation, starting the transition into a medical-care provider for people with HIV/AIDS.

1990: In LA, AHF opens a thrift store called Out of the Closet—the organization's first "social enterprise" business. Out of the Closet will turn into a nationwide chain.

1991: In LA, AHF opens its first healthcare clinic for people living with HIV/AIDS. Decades later, the organization manages more than 760 clinics in forty-five countries.

1992: AHF opens Carl Bean House in underserved South LA—the hospice facility serves terminally ill African American and Latino patients with AIDS.

1995: AHF launches the nation's first capitated managed care program, Positive Healthcare, for people living with AIDS.

1996: AHF opens its last hospice facility: Linn House in West Hollywood, California.

1996: To ensure that AHF patients have access to the new, lifesaving "AIDS cocktail," the organization pays for the expensive medication out of pocket with no government reimbursement. AHF faces financial ruin but pulls through.

2000: With nearly 8,200 clients, AHF becomes the largest nonprofit provider of HIV/AIDS medical care in the United States.

2000: In LA, AHF opens its first pharmacy—another social enterprise business. By 2014, AHF Pharmacy, which generates revenue that funds the organization's global program, expands to thirty-seven outlets across the US.

2002: Despite strong opposition from the South African government, AHF opens its first free HIV treatment clinic outside the US in Umlazi, South Africa. Started as a 100-person pilot program, the clinic serves more than 12,000 clients by 2014. Throughout South Africa, in 2014, AHF serves more than 44,000 clients.

2002: AHF opens a free HIV treatment center in Masaka, Uganda. It grows from a 100-person pilot program to serving more than 10,000

clients in 2014. Across the country, AHF serves more than 47,000 clients in 2014.

2003: AHF plays a key role in the creation of the President's Emergency Plan for AIDS Relief (PEPFAR), the landmark global AIDS program pushed forward by President George W. Bush. Millions of AIDS sufferers around the world now have better access to lifesaving antiretroviral drug therapy.

2004: AHF continues to fight aggressively for lower HIV drug prices so more people around the globe have access to antiretroviral therapy.

2005: AHF provides free HIV treatment services in the US, Latin America, Africa, Asia, and Eastern Europe.

2006: With an operating budget of $128 million, AHF serves more than 53,000 clients in more than fifteen countries.

2007: AHF's marketing department develops social media campaigns to educate a younger generation about the continued threat of HIV/AIDS.

2009: AHF creates its own brand of free, high-quality condoms and distributes millions around the globe.

2010: AHF conducts Testing America Tour, providing free HIV testing in forty-eight states and raising awareness about HIV/AIDS.

2010: AHF holds "die-ins" in the US to protest rising drug costs.

2010: AHF conducts more than 500,000 free HIV tests worldwide.

2011: AHF serves 166,000 clients in twenty-five countries.

2012: AHF launches the Condom Nation campaign, which distributes free condoms across the US and raises awareness about safer sex.

2013: AHF serves 276,000 clients in thirty-two countries and operates with an $857 million budget and 1,906 employees. AHF per-

forms nearly two million free HIV tests worldwide and distributes nearly thirty-two million free condoms.

2013: AHF kicks off 20×20 campaign, which challenges the world to bring twenty million people into HIV treatment by the year 2020. AHF pledges to provide care for one million of them.

2015: Twenty-eight years after its founding, AHF hits a major milestone, serving more than 500,000 clients around the globe.

2017: AHF establishes Healthy Housing Foundation, a housing provider division, and Housing Is A Human Right, a housing advocacy division, to address gentrification and the housing affordability and homelessness crises in California. Throughout the state, AHF patients have been negatively impacted by gentrification, rising rents, and housing instability.

2018: Two years ahead of schedule, AHF makes good on its promise to place one million people in HIV/AIDS care—a major achievement.

2020: AHF operates in forty-five countries, serving 1.5 million clients. It continues to bring lifesaving HIV treatment to people around the globe and to reach the ultimate goal of controlling the global spread of HIV/AIDS.

2020 and 2021: Taking aim at governments and major institutions, AHF strongly advocates for a smarter, quicker, and more transparent response to the COVID-19 pandemic. It's another example of AHF's work in the global public health arena beyond HIV/AIDS.

PART ONE

A New Year of Fighting for What's Right

Chapter 1

A Textbook for Righteous Rebels?

Michael Weinstein

FOR AS LONG AS I can remember, I have been drawn to a certain type of rebel. The one who catches my eye and gives me inspiration tends to be modest and thoughtful and selfless to some degree. He or she eschews fads and common wisdom and instead lives by a deep sense of what's right and just, even if that means being at odds with large swaths of the population, which happens often. He or she is smart but not overly intellectual or academic. That would prevent that person from seeing certain realities and then going about challenging them. But perhaps the overriding trait of this individual is an all-consuming desire, maybe even an obsession, to live a life that's true. This righteous rebel fears selling him- or herself out.

Sometime in the winter of 1998, in Los Angeles, I met Michael Weinstein, the cofounder and president of AIDS Healthcare Foundation. I had just moved to LA from New York City, and I was working as a reporter at the *Los Angeles Independent*, a community newspaper chain. Miki Jackson, a close friend of Weinstein's and a community activist whom I often talked with, introduced us at a civic event.

Weinstein had been leading AHF since its founding in 1987. He was fit and trim, sharp featured, and forty-six years old. He wore a dark suit and tie with his black hair slicked back. He looked like a Wall Street hotshot, not the president of an HIV/AIDS nonprofit. We only talked briefly, but Weinstein came across as smart and quick-witted, with touches of modesty and shyness. He also exuded a palpable energy that I associated with my favorite kind of New Yorker. I later learned he was born in Brooklyn. After our conversation, I decided to keep an eye on Weinstein and AHF. Every now and then, I wrote a story about the organization.

But it wasn't until January 25, 2000, that Weinstein popped up on my radar in a singular way. I'd picked up the *Los Angeles Times* that morning and read, with some confusion, that he was being vilified for advocating for condoms. Even more baffling was that the controversy was taking place in West Hollywood, a small city wedged between Beverly Hills and Los Angeles and considered one of the world's gay meccas.

Weinstein was Jewish, gay, and a longtime AIDS activist, but someone had gone to several gay bars in West Hollywood and put up wildly inappropriate posters that deemed him a "condom Nazi." The poster claimed that he was "an enemy of the gay community" who had "betrayed us," and he was compared to such anti-gay demagogues as Senator Jesse Helms and Jerry Falwell, cofounder of the Moral Majority, a conservative Christian political group. Weinstein's sin, I learned from the article, was that AHF had pushed for an HIV-prevention program in which nearly all West Hollywood bars and nightclubs—gay and straight—would be mandated by the

city to offer free condoms and safer-sex literature to customers. Bar and nightclub owners, however, wouldn't pay a cent.

The charged rhetoric aimed at Weinstein wasn't the only puzzling thing. For decades, West Hollywood had been a popular red-light district, where straight and gay people patronized the area's many bars and nightclubs. They partied hard and hooked up, but people who were drunk or high were less likely to practice safer sex—and were more likely to contract and spread sexually transmitted diseases. In the age of AIDS, which had killed more people in 1999 than in any previous year, a bowl of free condoms at a West Hollywood bar seemed sensible, if not obligatory.

In addition, West Hollywood's gay residents had been rocked by the deadly AIDS epidemic. In fact, in 2000, the city, which had only 35,874 residents and less than one-half of one percent of Los Angeles County's population, had a whopping 7 percent of the county's HIV/ AIDS cases. Local public health officials estimated that between thirty and forty thousand adults (eighteen to sixty-four years old) in LA County were infected with HIV/AIDS. That meant between 2,100 and 2,800 West Hollywood residents were living with HIV.

That alarming statistic didn't tell the whole story.

Most, if not all, of the HIV/AIDS cases in West Hollywood involved men who had sex with men. City officials believed that roughly one-third of West Hollywood's total population—or 11,838 people—was gay adults. The overwhelming majority were men—few lesbians lived in the city then. If 2,800 people had HIV/AIDS in West Hollywood, that meant a potentially devastating 24 percent of the city's gay and bisexual male population was HIV positive.

With those kinds of numbers, one would think that West Hollywood's community leaders, including politicians and bar and nightclub owners, would do anything to help protect people and lower the city's outrageous infection rate. Instead, they aggressively opposed the free condom program, particularly gay bar owners, who were probably behind the "condom Nazi" posters. They believed

that condoms and pamphlets would offend customers and drive them away. A perceived threat to profits, rather than a public health epidemic, was their chief concern.

In the months that followed the "condom Nazi" episode, Weinstein and AHF continued to stand up and take the heat. The West Hollywood City Council was another story.

Under heavy political pressure from bar owners, the council passed a watered-down "voluntary" condom program. The so-called compromise was far less sweeping, and the rollout would be problematic. In response, AHF pushed for a ballot measure so voters could override the city council and approve the organization's more effective proposal, but that failed in 2001—West Hollywood residents voted "no" by 53 percent.

"There is an underlying prudishness that came out in this," Weinstein told the *Los Angeles Times* after AHF's defeat. "A lot felt the government shouldn't play a role and business shouldn't be required to play a role in condom distribution, that it's a matter of personal responsibility."

Regardless of the outcome, Weinstein struck me as gutsy and principled, and I admired his outspoken, tenacious style. He not only clashed with bar owners and politicians to implement policies that protected the public's health but also with other activists and organizations within the AIDS movement, if necessary.

Many years after the West Hollywood condom battle, Peter Staley, a well-known AIDS activist, told *Slate* magazine, "If there's one thing that every AIDS activist knows, it's that Michael Weinstein is not an AIDS activist. Yes, he's the CEO of the 'largest AIDS organization in the country'—based on revenue—but from the get-go, his tactic for building this empire has been taking contrarian positions that assure his placement in almost any article that appears about the latest HIV/AIDS debate."

Sean Strub, a longtime AIDS activist and founder of *POZ* magazine, told me via an email interview, "It is like [AHF and

Weinstein] start from the position of figuring out how many people they can piss off rather than finding allies or finding where they share ground with others."

Those criticisms were typical of what I had heard about Weinstein, but they never rang true to me.

By 2007, I was a staff writer for *LA Weekly*, one of the top alternative newspapers in the United States. When I wrote about gay rights or gay men's health issues, I often contacted Weinstein. He had a different way of seeing things, and he could be counted on for thoughtful, if not provocative, ideas that needed saying but that few others had the courage to say.

After California voters passed Proposition 8 on November 4, 2008, I interviewed Weinstein. The ballot measure, which was later declared unconstitutional, had taken away the existing right of same-sex couples to marry in California. Numerous gay-rights groups had run the No on Prop 8 campaign to keep same-sex marriage legal, but many political observers believed they'd done a disastrous job. Few gay leaders, however, were publicly critical. Just coming off a shocking loss, they didn't believe the time was right for a thorough dissection of the "No on Prop 8" campaign. Weinstein wasn't so hesitant.

"When is the time to finger-point?" Weinstein said to me for an article. "After we lose again? Look at what the Republicans are doing [after Obama's victory]. They're sizing everyone up."

Weinstein urged younger gay-rights activists to hold "No on Prop 8" leaders accountable.

"It's important for people to tell the truth," he said, "and it's important for the young generation to demand the truth."

For a 2012 *LA Weekly* story about gay men's health, I asked Weinstein about a popular theory among academics called the "minority stress model." It essentially pushed the idea that the stress of living with discrimination and homophobia caused serious health problems among gay men. Gay-rights leaders and health experts then employed the theory to explain why gay men used drugs and

alcohol more than straight men, suffered depression at higher rates than straight men, and engaged in risky sexual behavior that resulted in high rates of HIV and STD infections. Weinstein thought the minority stress model was a cop-out.

"All the sociological factors are just an explanation after-the-fact," Weinstein told me then. "It's an excuse. It may even be a valid one, but it's still an excuse."

His remark flew in the face of the victimhood politics pushed by many gay researchers and activists, and it challenged gay men to honestly look at their own behavior rather than blame others for their health issues.

In fact, a sociology professor I also interviewed for the article made a strong case for a concept called "reference group theory," in which an individual's close friends and associates set the standard for what is acceptable behavior and then that person follows suit. For example, if a gay individual is surrounded by people who engage in risky sexual behavior, that person is more likely to engage in risky sex. On the flip side, if one's friends always practice safer sex, a person is more likely do the same. The stress of living with homophobia, according to the professor, didn't have as much impact on gay men's health and behavior as did their friends.

Too often, though, gay leaders refused to publicly confront the messy issues that affected the health of gay men. After decades of persecution, they reasoned, they didn't want to give homophobes any ammunition to demean the LGBTQ+ community and stop the gay rights movement. It was a public relations strategy that Weinstein wanted no part of. He once told me that saving lives, rather than saving face, was what mattered most—and you couldn't save lives without talking honestly and openly.

—

As time went on, I came to know more of AHF's story, the nut of which was mind-boggling and profound. It was also largely untold—

the Los Angeles press, except for a reporter or two, seemed unable to grasp that the organization was a hometown success story on a global scale.

In 1987, AHF started with only one full-time employee, had very little money in the bank, and provided hospice care to terminally ill AIDS patients in the Los Angeles area. A few decades later, everything had changed: AHF had turned into the largest HIV/AIDS medical-care provider in the world. It had not only saved millions of lives but also served many of the most vulnerable people on the planet: women, children, the poor, gay men, people of color, transgender people, and intravenous drug users.

By 2013, AHF worked in thirty-two countries, including the US, Russia, Ukraine, China, India, Cambodia, South Africa, Nigeria, Mexico, Haiti, and Argentina; provided lifesaving HIV drugs and medical services to more than 276,000 registered clients; and operated with an $857 million budget and 1,906 staffers. Additionally, in 2013, AHF had performed nearly two million free HIV tests around the globe, including 129,326 tests in the United States; identified 72,584 people who were HIV positive; and distributed nearly thirty-four million free condoms worldwide. These were big, bold contributions to the global AIDS fight that no other organization had come close to duplicating.

In my mind, someone had to write about this, so I approached Weinstein with the idea of a book. He was interested but said early on that he didn't want the focus solely on him. He also wanted an honest book, which was exactly what I wanted to hear. During the fall of 2013, Weinstein suggested that I do preliminary research while he decided whether or not to move forward with the project.

Between October and December, I interviewed AHF employees and saw the everyday work of HIV prevention and treatment; talked with Weinstein and high-level managers, such as senior vice president Peter Reis, global advocacy chief Terri Ford, and chief of public affairs and general counsel Tom Myers; and attended

several AHF marketing meetings where domestic and international advocacy campaigns were hashed out.

I also went to an AHF protest at the Chinese consulate general in Los Angeles over China's failure to make significant contributions to the Global Fund to Fight AIDS, Tuberculosis and Malaria; visited AHF's Rose Parade float, which generated national headlines and aimed to fight discrimination and stigma by celebrating same-sex marriage; and watched AHF kick off its ambitious 20×20 campaign, which challenged world leaders and AIDS organizations to bring twenty million people into HIV treatment by the year 2020, with AHF pledging to care for one million of them. To my mind, AHF was relentless, and restless, in its fight against AIDS—and with good reason.

More than thirty years into the epidemic, an estimated thirty-five million people are living with HIV/AIDS around the globe. Every day, four thousand individuals die from AIDS-related illnesses. In the US, about fifty thousand people are newly infected each year, and UNAIDS estimated that between sixteen thousand and twenty-seven thousand Americans died from AIDS in 2012.

Worldwide, 2.1 million people are newly infected with HIV annually. Since the early 1980s, according to UNAIDS, seventy-eight million people have contracted HIV/AIDS and thirty-nine million have died from AIDS-related illnesses. There is still no vaccine for human immunodeficiency virus, also known as HIV, which causes acquired immune deficiency syndrome, or AIDS.

Since the early 1980s, when HIV was discovered, the transmission of the virus has not changed. According to the Center for Disease Control (CDC), Americans are most often infected by engaging in anal sex ("the highest-risk sexual behavior") or vaginal sex; by sharing needles, syringes, or other equipment with an HIV-positive injection-drug user; or (less commonly) by receiving a blood transfusion contaminated with HIV. Being born to an HIV-positive mother who is not taking HIV medications is another way to be in-

fected by the virus. Having multiple sexual partners or having other sexually transmitted diseases increases the chances of a person getting HIV through sex. These modes of transmission take place in the US and around the world, and vaginal sex or shared needles are the primary ways people are infected in such places as Africa and Eastern Europe.

The global problem now is finding people who are HIV positive and getting them on lifesaving, highly effective antiretroviral therapy, also known as ART. In 2013, UNAIDS estimated that only thirteen million of the world's thirty-five million HIV/AIDS cases had access to ART, and nineteen million were unaware that they were infected with HIV. In the United States, only 37 percent of the people living with HIV are taking antiretroviral therapy.

Treatment is an essential tool to stop the global spread of HIV and AIDS. A landmark study known as "HPTN 052," which was published in 2011, found that if a person living with HIV dutifully takes his or her medication, that individual is 96 percent less likely to infect other people than someone who is not taking medication. So, treatment not only keeps people from dying but also stops the spread of HIV. Within the global AIDS movement, such a concept is known as Treatment as Prevention, or TasP.

The AHF team, which works on the front lines of the worldwide AIDS epidemic, is keenly aware of these statistics and challenges. Sounding a note of urgency that's typical within the organization, Terri Ford told me, "There are thirty-five million people with HIV, and only thirteen million have treatment. So what are we going to do about that? Just let them die? That is not acceptable."

—

By mid-December of 2013, Weinstein gave me the green light. I would dig into AHF's history, but I'd also follow it over the course of 2014—from January 1 to December 31—and write about what unfolded. AHF would pay me a salary and pick up the tab for my

traveling expenses and an assistant. In terms of what I could research or write about, Weinstein placed no restrictions on me.

I had always thought highly of Weinstein, but now I was heading into the nitty-gritty. With inside access granted to me for a year, I knew that the truth about AHF would reveal itself, and I had no intention of looking the other way if something scandalous popped up—too many people had put their lives into its care. If that happened, I wondered if Weinstein would go back on his word about wanting an honest book. I was prepared to quit or be fired rather than betray AHF clients.

Whatever played out, I knew I was embarking on an uncharted, worldwide journey, and I had no idea what I was going to find. But I had a hunch after the preliminary research: AHF's story could be incredibly inspiring. Not just for people combating HIV/AIDS and living with the disease, but for anyone in any country who wants to challenge the status quo and make the world a more just and compassionate and fair place to live. The AHF story, I thought, could be a textbook for the world's aspiring righteous rebels.

Chapter 2

The Core of AHF

AHF senior management: (left to right) Mike Kahane, Anita Castille, Scott Carruthers, Tom Myers, Lyle Honig, Donna Tempesta, Whitney Engeran-Cordova, Michael Weinstein, Dr. Michael Wohlfeiler, Donna Stidham, Dr. Penninah Iutung Amor, AJ Alegria, Terri Ford, Peter Reis, Laura Boudreau, and Tracy Jones

AIDS HEALTHCARE FOUNDATION IS not simply a provider of medical care. Instead, and perhaps more accurately, AHF senior managers consider the organization to be a global movement, in which HIV testers, doctors, advocates, and thousands of others, in dozens of countries, work together to control the spread of HIV/AIDS. It is no small job.

AHF's work and influence extends across the United States and around the globe, including such cities as Amsterdam, Moscow, and Mexico City and rural, remote towns in such countries as Uganda, Cambodia, and Kenya. The global sites reside, for the most part, in four AHF bureaus: Africa, Asia, Europe, and Latin America.

AHF's headquarters (HQ), however, are not based in traditional power centers such as New York City or Washington, DC, although it has clinics in both places. The center of the AHF universe is Los Angeles, or, more specifically, the neighborhood known as Hollywood. On the corner of Sunset Boulevard and Argyle Avenue, AHF's administrative headquarters is located on the twenty-first floor of a steel-and-glass skyscraper called Sunset Media Center. Michael Weinstein works here, in a corner office.

Three minutes south of HQ, on an industrial stretch of Santa Monica Boulevard, AHF Worldwide operates on the second floor of a green, two-story building. Global advocacy, domestic and international marketing, and communications departments are housed here. Hollywood Center Studios, where such movies as *When Harry Met Sally*…and *The Karate Kid* were made, is a next-door neighbor.

Four minutes west of HQ, the Public Health Division resides in a sleek, two-story building on La Brea Avenue, where AHF's local and national HIV testing, client linkage, and clinic programs are managed. The world-famous Hollywood Walk of Fame is a half-block away.

And four minutes east of HQ, the Department of Medicine and Research Institute is located in a former bank, two blocks from LA's sprawling Griffith Park. The department oversees medical providers at AHF clinics, while the institute conducts research on new ways to treat and prevent HIV/AIDS.

The AHF story is very much a Los Angeles story. It is a city in which anyone from anywhere can be extraordinarily successful if one is passionate, works hard, and comes up with a smart idea. Weinstein and his friends, for example, were not wealthy or politically connected, but they knew that terminally ill AIDS patients needed a safe place to live. So, they opened a twenty-five-bed hospice near Dodger Stadium. From there, AHF constantly reassessed itself and adjusted and grew.

—

YEARS AGO, WEINSTEIN CAME up with the official AHF vision: "to achieve global AIDS control through policy change, quality programs, and expansion." To make that happen, AHF employs an international staff of HIV testers and lab technicians, doctors and nurses, managed healthcare professionals and data collectors, pharmacists and salespeople, grassroots organizers and policy advocates, retail clerks and drivers, marketers and communications experts, computer technicians and human resources staff, and lawyers and financial wizards, among others.

Attempting to control the worldwide spread of HIV/AIDS is expensive, especially when hiring doctors, lawyers, and pharmacists. Like other AIDS organizations, AHF secures government grants to pay for the operation of a medical clinic or to carry out an HIV testing program. But the government only provides so much money, and politicians sometimes take it back through budget cuts. So early on, AHF decided to not rely on government funding and started a number of "social enterprise" businesses.

"Social enterprise isn't about asking for donations and praying that you get them every year," Jonathan Petrus, the chief financial officer of performance and investments at AHF, told me.

Instead, AHF's businesses generate revenue so the organization can pay for daily operations, growth, and sustainability.

"There is a stereotype that do-gooders have no business sense," Weinstein told me, "and people with business sense have no heart. The reality is, we are going to have to combine the two."

Social enterprise has another benefit: AHF is uniquely independent. Since the organization is mostly self-funded and doesn't rely on government money, it can more freely criticize bad policies and take bold stands on behalf of people impacted by HIV/AIDS.

It all adds up to an extraordinary business model that focuses on saving lives. The more lives AHF saves, the more revenue it generates. The more revenue AHF generates, the more money it can spend on

saving lives. More than thirty years into the AIDS crisis, there is still much need for the organization's services.

"There are too many people out of care," Petrus said. "There is a huge market for us, and that is a sad fact."

Today, AHF's businesses in the United States include a specialized managed care program, called Positive Healthcare, for people living with HIV; a popular chain of twenty-two thrift stores known as Out of the Closet; and a chain of thirty-seven pharmacies. In October 2014, AHF started up the Liver Institute, a clinic that treats people with hepatitis B and C. The income from these businesses provides funding for advocacy campaigns, HIV testing, and HIV treatment and prevention around the world. In fact, AHF has determined that ninety-six cents of every dollar earned at thrift stores and pharmacies are cycled back into those services, a dramatic fiscal and humanitarian success.

But much different from other successful businesses, AHF's senior management team doesn't receive enormous salaries and multimillion-dollar bonuses. In 2013, Weinstein earned $396,161 in total compensation—a reasonable sum for a man leading a global, billion-dollar nonprofit that gets results. Compared to other influential AIDS and gay-rights leaders in the United States, Weinstein's earnings may even be modest. Human Rights Campaign, a Washington, DC, gay-rights lobbying group, had $38.5 million in total revenue in 2013, and president Chad Griffin received $429,411; the Los Angeles LGBT Center had $66 million in total revenue in 2012, and chief executive officer Lorri Jean got $425,651; and the San Francisco AIDS Foundation had $30 million in total revenue, and chief executive officer Neil Giuliano received $327,447 in 2013.

No other AIDS organization in the US, including the Elizabeth Glaser Pediatric AIDS Foundation or Gay Men's Health Crisis, generates revenue that comes close to AHF's. In fact, it generates more annual revenue than many of the largest charities in America,

including Doctors Without Borders USA, United States Fund for UNICEF, and the American Heart Association.

What drives AHF's success is its pharmacy division, the overwhelming breadwinner among AHF's businesses. In 2014, that social enterprise brought in nearly $700 million. AHF Pharmacy utilizes a federal program called 340B, which was signed into law by President George H. W. Bush. It mandates that pharmaceutical companies must give major discounts to eligible healthcare organizations, such as AHF, that buy medications from them. AHF then distributes the drugs to uninsured and insured patients and is allowed to charge a private insurance company or the government the retail cost of the medication. Under 340B, an organization is permitted to keep the difference from the low price paid for the drug and the higher amount reimbursed.

"The intent of the program from the government point of view is to create an opportunity for organizations like ours to have extra resources for programs," AHF senior vice president Peter Reis explained to me.

Out of AHF's $903 million budget in 2014, only $20 million was tied to government grants. In fact, by 2014, AHF had turned into a donator, giving out more than $2 million in grant money to sixty organizations worldwide.

Despite such abundance, AHF doesn't spend without purpose. What keeps things in check is a term that's used throughout the organization: "return on investment" or "ROI." Many people in the nonprofit world might cringe at such a corporate-sounding term. At AHF, it's acknowledged as a good thing—ROI keeps management and staffers money-conscious so the organization can remain sustainable. It's also used as a measurement for whether or not a program is getting results and needs to be changed or abandoned. Since AHF will serve hundreds of thousands of patients over a lifetime, it would be reckless to not think about ROI.

The ROI for HIV testing, for example, is twofold. First, testing helps people to know their status and starts the process of getting them into treatment. Second, it brings individuals into AHF's global system of care, which benefits the individual's health, the public's health, and the organization economically. Yet, what Weinstein considers a good return on investment is not always about making more money. Every year, AHF throws a big holiday party in Los Angeles for employees, who spend large chunks of their lives carrying out its mission. The party is hugely popular and fun and builds up morale and camaraderie—another return on investment, Weinstein believes.

From the beginning, AHF took the stance that AIDS was not just a gay issue—it was a public health disaster and should be urgently addressed that way. That position hasn't changed. AHF, as a result, has never been a gay-focused organization. Whoever is impacted by HIV/AIDS—a mother in Uganda or a recovering drug addict in Russia or a gay man in Florida—that's who AHF will serve.

"AHF doesn't have the luxury of looking at this issue through the eyes of one group," Weinstein explained. "I don't think that you can look at it only through the eyes of gay men or bisexuals or sex workers or drug addicts. You have to look at it universally, and then you really have to look at it from the point of view of how do you contain this? The most effective message is one that is universal. When it comes down to it, it is about human sexuality; it is about life and death; it is about access to lifesaving medication. And these things are not in one particular group. That is another struggle that you have, is how do you balance the needs for society versus any specific minority? I think you're going to be seen as a special interest if you're representing one group. I think the AIDS movement has not represented the society at large, even in the United States."

To fulfill its vision, AHF is guided by a mission statement and accompanying core values, which were written by Weinstein. He gets directly to the point: AHF provides "cutting-edge medicine and

advocacy, regardless of ability to pay." The core values are fivefold: patient centered, respect for diversity, value employees, be nimble, and fight for what is right. On a prominent wall in nearly every AHF building, you'll see the AHF mission statement.

"A mission statement is useless unless people can recite it or know what it is," Weinstein explained. "If you have a mission statement with clauses and paragraphs, it is useless." He added, "The mission statement doesn't explain what you do, it is what you aspire to be."

—

WEINSTEIN RELIES ON THOUSANDS of employees and a team of veteran managers to carry out AHF's work. But, when it comes to any program or advocacy campaign of major consequence, Weinstein will have his fingerprints all over it. Jerry Baughman, a former AHF finance director, sums it up best. "AIDS Healthcare Foundation is the direct expression of Michael Weinstein," he told me. "It's all his hopes and desires and what he wants the world to be."

Public Health Division director Whitney Engeran-Cordova explained, "He is the pulse of this organization on every level. He sets the tone and sets the agenda in every way."

And Africa Bureau chief Dr. Penninah Iutung Amor told me, "More than anyone, Michael really lives our mission on a day-to-day basis."

When Weinstein hears such praise, he often looks uneasy or slightly embarrassed and will quickly point out the contributions of other leaders at AHF. Such as Peter Reis, the forty-nine-year-old senior vice president of AHF. Reis, a former college football player from South Hadley, Massachusetts, moved to LA to be a television writer but had a background in finance. In 1995, when Reis was thirty, AHF hired him to be a financial analyst for Positive Healthcare. Five years later, Reis became AHF's chief financial officer, overseeing a multimillion-dollar nonprofit and helping with AHF's expansion into Africa.

"We are pioneers," Reis told me. "We are the first AIDS organization to do work overseas in ways it wasn't being done."

Over the past nineteen years, Reis has guided AHF through all kinds of peaks and valleys—from hard-fought battles with governments to tight financial times when the organization was expanding to the start-up of AHF Pharmacy. Throughout, he and other AHF veterans were obsessed with providing care wherever it was needed.

"We care about people," Reis explained. "We are aggressively focused on getting them what they need."

There's also Terri Ford, chief of global advocacy and policy. She started at AHF in 1990, serving as the director of dietary services at the organization's first hospice facility. Ford quickly proved to have a special talent for getting things done—from completing messy construction projects to organizing advocacy campaigns all over the world.

Today, Ford, a fifty-three-year-old Los Angeles native, travels constantly, meeting with AHF staff in numerous countries, talking with government officials, and learning about policy issues that the organization must address. Of all the top managers at AHF, Ford and Weinstein probably earn the most frequent-flyer points, and he relies on her judgment when figuring out strategies for AHF's global advocacy.

Like Reis, Ford has constantly joined Weinstein in battle, such as trying to bring free condoms to West Hollywood bars, opening a free HIV treatment clinic in South Africa against the wishes of the South African government, and demanding that the Estonian government provide free antiretroviral therapy to AHF clients.

"In many countries around the world," Ford told me, "we are the safety net for HIV treatment. We're also the ones pushing the governments to do better. If we were not in many countries, the government public health systems would be worse."

And there's Tom Myers, chief of public affairs and general counsel. Based in Washington, DC, Myers, a Harvard Law School graduate, began at AHF in 1998. He now leads a feisty staff of in-

house attorneys and guides AHF's legislative agenda in the nation's capital, working on lower drug prices and reforms of federal AIDS programs such as the Ryan White CARE Act.

Raised in Cherry Hill, New Jersey, and a fifty-year-old father of two, Myers often appears as if he's poised to poke a hole in anyone's argument. And he thoroughly enjoys a righteous fight, which he's carried out time and again over the past sixteen years.

"At AHF," Myers told me, "at the end of the day, if we do our job right, more people get access to lifesaving drugs. That is what it is all about."

He added, "The federal government is pretty darn big. The drug companies are pretty darn big. So there needs to be a group that has the resources to effectively advocate to make sure that the interest of people with HIV comes first, and we want to be bigger so we can effectively advocate against these larger institutions."

There's also Donna Stidham, chief of managed care. Before joining AHF in 1994, Stidham, a sixty-three-year-old native Californian, was a nurse who worked with some of the first AIDS patients in Los Angeles.

"Our patients were young, and they were dying quickly," Stidham told me. "It was difficult to see young people die and not be able to do anything. The only thing we had to offer them was good nursing care and to try to fight some of their infections or their opportunistic cancers."

Stidham, known for her warmth and empathy, has a vast know-ledge about managed care systems and was hired to run AHF's Positive Healthcare. She helped turn the business into a major revenue source for the organization while also giving HIV patients quality, specialized medical treatment.

Stidham said, "AHF is here to take care of patients. It isn't about being part of the AIDS industry. It's about the AIDS patient."

And there's Mike Kahane, the Southern Region chief. A fifty-two-year-old former corporate attorney, Kahane started at AHF in

2007, overseeing its expansion in Florida and other southern states, where the AIDS epidemic is especially troublesome.

"The general population or the elected officials or health departments don't seem to realize the crisis that we are still in," he told me.

Kahane, a native Floridian, is now working to bring more of AHF's services to Latin America, constantly flying to Panama and Nicaragua and Guatemala to create government partnerships. "Sometimes the governments are slow to be trusting," he said, "but people on the ground desperately want our help."

There's also Dr. Penninah Iutung Amor, the Africa Bureau chief. Amor, a thirty-nine-year-old Ugandan, joined AHF in 2004. As a young doctor, she worked at the organization's HIV clinic in Masaka, Uganda, where AIDS was decimating the population.

"We'd receive patients from many different places," Amor said. "There were so many people lined up outside the clinic because it was their only hope for living."

As the Africa Bureau chief, Amor supervises AHF's country programs in West and East Africa and sub-Saharan Africa, where many of the world's worst AIDS hotspots are located. "We are going to the heart of the problem," she said.

Other members of the senior management team include chief financial officers Jonathan Petrus and Lyle Honig, chief pharmacy officer Scott Carruthers, senior director of marketing and sales Samantha Granberry, chief counsel for operations Laura Boudreau, chief of medicine Dr. Michael Wohlfeiler, senior director of human resources Anita Castille, chief information officer Wayne Mackert, and director of public health Whitney Engeran-Cordova. Many have worked at AHF for years. During their tenure, the organization has gone through its greatest period of expansion.

Leading them, of course, is Weinstein, the sixty-one-year-old president of AHF. People within the organization described him to me as "not willing to compromise himself," a "genius," "innovative," a

"social activist," "very passionate," "impatient," a "take-no-prisoners kind of guy," "tough," "not always right," "almost always right," "likes to be right," "controversial," "loyal," "truthful," and a man of "integrity." No one said he was rude or self-centered or mean.

Asked to describe himself, Weinstein, who dislikes tooting his own horn, told me that he's "loyal," an "innovator," "not very diplomatic," "impatient," "impetuous," "creative," and someone who doesn't "suffer fools gladly." He added, "It is hard for me to understand extreme vanity. The vanity thing is where I get really hung up."

Just as all roads once led to Rome, all roads in the AHF universe—whether you're standing in Dallas or Beijing or Mexico City—lead to Michael Weinstein.

Chapter 3

January 2014—Los Angeles

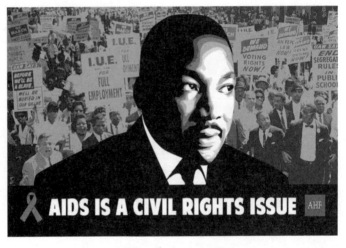

AIDS IS A CIVIL RIGHTS ISSUE

AHF marketing campaign

ON JANUARY 8, THE same day that AHF opened a new clinic in Brooklyn, Weinstein and his staff met in a dimly lit conference room at AHF Worldwide. It was the first marketing meeting of the new year. Unlike other nonprofits, AHF operated an in-house marketing department, using advertising agencies only when necessary. Things didn't always work that way.

"We'd have meetings [with outside agencies], and Michael would explain what he wanted changed or his idea," Jason Farmer, AHF's creative director, told me, "and they'd come back a week later with something completely different, and that kept happening."

Farmer, who's thirty-three years old, was born and raised in Birmingham, Alabama. He is bearded and tattooed and creates the artwork for an endless stream of AHF marketing campaigns. Influenced by artist Keith Haring and Joe Strummer of The Clash, Farmer believes AHF embodies a do-it-yourself, punk-rock ethos: if things in the outside world are not getting done to Weinstein's satisfaction, he'll have AHF do it.

It's a mindset that's given birth to hospice facilities, a managed healthcare program, a global network of medical clinics, an in-house marketing team, and many other programs and departments at AHF. At the same time, it generates an enormous amount of work for staff.

"We look at ourselves as an [advertisement] agency," Samantha Granberry, senior director of AHF Worldwide marketing, media, and special projects, told me. "An agency that, for what we do, would have a staff of fifty to sixty people."

Granberry wasn't exaggerating. Her fifteen-person team works on at least nine new marketing campaigns each month—an incredible output that must be created, edited, and finalized. Then depending on what's needed, they'll buy billboard space or newspaper space or TV time for the campaign—sometimes they'll buy all three. They may also hold a public event connected to the campaign, such as kicking off a new push to distribute more condoms. And these events take place all over the United States, not just in Los Angeles. Terri Ford, the global advocacy chief, and her team do similar work for marketing campaigns outside of the US.

—

Before the marketing meeting got underway, Jacquie Burbank, the marketing and communications assistant who sat at the head of a long table in the middle of the conference room, tapped a few keys on her computer, which was connected to a projector. In an instant, AHF employees and managers from around the country appeared

on a white wall in front of us. In addition to those who attended by video, another fifteen had called into the meeting.

Ged Kenslea, the fifty-five-year-old communications director and an eighteen-year veteran of AHF, stood near the white wall, holding a microphone. Every Wednesday, he led the meeting as a kind of timekeeper, master of ceremonies, and stand-up comedian. Weinstein sat at the long table near Burbank, and he was surrounded in the room by some twenty employees who were straight and gay; young and middle aged; men and women; and white, Asian, Latino, and African American. The diversity of staff reflected the diversity of the people whom AHF serves. With everyone settled, Kenslea brought the microphone to his mouth and asked for a roll call.

Beyond the discussions of artwork and advertisement buys, the marketing meeting is an excellent way to get a quick, ninety-minute report on AHF's work around the world. At previous meetings, Weinstein and his team had talked about an advocacy campaign that targeted the Estonian government, which had failed to follow through on a promise to provide antiretroviral drugs to an AHF clinic. They also discussed a worldwide AHF protest that called for the Chinese government to contribute more money to the Global Fund to Fight AIDS, Tuberculosis and Malaria, and they talked about placing HIV and STD testing advertisements on Grindr, a gay dating app.

Weinstein comes up with most of the marketing concepts, and he obviously relishes this part of his job. He often cuts loose with witty one-liners, pays attention to the smallest of details, figures out simple solutions for seemingly complex problems, and constantly throws out ideas.

During an earlier discussion about AHF's Rose Parade float, which featured a giant wedding cake made from coconut chips and red kidney beans, Weinstein went into a somewhat quirky stream of consciousness, already thinking about future campaigns. "The cake is great," he said. "Can we take it? Like with the Elizabeth Taylor float?

Can we remove the cake and use it for other parades? We should try. Because the cake is 90 percent seeds and beans, so it's not perishable. But it might sprout something. But we could clip it!"

Perhaps more than anyone in AHF, Weinstein believes that marketing is an essential tool to influence the public. In addition to directing people to AHF's services, the marketing campaigns implore the public to practice safer sex, get tested, and get into treatment if infected by HIV or other STDs. AHF marketing also tries to knock down the fear and shame that stop people from getting tested or receiving treatment.

Although the HIV/AIDS crisis is more than thirty years old, stigmas continue to linger in suburbs, small towns, and inner cities around the world. People of all ages, for example, fear that if they take an HIV test, they'll be labeled immoral or promiscuous. And if they test reactive for HIV, they'll be deemed damaged goods. Since HIV most commonly involves sex or injection drugs, cultural, religious, and moral baggage often come with the disease. To this day, experts cite stigma as one of the major problems that continues to hinder the fight against AIDS.

AHF marketing, as a result, continually reminds people that there's "no shame" in getting tested, that they'll feel "less stress" after getting tested, and that they won't deal with "judgmental bullshit" when they get tested at an AHF clinic. In one AHF billboard campaign that challenged religious stigma, people wore a red T-shirt saying "HIV+" and stood next to the slogan "God Loves Me."

"The only way to get at saving lives and stopping infections is through the culture," Weinstein explained to me. "That's what people pay attention to. We can have all kinds of battles on all kinds of issues, like drug pricing and patents. No one is listening. Some opinion leaders are, but the public is not listening. But when it is the Rose Parade or billboards, then people listen. And they listen because these things are cultural hallmarks, and that's what defines a lot of people's lives and their consciousnesses."

AHF also uses marketing as an advocacy tool, whether it's pressuring politicians to fix a problem or putting the spotlight on bad policy decisions. One campaign targeted President Barack Obama for proposing to cut more than $200 million from the President's Emergency Plan for AIDS Relief (PEPFAR). The global AIDS program, which has saved millions of lives in poor countries by greatly improving access to antiretroviral therapy, was established by President George W. Bush.

For the 2012 International AIDS Conference in Washington, DC, AHF created a poster that showed split headshots of a smiling Obama and a smiling Bush, with the provocative question, "Who's Better on AIDS?" The organization placed the poster at sixteen bus shelters near the White House. Many AIDS activists, whose allegiance often aligns closely with the Democratic Party, were aghast. "People were furious with us," global advocacy chief Terri Ford told me with a shrug.

But AHF had good reason to put Obama on notice. In a 2013 HuffPost column, Chris Collins, the director of public policy at amfAR, noted that since 2010, PEPFAR spending had dropped 12 percent under Obama. The president's consistently weak support even unnerved Archbishop Desmond Tutu, the South African civil rights leader and Nobel Peace Prize winner. In a YouTube video produced by AHF, Tutu said that a "scale down in PEPFAR would have devastating consequences" in Africa, and he urged the president to "continue to fund and support" the program. Obama, whose father was born in Africa, didn't listen to AHF or Tutu and kept proposing budget cuts.

Over the past three years, AHF has spent $15 million on billboard campaigns, media advertisements, YouTube videos, and Google and social media ads. AHF's critics sometimes complain that an AIDS organization shouldn't spend so much on marketing—a charge that's usually made when a campaign is controversial.

In Weinstein's mind, one should consider how Apple sells five hundred million iPhones or how a movie studio rakes in hundreds of millions from its latest blockbuster. Those companies spend enormous sums on marketing, which grabs people's attention and moves them to buy. In the fight to control the global spread of HIV/AIDS, Weinstein thinks such successful business practices by Apple or Disney should be replicated, not ignored.

"The vast majority of people don't understand the importance of marketing or what it does," Weinstein told me. "They kind of recognize that certain companies do it well, and it contributes to their success. But people like to think they're not influenced by marketing—that they're not being hypnotized, which is essentially what marketing does. It invades your subconscious, and it plants ideas there."

—

WITH ROLL CALL COMPLETED, Ged Kenslea turned over the marketing meeting to Weinstein. He broke away from the planned agenda to talk about goals for the coming year. Unequivocally, and in conflict with his critics, Weinstein declared, "We are not doing enough marketing."

The room went silent, but nobody visibly disagreed.

Over the past few years, AHF had been aggressively opening clinics and pharmacies all over the United States. From Weinstein's point of view, the marketing division needed to plant more ideas and invade more minds in the new service areas, which included New York; Washington, DC; Ohio; Louisiana; and Nevada. And, according to Weinstein, AHF's numerous divisions, such as media, pharmacies, clinics, and thrift stores, needed to work together better.

"Integration needs to be national," he told everyone.

To Weinstein's right, at the long table, Samantha Granberry was scribbling notes on a pad of paper. Granberry, a purposeful, thirty-seven-year-old African American woman from Pasadena, California,

had been working at AHF for nearly five years. She strongly believed in the power of AHF's marketing, and understood that she had just received her charge.

"He sets the bar," Granberry later told me. "You might not always hit that bar, but if you don't hit it, you'd better let him know ahead of time."

Talk switched to the Rose Parade. A week earlier, in front of a national TV audience, two gay men, Aubrey Loots and Danny Leclair, got married on top of AHF's award-winning float. It was a celebration of the recent legalization of same-sex marriage in California and another high-profile effort to break down stigmas.

"We got so much unflinching support from the Tournament of Roses," Weinstein told everyone at the meeting.

But it didn't go off without trouble.

In the days leading up to the wedding, an anti-gay-marriage group called for a boycott of the Rose Parade. Even worse, AHF received phone calls and emails from people who threatened violence. Kenslea hired private security to protect everyone on the float, including Mina Meyer and Sharon Raphael, a married lesbian couple who are close friends with Weinstein.

In the end, AHF's float was glowingly received. The *New York Times* ran a supportive editorial, and the *Los Angeles Times* noted, "There is simply no better way to illustrate the country's advances in gay civil rights than to celebrate a same-sex marriage on the first day of the new year atop some of the most sentimental turf in America: a Rose Parade float." Kenslea said that the combined TV, radio, and newspaper coverage, which got people around the nation talking about same-sex marriage and AIDS Healthcare Foundation, was the equivalent of $6.5 million in advertisement placements. It was a marketing grand slam.

Next on the agenda was AHF's newest billboard campaign, which honored the fiftieth anniversary of the Civil Rights Act of 1964 and the national holiday for Dr. Martin Luther King Jr. Projected

on the white wall in front of us, the billboard featured a black-and-white photo of King, a red AIDS ribbon, the AHF logo, and the slogan "AIDS Is a Civil Rights Issue." The campaign would run in Los Angeles; Columbus, Ohio; Washington, DC; Baton Rouge, Louisiana; Jackson, Mississippi; Atlanta; and South Florida.

Most people in the conference room looked impressed. But a few were worried that connecting King and civil rights to AIDS would stir up an African American backlash, and they asked how AHF staff would handle that. Kenslea and Weinstein were already on it.

"We showed this billboard to all our advocates and mobilizers that work with us nationally," said Kenslea, referring to the grassroots organizers hired by AHF. "The majority are African American, and they all thought it would spark the debate we want." The overall response, Kenslea added, was very favorable.

Weinstein, who thought up the campaign, ran through some talking points.

"What made Martin Luther King a transcendent figure was the fact that he opposed the war in Vietnam and spoke to universal issues," said Weinstein. "The other thing we would have to say to back this up is that if AIDS had affected white suburbs, there would have been a response from day one. After that, we have to address the inequalities that have to do with stigma and medical care."

In 2014, Weinstein wanted to unleash a major offensive against stigma. He was particularly moved into action after talking with AHF Associate Director of Community Outreach Phil Reh, who supervised the mobilizers. Reh explained that nearly everyone on his team considered stigma a high-priority problem among African Americans, who suffered HIV infection rates at shocking levels. Although African Americans make up only 12 percent of the total population in the US, they accounted for 44 percent of all HIV/AIDS cases. Stigma within the Black community wasn't the only reason for that disturbing statistic, but it played a part—and needed attention. "AIDS Is a Civil Rights Issue" was AHF's opening salvo.

Weinstein kept staring at the image of King on the wall, thinking aloud that Cesar Chavez, the Mexican-American labor leader, or Nelson Mandela, the former president of South Africa, could be switched into the campaign at some point. But Weinstein and his team wanted to first see the reaction to King. In twelve days, on January 20, the billboards would go up.

—

A FEW WEEKS LATER, I drove to Sunset Media Center. Corina Pop, Weinstein's longtime executive assistant, ushered me into her boss's corner office. Weinstein sat behind his desk and finished reading an email. I took a seat at a conference table and looked around.

Outside, the LA skies were again blue and cloudless, and twenty-one stories below, numerous construction projects were turning Hollywood into a trendy neighborhood with luxury condos and high-end restaurants. Beyond that, looking northeast, I could spot Weinstein's home nestled in the Hollywood Hills, not far from the Hollywood sign. From that living room, Weinstein could easily see Sunset Media Center, which was all too appropriate—his mind rarely, if ever, drifted far from work. Or, as he liked to put it, his "life's work."

Weinstein's office, as with all the offices at Sunset HQ, was painted an institutional green—a lighter shade of green that one might find at a county hospital. One wall, however, was completely covered by a gigantic world map, which Weinstein could easily consult from the nearby conference table. Behind his large wooden desk were framed proclamations, a framed photograph of Weinstein sitting in front of the Taj Mahal in India, and, perhaps most significantly, a vibrant yet haunting painting of Chris Brownlie, a cofounder of AHF and Weinstein's best friend. Brownlie died from AIDS on November 28, 1989, at the age of thirty-nine.

Around the office were miniature AHF billboards (gifts from an outdoor advertising company), framed newspaper and

magazine cover stories, framed posters from AHF's early years, and photographs of Weinstein with such people as President Bill Clinton, actor Edward Olmos, basketball star Magic Johnson, actor Blair Underwood, performer Harry Belafonte, and singer Alicia Keys. There were also pictures of Weinstein leading a protest march and yelling into a bullhorn at a rally.

On the carpeted floor next to a brown leather sofa, there was a toy Kawasaki ATV. It wasn't for children but rather to show people what drove AHF's success. On each black plastic wheel Weinstein had put a sticker with a word or two. One wheel read "business," another "policy," the third "operations," and the last one "mission" and "philosophy."

As a complement to that, Weinstein had positioned on top of his desk a small plaque—similar to a nameplate—that Whitney Engeran-Cordova had given him. It read, *"Aut viam inveniam aut faciam."* Attributed to the ancient military commander Hannibal, the Latin phrase translates as, "I shall either find a way or make one." It described Weinstein perfectly.

At the time of our meeting, in late January, AHF was working in thirty-two countries with 282,292 registered clients—211,524 were taking antiretroviral therapy. And the organization was already charging hard in the new year—a mode that Weinstein not only preferred but craved.

In just the first few weeks of January, Weinstein had been the subject of a front-page profile in the *Los Angeles Times* ("Supporters call Weinstein a 'genius'; detractors label him a 'dictator.' All agree that the hawkish-featured advocate remains uncompromising."); AHF had been prominently cited in a *New York Times* article and a *Slate* column about a controversial HIV prevention drug regimen called PrEP that the organization didn't fully support—a position that was also controversial; the California Assembly passed an AHF-sponsored bill that sought to distribute condoms to California prison inmates, who faced greater risk of getting infected with HIV

and other STDs than the general public; AHF general counsel Tom Myers and director of domestic policy Tim Boyd had started the push, against the wishes of the Obama Administration and other AIDS organizations, to change the way money was distributed through the federal Ryan White CARE Act, a source of funding for HIV/AIDS medical-care programs and social services; and Terri Ford and her global team were gearing up for the 20×20 campaign. Only weeks earlier, in December 2013, AHF had successfully pushed through a reauthorization of PEPFAR, which many AIDS groups thought would be impossible.

And, on January 31, California State Assembly member Isadore Hall III introduced "Condoms in Porn," an AHF-sponsored bill that required condom use in all adult films made in California. AHF had been involved in the issue for years, and Engeran-Cordova had been coordinating the most recent effort. The adult film industry was loudly opposed to the legislation, saying it would wreak financial havoc (people don't want to pay for pornography in which a man is wearing a condom, the reasoning went) and force the multibillion-dollar industry out of California, with thousands of film production jobs going with it. Their argument sounded eerily similar to what West Hollywood gay-bar owners had pushed fourteen years earlier.

Engeran-Cordova later told me, "Adult film actors are taken advantage of, run down, and disposed of, and their health is not thought of in the least. That infuriates me as a social justice issue. It also corresponds, quite frankly, with what we see with people who are living with HIV—people who have been set aside and discounted."

All the proposed legislation, battles, and advocacy campaigns added up to a mind-boggling load of work. In addition, AHF had its day-to-day global operation of clinics, HIV testing programs, thrift stores, and pharmacies. And after a generally positive response to the AIDS Is a Civil Rights Issue campaign, Samantha Granberry was leading an expansion of it by creating a nationwide series of town

hall meetings in African American communities. AHF was lining up Reverend Al Sharpton, the civil rights leader and talk show host, to be the featured speaker.

Weinstein, who'd recently gotten married to his longtime partner, Kevin Tran Nguyen, now sat with me at the conference table with a bottle of Snapple iced tea in front of him. He took good care of himself and worked out regularly and stayed fit and trim, which helped him to carry out a demanding work schedule. Between 1998 and 2014, for example, Weinstein constantly flew all over the world in economy class (under his own rule, AHF doesn't pay for business or first class) to turn AHF into a global organization. He also took early-morning and late-night phone calls from far-flung places, and he was constantly putting out fires. And he was routinely starting up, and closely engaged in, AHF's advocacy battles around the globe. It would be exhausting work for most people, but Weinstein always gave off a youthful energy, and his mind was sharp and fertile and encyclopedic. He was usually the most intellectually engaged person in any meeting and the most active listener.

As we sat at the conference table, I asked how he saw things shaping up for AHF over the next twelve months. Without hesitation, he launched into an all-encompassing answer:

"On the money front, the global program and our advocacy relies on the money that we generate from the businesses, and we expect to grow the budget about 20 percent, which is in keeping with what we've been doing. It is less in some years, but the point is that we have to execute on that in order to both afford everything that we're paying for now, plus investments that we make to grow in the future.

"When it comes to the mission, we're planning on adding one hundred thousand patients in 2014. That's always a management issue—also cutting through the red tape. There are new countries that we want to do things in and also there are individual sites.

"From the policy point of view, there's the reprioritization of Ryan White, which is controversial. There are drug-pricing issues

that are hot. There's the continued stuff with porn and PrEP. There are policies around testing. Part of the growth with the revenue comes from domestic expansion. So we'll have discussions in marketing about putting more emphasis on these new places in terms of having them grow.

"I'd say also with the advocacy, we have a much bigger focus on global institutions like the Global Fund and the World Health Organization and UNAIDS and the G20 and the G8. So I think we'd like to continue to ramp up both our own influence but, more importantly, create a global focus on AIDS and other infectious diseases.

"A very good discussion we had at the AHF board meeting last Saturday was on the subject of public health, in putting HIV and AHF in the context of public health. We've had that discussion periodically, most recently about three years ago, and that resulted in the renaming of our prevention and testing department as the Public Health Division.

"So, in this discussion, I'd say what we were talking about was to take yet another expansion of our interpretation of HIV and being an HIV/AIDS organization and embracing more of a public health operation. There's a breakthrough drug for hepatitis C, but it's very costly. About half a million people die every year from tuberculosis, and they're also HIV positive. There are tariffs in some countries on HIV and STD test kits or condoms. Or the approval processes take too long or are too diverse.

"In the operational aspect, as we grow larger, the patient can't get lost in the shuffle. We have to pay attention to client satisfaction, specifically the things that contribute to patients not being retained in care, like canceling appointments or not calling them when they don't come.

"On the outer frontier, we've set up this research institute, and we're looking at trying to get human trials started for treatments that maybe other people wouldn't fund. And, at the same time, we're looking at our database of our patients who have been long-term nonprogressors and understanding more about their characteristics

and also having a repository for blood samples that could be used for future research.

"Also, in the research area, we have a lot of people who are called 'acute infection.' That means we're catching them right after they're infected and maybe even in a window period where the less-sensitive tests won't pick up that they are positive. And maybe there's some information in that population that will give us clues to either slow or stop the progression of the disease. A lot of what we're looking at in terms of collaborations with other institutions has to do with gene therapy. It's interesting, but there are no guarantees. Most research finds dry holes.

"But I think we have the possibility, because we will fund it ourselves, and because of the large population of patients that we have, I think we can make a potentially unique contribution."

It was a bold agenda: taking care of hundreds of thousands of patients and adding another 100,000; influencing the wealthiest countries in the world; striking out into global public health beyond HIV/AIDS; and backing research that few other organizations would fund. This man from Brooklyn and this organization based in Los Angeles were playing for keeps. I asked if what AHF hoped to do in 2014 was part of a larger strategy for the next six years as it forged ahead with the 20×20 campaign.

Weinstein replied: "In the last six months to a year, we've come to define everything we are doing under this umbrella of 20×20 and under the umbrella of global AIDS control. I think that concept— those two concepts—are picking up a lot of traction.

"I think, first of all, that 20×20 is catchy. It is doable. The idea of global AIDS control, which we've been talking about for a bunch of years, is not easily understood by people. But now I think it's coming into focus. The other important thing we're trying to do in 2014 is this: if we're going to get to these higher numbers for global AIDS control, we have to deal with these troublesome countries when it comes to HIV. Nigeria, with the second-highest number of cases,

and India, with the third-highest number of cases, are both doing a terrible job. Russia's numbers are exploding."

We talked more about Russia and other countries and how an AIDS organization should deal with stigma.

"Tackling it head-on doesn't usually work," Weinstein said. "So AIDS Is a Civil Rights Issue is a way of getting at stigma, but in a more creative or different way. Even our campaigns like Sexual Revolution are a way of getting at it, because it's talking about the fact that you shouldn't be ashamed of sexuality."

Weinstein had clearly been putting a great deal of thought into solving global problems. But he didn't sound angry or bitter or overwhelmed, although he once told me that he felt at times as if he was "juggling chainsaws." Instead, he sounded optimistic, truly believing that AHF could change things. It was hard to not feel hopeful or inspired around such a person.

As we wrapped up our talk, Weinstein suggested that I leave Los Angeles to learn about what was happening "out there" in the AHF universe. In the coming months, I would travel thousands of miles to meet with AHF employees and clients in such places as Washington, DC; Baton Rouge, Louisiana; Dallas, Texas; Kampala, Uganda; Delhi, India; and Phnom Penh, Cambodia. But my first trip would take me to Florida for five days and then Mexico City for three.

On the day of my departure, February 4, AHF had taken off its gloves once again. In a blistering press release, it blasted Gilead Sciences, Inc., the pharmaceutical giant that makes billions off antiretroviral drugs, for "unbridled" corporate "gluttony" and "greed." For a twelve-week treatment for hepatitis C, the company was charging $84,000—or $1,000 per pill. By restricting access to only those people who could pay, Gilead Sciences was making mass treatment of a public health problem too expensive and therefore impossible. AHF could never stay silent.

Chapter 4

February 2014—South Florida & Mexico City

International Condom Day in Mexico City

ON A RED-EYE FLIGHT to Miami, I continued reading a book that I considered a masterpiece: *Sexual Ecology: AIDS and the Destiny of Gay Men.* Written by former *Newsday* columnist and AIDS activist Gabriel Rotello, *Sexual Ecology* stands alongside such landmark AIDS nonfiction as Larry Kramer's call-to-arms essay "1,112 and Counting" and Randy Shilts's investigative tome *And the Band Played On.* Kramer, the undisputed godfather of AIDS activism, wrote about *Sexual Ecology*: "One of the most important books ever written for and about gay men. Buy it and read it immediately." That's exactly what Michael Weinstein did.

In fact, Weinstein told me that the book had shaped his understanding of AIDS and, therefore, how to combat the disease, which was why I was reading it. Published in 1997, a year after the lifesaving drug treatment known as the "AIDS cocktail" became available, *Sexual Ecology* explained in straightforward prose why gay men got HIV/AIDS, why gay men continued to get HIV/AIDS, and how gay men could decrease their chances of getting HIV/AIDS. Thoughtful and passionate, with an extraordinary amount of data, the book was written by a man who clearly wanted to save his gay brothers.

"My goal in writing *Sexual Ecology* was to try to imagine a sustainable homosexuality," Rotello wrote in the book's afterword, "one in which gay men can be open and proud and proudly sexual— but also healthy. I am seeking to imagine a gay world that has banished the association between homosexuality and disease, and to start a conversation on how to gain that world, if we want to."

Rotello, now a Los Angeles–based documentary filmmaker, argued that the sexual ecology of the US was transformed dramatically by the sexual revolution of the 1960s and '70s, when young Americans, straight and gay, started having multiple sexual partners. Sexually transmitted diseases could now spread like wildfire, particularly among very sexually active gay men who were having more anal sex than previous generations of gay men, who did not use condoms, and who were hooking up with prodigious numbers of partners at sex clubs and bathhouses.

Those men then spread HIV to others, some of whom also had numerous sexual partners. A vicious, lethal circle emerged. Even if one did not ordinarily frequent a gay bathhouse or engage in risky behavior, all it took was one unprotected sexual encounter with a high-risk individual to become infected with HIV, which enlarged the circle.

Based on interviews with top epidemiologists and other in-depth research, Rotello concluded that if gay men wanted to dramatically

reduce death and disease and flourish as a community, they needed to understand how sexual ecologies worked, and then change by cutting down their number of partners, rejecting risky sexual behaviors, and utilizing serial monogamy.

Rather bravely, Rotello took aim at cherished aspects of gay culture: sex without condoms, multiple partners, and sex clubs. His suggestions struck some gay critics as moralistic and a threat to gay liberation, which was partly founded upon people wanting the freedom to engage in same-gender sex without getting fired or evicted or arrested. Rotello was labeled as a betrayer, a stigmatizer, and/or a distorter of gay life.

As I read *Sexual Ecology*, I couldn't help but think of Weinstein, who's had similar insults hurled at him by the same kind of critics. Also like Rotello, Weinstein believed that confronting hard truths, coming up with clear-eyed solutions, and taking decisive action were the only ways to get a handle on AIDS. In Weinstein's case, that approach extended to all vulnerable populations that AHF served, not just gay men.

Months later, I would meet up with Rotello. He was still knowledgeable and passionate, and he told me something both significant and chilling: not only did Weinstein have "an understanding of the dynamics of sexual epidemics that most AIDS prevention leaders don't have," but he was "one of the only" heads of a major AIDS organization who had "the correct perspective on the AIDS epidemic, both in the perspective on treatment and the perspective on prevention."

—

JUST BEFORE DAWN, MY plane touched down at Miami International Airport. I drove thirty miles north to AHF's Southern Region headquarters, in Fort Lauderdale, arriving in the middle of the balmy tourist season. South Florida, which includes Miami and Fort Lauderdale, has long attracted tourists who hit the beaches, drink a

few too many mojitos, and let loose. Fort Lauderdale, in particular, has one of the busiest cruise-ship ports in the world, with more than four million people arriving each year to travel to Mexico or the Caribbean.

South Florida's chambers of commerce, however, don't publicize, a fact that public health officials know all too well. Between 2003 and 2012, Miami-Dade and Broward counties, where Miami and Fort Lauderdale are located, had the highest numbers of chlamydia and syphilis cases in Florida. It was a trend that showed no signs of diminishing.

And in 2014, Miami-Dade and Broward ranked first and second, respectively, for the most new HIV infections and most HIV/AIDS cases in Florida. In 2013, the CDC reported that Florida had the second-highest number of new HIV diagnoses among all fifty states.

AHF employees gave me a laundry list of reasons explaining such high rates of HIV and STDs in South Florida—from locals and tourists living recklessly in Miami's drug- and alcohol-fueled party scene to risky sexual behaviors among young gay men. The AHF team, for example, had learned that gay men would meet up to have sex, test each other for HIV through a home-testing kit, and then have unprotected sex if their results both came back HIV negative. That might appear responsible, but it was actually quite risky. "Acute" HIV infections, in which someone has just been recently infected, often aren't detected by the home-testing kits. As a result, the infected man would unknowingly give his partner HIV. In addition, since they weren't using condoms, they were still susceptible to such STDs as gonorrhea and syphilis, which were spiking in South Florida.

The bottom line for everything was, first, too many people were having unprotected sex and, second, the local government response was neither urgent nor adequate.

AHF arrived in Florida in 1999—the first time it had offered services outside California. It was a significant moment for the organization: the state had contracted AHF to run the nation's

largest HIV/AIDS disease management program, known as Positive Healthcare/Florida, which initially served around 7,500 Medicaid patients. The work involved such things as helping patients comply with their HIV treatment and educating primary care physicians, who were often uninformed about the best kinds of HIV treatment.

Eight years later, by 2007, AHF had one clinic, five pharmacies, and sixty employees in Florida, but operations would soon expand even more. In 2008, Northpoint Medical Center, a Fort Lauderdale HIV/AIDS medical practice that was the largest in Broward County with over 6,000 clients, faced financial ruin. If Northpoint closed, thousands of patients could fall out of treatment. AHF, which now worked with a $178 million budget, bought the medical center.

Overnight, Northpoint became AHF's largest clinic in the US, and eventually one of the premiere HIV/AIDS clinics, private or governmental, in Florida. In addition, AHF Pharmacy could utilize the federal 340B program at the medical center, which would generate impressive revenue. Taking notice of what AHF had pulled off at Northpoint, other financially challenged medical providers in Florida reached out to AHF, which then acquired those practices.

Critics hold up such acquisitions to argue that AHF is the Walmart of the AIDS movement. It's a barb that smaller AIDS organizations, some of which view AHF as a competitor, love to sling. Weinstein makes it a rule to never criticize other AIDS activists and organizations by name, but he will speak up in more general ways. When I asked him about the Walmart label, he dismissed it as empty rhetoric and countered that some AIDS groups "could use the competition"—his way of saying that they could do better work. He then pointed to a measurement used by the US government called the HIV Care Continuum.

In the US, according to the HIV Care Continuum, 14 percent of the 1.2 million people living with HIV do not know they have it. In other words, these 168,000 Americans are not getting treatment. Additionally, of that 1.2 million with HIV, only 40

percent are "engaged in care," meaning that 720,000 are not. Also, only 37 percent have been prescribed ART and only 30 percent are "virally suppressed." That last statistic means that 70 percent of the 1.2 million people living with HIV have levels of the virus that are detectable and are therefore infectious. That's 840,000 people. These are staggering numbers, and they show how much more still needs to be done. Put simply, there's plenty of work to go around.

Also, Weinstein wants AHF to directly impact the troubling statistics of the HIV Care Continuum by expanding into towns and cities across America and providing quality services that specifically address the issues of nontreatment and patient adherence to antiretroviral therapy. And in his mind, by undertaking such a nationwide effort, AHF's mere presence in a city or town might force other organizations to improve their HIV testing and patient services. That last line of reasoning often offends certain people in the AIDS movement, but that doesn't mean it's not valid.

AHF's critics fail to mention something else. Medical practices in the US that specialize in HIV care are struggling to make ends meet due to extra regulatory burdens placed on doctors and low reimbursement rates from insurance companies. In fact, many practices have gone out of business, and AHF has noticed that fewer young doctors are going into the field of infectious diseases. This dangerous trend not only threatens the treatment and health of individuals with HIV but the public's health. By acquiring other medical practices in Florida, AHF was certainly expanding, as its critics claimed. But it was also ensuring that far more people stayed in treatment.

By 2014, six years after the Northpoint deal, AHF had grown dramatically in Florida, having opened four Out of the Closet thrift stores, operating fifteen clinics and thirteen pharmacies, and employing 396 people. Beyond Miami-Dade and Broward counties, AHF also had clinics in Tampa, Orlando, Pensacola, Fort Myers, Delray Beach, and Jacksonville. Its operation in Florida was now

serving more clients and testing more people than AHF's system of care in California.

The man who led that extraordinary expansion over seven years was Mike Kahane, a former corporate attorney who had represented, among other publications, the *National Enquirer*. When he arrived at AHF, Kahane was a complete newcomer to the AIDS movement.

—

IN DOWNTOWN FORT LAUDERDALE, about three miles from the Atlantic Ocean, AHF is headquartered on the seventeenth floor of the 110 Tower building, where Kahane has an office. As AHF's Southern Region chief, he oversaw programs in Washington, DC, the American South, Florida, and the Caribbean. He also helped supervise work in Latin America. Kahane and I sat at a round table near his desk, on top of which sat a little paperweight that read, "No act of kindness, no matter how small, is ever wasted." Directly behind him, a bookshelf was neatly arranged with legal books, a thick, spiral-bound AHF client satisfaction survey, and a coffee-table book of celebrity photographs from the *National Enquirer*.

Kahane was tan and muscular, with an unflinching gaze. He had a precise way of speaking, and the same kind of youthful energy that Weinstein exuded, although Kahane appeared a bit worn out from constantly traveling for work. As we started to talk, he came across as a battle-tested attorney only willing to give the necessary facts and ready to pounce if he heard something that, in his mind, was inaccurate or not specific enough. Sleep-deprived, I was spooked by such a human buzz saw. Apparently, my mere presence as a writer had brought out a side of him that wasn't always on display. But within minutes, he was engaging and polite and bubbled with a kind of happy playfulness. He even apologized for "being a lawyer."

"Most people think I'm pretty easy and laid-back," he'd later explain to me. "So most people tend to be surprised when they see me be extremely firm and assertive, usually done in a respectful way."

Kahane grew up in Hollywood, Florida, where his now-deceased father, Alfred Kahane, was a well-known sportscaster and owner of a commercial real estate firm. Mike had an enjoyable childhood and followed a path typical of a well-to-do American: he graduated from Purdue University, then graduated from law school at Northwestern, and then earned another law degree in intellectual property from John Marshall Law School.

By 1987, Kahane was working at a boutique law firm, eventually becoming executive vice president and general counsel for American Media, one of the largest publishing companies in the country. Headquartered in Boca Raton, it owned the *National Enquirer*, *Star* magazine, *Muscle & Fitness*, and other popular publications. Kahane practiced First Amendment law and, he told me, made a "ridiculous" amount of money.

In 2003, he was having drinks, in Washington, DC, with a man named Romano Romani and mentioned that someday he'd like to work for a nonprofit. Kahane had no idea that Romani was AHF's lobbyist, and they never spoke about AHF. Four years later, out of the blue, Kahane received a call from Romani, who'd just gotten word from Weinstein that he needed someone with a business mind to run the Florida operation. Romani told Kahane that he instantly thought of him. A few months later, Kahane took a 90 percent pay cut and went to work for AHF.

His boss at American Media was stunned, thinking Kahane was going through a crazy do-gooder phase. Kahane didn't think so, especially after he talked with Donna Stidham, the well-respected chief of managed care at AHF.

"She was telling me about a project that AHF did in Guatemala," he explained to me. "She said that they do needs assessments before they open a clinic and after they open it. Before that particular clinic opened, the number-one need for about 80 percent of the client base was money for a coffin. Six months after opening the clinic, the number-one need was for a job. That had a profound impact on me.

I walked out of the meeting and thought, 'This is something I want to be a part of.'"

Kahane took a gamble on AHF, but Weinstein was also throwing the dice. Kahane was a novice in the AIDS world, had never worked for a nonprofit, and had never attended a political protest in his life. Seven years later, after the tremendous growth of care that AHF provided in the Southern Region, the bets on both sides paid off.

In my conversations with Weinstein, he couldn't praise Kahane enough. He told me that Kahane was dedicated and passionate, with a keen sense of vision, and he had a special talent for getting the best out of his employees. Kahane, in return, described Weinstein as a "role model" and a "close personal friend" who engages him in "intellectual gymnastics," which he enjoys. "You'll start out at this conversation about A and B," he said, "and you end up at X and Y."

Kahane also frankly described his boss as "cantankerous" but not as cantankerous as other high-powered bosses he had worked for. He added that Weinstein's irritability was rarely without reason. "Usually there's something in the internal or external bureaucracy that is inhibiting patient care, or people aren't challenging government systems that should be challenged because they aren't delivering the best patient care possible," he said. "So usually it is patient focused."

Only a few weeks into 2014, Kahane was already engaged in a busy year. He was closely watching how the Affordable Care Act, also known as Obamacare, would impact AHF clients and other people with HIV, and he was working with his legislative-affairs team to help with AHF's big move to reprioritize the Ryan White CARE Act. That effort, which involved AHF policy experts and community-based advocates from around the country, was seeking a more humane and sensible distribution of federal funding to regions that were hardest hit by AIDS.

"The epidemic is in the South right now," Kahane explained. "But the funding is not in the South. We have to correct that. We have to get more funding for testing, more linkage, more access to care throughout the southern United States."

Kahane continually works on the expansion of treatment. When we met, he had just returned from Jamaica, where AHF had finalized an agreement with the ministry of health to become the country's national partner in fighting AIDS—a massive and complex undertaking. He said, "The Jamaican Ministry of Health has said, and it was actually refreshingly candid, that the problem is a little out of control, and they don't know what to do."

Though it gets little media attention compared to Africa, the Caribbean, which includes Jamaica, Haiti, The Bahamas, and Puerto Rico, suffers the second-highest HIV prevalence rate among adults in the world—1.1 percent of its people, or 250,000 individuals, are living with HIV. Only sub-Saharan Africa has a higher adult prevalence rate, at 4.7 percent. In Jamaica, 1.7 percent of the adult population lives with HIV—nearly three times higher than the US rate of 0.6 percent. Among Jamaica's gay and bisexual population, also known as men who have sex with men or MSM, an alarming 20 to 30 percent have been infected with HIV. ("Men who have sex with men" is a catch-all phrase used by AIDS scientists, doctors, and researchers, because some men don't identify themselves as gay or bisexual, even though they have sex with other men.)

In Jamaica, intolerant cultural and societal attitudes toward gays and people living with HIV have contributed to the AIDS epidemic there. "Jamaica is probably one of the most stigmatized countries in the world," said Kahane, noting that people in the American South face similar intolerant attitudes. "There is stigma against HIV, and, on top of that, there is gay stigma."

Like Weinstein, Kahane wanted to dramatically diminish the stigmas attached to AIDS. He thought it was critical for the success of AHF's global 20×20 campaign. "The only way you're going to get people to access care and get tested is to address the stigma issue," Kahane explained.

There was already talk within AHF that an AIDS Is a Civil Rights Issue town hall would roll into South Florida in the spring.

Kahane was one of the people initially worried that the campaign would offend the African American community—that it would be perceived that AHF was making a naked grab for publicity using King's federal holiday. A backlash never happened. "People saw immediately that wasn't the case," he said.

As we talked, a delivery person came in carrying an unmarked brown paper bag. Kahane was nervous—he worked at American Media in 2001 when the company famously received an envelope filled with anthrax that killed an employee. But this bag contained donated medications for AHF's operations in Haiti. "Just another day at AHF," he said. "Doing great things!"

He added, however, that he wasn't blind to what needed to be improved at AHF. The fast expansion in Florida and other parts of the Southern Region, he said, had caused growing pains. He was particularly concerned about new hires thrown into work without knowing enough about the AHF way of doing things, and he thought that new clinics sometimes experienced a sense of disconnection.

"I don't want them to feel like they're an island unto themselves," he said. "I want them to feel like they're a part of the bigger mission, and that includes global and that includes all the things we do. So our communication skills have to be very good. I don't think we're as good at that as we could be."

Even though Kahane had left corporate America, he was still working long hours and replying to emails in the middle of the night. The difference between then and now, he said, was that he didn't feel as if he was working for a living. "You're fighting for what is right and fighting for what patients need," he said, adding that he has never regretted leaving American Media and his big paycheck. "I can honestly say that there has not been a single day," he said. "Not one."

—

In Florida and around the world, AHF is a "safety-net provider," a term used often in the public health world. Safety-net

providers, which usually care for the poor, essentially do the work that government does not. They often step in to help because of government incompetence or government disinterest or because a government has set up a partnership with the organization. The growth of AHF is largely due to the failure of governments around the world to do things correctly or to act at all.

Yet, AHF wants governments to work more effectively in tackling AIDS because safety-net providers can only do so much. A competent government, with all its financial resources and power, can have a greater impact on controlling the spread of AIDS than any nonprofit.

"One of my concerns is that we don't want to become a replacement for governments' inefficiencies," Weinstein said during a biweekly advocacy conference call, in which AHF's domestic-policy advocates and managers discuss strategy.

But, at the same time, Weinstein and other key decision makers at AHF know that governments are slow to respond to AIDS, and they're not waiting for politicians and bureaucrats to do the right thing. So AHF not only pressures governments into action but has also been constructing its own global network of care. As early as 1997, Weinstein saw the need to do what he doesn't really want to do—to be a replacement for government.

"We need to build a system of coast-to-coast, border-to-border care with a clinic in every community that has more than two hundred HIV/AIDS cases," Weinstein wrote in AHF's 1997/1998 annual report.

In the US and other countries, AHF works a model called "test and treat." On the face of it, it seems simple. First, AHF staffers test people at a clinic or at an Out of the Closet thrift store or at a mobile testing site, such as a music festival or a busy nightlife strip. If a person tests positive, an AHF linkage specialist gets him or her into treatment as soon as possible with an AHF medical provider— the goal is to place a person in care within seventy-two hours. The medical provider then gets the person on HIV medications at an

AHF pharmacy and reduces his or her viral load to undetectable so he or she is healthy and not infectious. AHF then tries its best to keep that person from falling out of treatment.

"Years ago, we did focus groups," Weinstein told me, "and people said that I'm scared, and I don't want to do it. They had these excuses. I don't want to be waiting; I don't want to be asked a lot of questions; I don't want to be judged; I don't want to go to a skanky free clinic. But if you took away the excuses, then they'd be more likely to test and get treated. So one by one, we've addressed all of those issues and taken away as many barriers as we can."

No other AIDS organization in the world offers such comprehensive services. AHF provides its patients, whom include children, not only HIV and STD testing, but promotes safer sex practices, brings clients to doctors and onto antiretroviral therapy, provides specialized medical care and pharmacy services, advocates on behalf of patients, and conducts AIDS research all under the same highly organized umbrella.

The Elizabeth Glaser Pediatric AIDS Foundation, on the other hand, a well-respected international group, focuses exclusively on ending pediatric AIDS. AmfAR, the much-applauded organization that Elizabeth Taylor championed, zeroes in on international AIDS research. And the Elton John Foundation, another international AIDS nonprofit, offers grants for prevention and public policy programs. They all do great work but with a tighter focus.

"We have always had a sense of urgency," Weinstein explained, "and we still do. That is still important. I think other AIDS groups think that they're doing good work, they're serving people, meeting a need, and you can't do everything. And they kind of say, 'Okay, this is what we've carved out, and we're going to work to make sure that we get funding and tend to that garden.' I think that we've looked at it more than just tending to our vegetable garden. We had to figure out how to feed the city or the nation or the world as a whole."

—

ONE EVENING, KEPLER VERDUGA, a thirty-seven-year-old mobile testing program manager at AHF, picked me up at my hotel in Fort Lauderdale. He drove a gray Nissan Juke and wore a full, fuzzy beard and short, black hair. Muscular and compact, he looked as if he could be a free safety for the Miami Dolphins. Verduga had moved to Florida from Ecuador in 2001 and quickly became a popular fixture in South Florida's gay party scene. His passion, though, was medicine; he had finished medical school in Ecuador. By 2007, Verduga moved away from the parties and started working as an HIV tester for a local AIDS organization. In 2012, he joined AHF.

Verduga showed me how AHF carried out the "test" of its "test and treat" model. We visited several mobile testing sites in South Florida, where his teams parked a customized AHF motor home and stood outside for hours and conducted one-minute rapid tests. One stop took us to a mobile testing site outside an adult video store in Miami ("I'm friends with the guys who work there," Verduga said, "as long as I bring them condoms"), another site was in front of a gay bar on a busy street in South Beach, and still another site was on a street corner near a popular nightlife strip in a gay enclave called Wilton Manors.

"We're in a constant search to find new places to test," said Verduga.

"South Florida, especially Miami, is a party town," Verduga explained. "But the people who engage in risky behavior, especially men who are not openly gay, are unlikely to visit an AHF clinic or an Out of the Closet thrift store to get tested. So," Verduga said, "the mobile testers, who work day and night shifts, go to them."

In South Florida, AHF's mobile unit program averages 1,400 tests per month and finds around 160 reactives per year—testers tell a person he or she is "reactive" rather than "positive" in case of a test malfunction, and then allow a doctor to make the final diagnosis.

As part of its larger mission to control the global spread of AIDS, every time a mobile van heads out, AHF wants to find as many people living with HIV as possible and get them quickly into care.

In the US, AHF budgets $2.7 million for its mobile programs with a fleet of seventeen testing vehicles. It also has three mobile units in Mexico, two in India, one in Russia, and one in the Netherlands.

Mobile testing is not easy work: imagine if you were conducting a test that, within a minute, revealed to a person that he or she has tested reactive for HIV, and sometimes that person is a teenager. But many AHF testers find the work rewarding—they're helping people find out their HIV status, then getting them into care. "I've never worked at a place where people work so hard," said Verduga. "They want to be the best, and it's contagious."

At one point, Verduga and I visited a mobile testing crew at Sunshine Cathedral in Fort Lauderdale, a Christian ministry that serves the LGBT community. It wasn't a regular testing site for AHF, but the church was throwing a Valentine's Day dance for gay and lesbian teenagers—a golden opportunity to educate a younger generation. "We can reach out to these youths and hopefully prevent them from getting HIV," Jamie Rudd, an AHF program manager who was working the event, told me.

Under a bright moon, a sparkling red AHF motor home was parked near a small auditorium where the dance was taking place. On each side of the vehicle, a sign read in huge letters, "1 Minute Results," under which was written "freeHIVtest.net." As teenagers walked in and out of the dance, they couldn't miss the motor home—or its message. "We're letting them know that HIV is out there," said Rudd. Here and there, a teen got tested, especially if a friend did so first.

Thankfully, none of the teenagers at Sunshine Cathedral came back reactive. Neither did anyone else that AHF tested that night in South Florida. But when a person is found reactive for HIV at a mobile site or thrift store, a linkage specialist is immediately summoned to the scene—another key part of AHF's "test and treat" model.

In the past, AHF had found that people who had tested reactive at a mobile testing site wouldn't always go to a clinic—they

would often be scared or angry or in denial. That wasn't good for their health, and they could keep spreading HIV. So, AHF made an adjustment and hired linkage specialists, who are always on call and ready to move.

Once a specialist arrives, he or she does a lot of handholding and consoling while also collecting personal information from the new client. "You have to have the ability to empathize with someone," Mena Gorre, AHF deputy director of linkage to care, told me. The specialist must then place the person in front of an AHF medical provider and later deliver him or her to a follow-up appointment. In South Florida, that individual may end up in the office of Dr. Esther Schumann, considered one of the best doctors at AHF. She handles the "treat" of the "test and treat" model.

One afternoon, I met Schumann at her office in downtown Fort Lauderdale. She is one of sixty-three AHF doctors in the US—the organization employs or provides funding for the salaries of 720 doctors at more than 250 facilities around the globe. Schumann, who's fifty-five and witty and doesn't put up with nonsense, was born in northwest Germany in Lippstadt, where her father was a schoolteacher and principal and her mother was a forensic psychiatrist who regularly worked with people in legal trouble. As a young girl, Schumann dreamed of being a doctor at a Native American reservation in the US.

By the mid-1990s, however, she found herself at the Montefiore Medical Center in the Bronx, where she treated HIV/AIDS patients. She always wanted to practice "social medicine"—helping those in dire need—and continued her HIV work when she moved to Florida in 2005. Four years later, she joined AHF.

Schumann became known for handling AHF's most challenging patients in South Florida—people who had learning disabilities or mental health issues or substance abuse problems, any of which can cause them to not take their HIV medication routinely. But Schumann was not one to enable—or throw them away.

"We have a lot of socially not-gracious patients," she told me. "They will come in and try to bulldoze you down. I can recognize the pattern because it is often people who don't read and write, and they will try to bulldoze you down so that you won't question anything. I can deal with that. I say, 'Sit down, be quiet, and listen to what I have to say.'"

Possibly because of her tough-love approach, Schumann was well known in South Florida—newly diagnosed HIV clients often requested her. "The word is out on the street about Dr. Schumann," Michelle Morgan, an AHF program manager, told me.

During my visit, Schumann asked me to join her in an examination room, where she would see a female patient, who gave me permission to observe. Schumann wore a white doctor's coat and sat next to a computer and talked in a German accent that somehow seemed fitting. As the patient took a seat, the doctor said with a smile, "I haven't seen you since September!"

The middle-aged woman was not only HIV positive but racked with other medical and mental health issues—from carpal tunnel syndrome and hepatitis C to diabetes and depression. And, apparently, she used drugs from time to time.

"I was at a Super Bowl party and there were drugs there," she told Schumann.

"Cocaine?"

"Yeah."

"Cocaine is a bit strong for you," Schumann said matter-of-factly. "It is not good. Your body is taxed enough. It's no good."

The woman nodded and said nothing.

Schumann went through the woman's medications, which she brought in a small gym bag. The doctor found bottles and bottles filled with pills, a sign that the woman was not taking her medications.

"This is a total mess," Schumann said. "Are you sure you've been taking your pills?"

"For the most part, yes; I'm on it all the time."

"What would your viral load be if we draw it today?" asked Schumann, knowing that a viral load count above "undetectable" would indicate that the woman wasn't taking her pills.

The woman paused. "I feel confident that my viral load is low," she finally responded, sounding like a defense attorney.

Schumann looked at her skeptically and called a colleague at the AHF pharmacy at Northpoint Medical Center to figure out a way to better manage the woman's medications. The problem, they figured out, was that she was seeing more than one doctor and using multiple pharmacies.

"That doesn't fly," Schumann told the woman. "You have to go to one single pharmacy."

At one point, the woman, who talked about living with an alcoholic mother and having drug addicts come in and out of the house, started to cry. Schumann looked sympathetic but tried to keep things real.

"You need to be careful," the doctor advised softly. "The more you cry, the more you get back into that vicious cycle."

The woman lifted her head and looked back with wide eyes. By the end of the examination, she promised Schumann she would do better. "I hear you," she said. "I do."

Schumann worked with a small team that included a medical assistant, Nichell Robbins, and an office manager, Harry Watters. Together, they handled a packed roster of 650 patients, which included single African American mothers, married and single Haitian men and women, married and single Hispanic men and women, young African American men, and gay white men. Since Schumann could speak English, German, French, Spanish, and some Creole, she could communicate with them all.

To better accommodate her patients, many of whom took public transportation, Schumann had moved from Northpoint Medical Center to her current office in downtown Fort Lauderdale, where a bus stop was only a block away. Some of those patients traveled far

distances so their neighbors and coworkers wouldn't know they were being treated for HIV.

Schumann also called patients personally when they didn't show up for an appointment, spent any time necessary with them during an appointment, and started work early in the morning and ended late at night. She was desperate to keep people healthy, and sometimes her personal life suffered. "It's not easy when you care so much about your work," she told me at one point.

In fact, Schumann confided, with some amusement, that she had become increasingly obsessive and compulsive, always making sure, for example, that forks and knives were set perfectly next to a plate before she sat down to eat. "I'm striving for a more organized environment in my life because of the mess with our clients," she said with a laugh.

But Schumann wasn't looking for sympathy, and she didn't dwell on her sacrifices. She just got up and saw another patient.

—

IN SOUTH FLORIDA, AHF's work continued to expand. A few blocks from Kahane's office, AHF had bought a four-story office building, where they'd locate a dental office, the new Southern Region headquarters, and an automated pharmacy for twenty-four-hour refills. AHF's Broward Wellness Center, which provided free HIV and STD testing and treatment and was always busy, had already opened there.

AHF's growth in Florida was impressive, but something else also caught my attention: the same urgency and passion that I'd seen in Los Angeles was evident in South Florida. In other words, urgency and passion appeared to be the norm at AHF, not the exception. Mike McKany, a Fort Lauderdale–based deputy director at AHF's Public Health Division, explained best why staff put so much into their work. "It's about the underserved," he told me. "It's about people with HIV. It's about people who need care. It's about people

who live in Africa who need care. It's definitely not 'me-centric.' It's about everyone else, which I love. It is extremely rewarding."

As I flew out of Miami, I wondered if that urgency and passion would also be found in other AHF outposts.

—

AHF Mexico is headquartered in a three-story walk-up in a Mexico City neighborhood called Zona Rosa, or "Pink Zone," where gay bars and clubs come to life at night. In Mexico, men who have sex with men, male and female sex workers, and injection drug users have been hardest hit by the AIDS epidemic. This is particularly true in Mexico City, where HIV/AIDS is most prevalent in the country. It's one major reason why AHF is based there.

In Mexico, an estimated 180,000 people aged fifteen to forty-nine are HIV positive. In Latin America, which stretches from Mexico to Argentina, there are approximately 1.6 million people who live with HIV/AIDS. Yet, during this era of lifesaving antiretroviral therapy, according to UNAIDS, 47,000 people out of that 1.6 million died from AIDS-related illnesses in 2013.

AHF's Latin America Bureau includes Guatemala, Mexico, the Dominican Republic, Jamaica, Peru, Argentina, and Paraguay. Mexico is the largest program out of the group. In February 2014, AHF Mexico had 17,672 registered clients—11,157 were taking antiretroviral therapy.

The organization started work in Mexico in 2004 and opened its first clinic, in 2005, in Tijuana, whose border with California is crossed daily by more than three hundred thousand people. Many of those travelers are low-income migrant workers from Central American countries such as El Salvador, Guatemala, and Honduras—they pass through Mexico to reach the United States. In Mexico and the US, they are considered illegal immigrants and mostly live an underground existence to avoid deportation. They are extremely hard to find and test and treat in order to prevent them from spreading HIV.

To make matters worse, the Mexican government refused to pay for HIV medications for migrant workers. So in 2005, AHF picked up the expensive tab and offered free antiretroviral therapy at its Tijuana clinic. (By 2014, however, the Mexican government had changed its policy and offered HIV medications to migrant workers.)

At the same time, doctors in Tijuana were illegally hoarding HIV drugs meant for free distribution at a public hospital for lower-income people. Doctors told patients that if they wanted HIV medications, they had to visit the doctor at his private practice—and pay a small fee. Greed and corruption are all too common in the worlds of public health and AIDS. The AHF clinic in Tijuana, which was opened in partnership with the Mexican nonprofit Agencia Familiar Binacional, became a way to counter that.

As AHF Mexico grew, it started to offer, nationwide, free HIV testing kits and training to its partners among nongovernmental organizations (NGOs) located near government HIV clinics. Then those who tested positive could be easily offered nearby treatment. AHF supports this work today. In addition, in Mexico City, AHF partners with Clinica Condesa, the largest HIV clinic in Latin America, treating more than eight thousand patients.

AHF's approach in Mexico is different from its approach in the US. It doesn't operate pharmacies or Out of the Closet thrift stores, and it cannot get reimbursed from the government for supplying HIV medications to patients. Instead, AHF focuses on HIV testing—conducted both by the organization and fifty-one partner groups—and brings people who test reactive to government clinics for treatment.

Even though AHF works with government clinics, it doesn't hesitate to cut ties with a treatment center if non-AHF staffers refuse to operate according to AHF's standards or if the government is not fulfilling its responsibilities. AHF, as a result, has stopped working with clinics in Puerto Vallarta and Pachuca. It still supports health centers in Tijuana, Mexico City, Cancún, Mérida, San Bartolo

Coyotepec, Coatzacoalcos, Nezahualcoyotl, and Jiutepec, and it operates a mobile clinic in Veracruz.

Jessie Gruttadauria, an AHF veteran who started in 1990, did much of the initial legwork in Mexico. In 2006, she helped bring in Dr. Patricia Campos, the former director of an HIV/AIDS program in the state of Jalisco, about three hundred miles west of Mexico City and home to Guadalajara. Within a few years, Campos built up AHF's operations in Mexico and became the country program manager, then worked on AHF's expansion into other Latin American countries and turned into the Latin America Bureau chief. Mike Kahane, in Florida, is her supervisor.

—

ON A BRIGHT MONDAY morning, I met with Campos and her staff at AHF headquarters in Zona Rosa. Campos was sharp and jovial and excited to tell me everything about AHF's work in Mexico. I also learned that she was a workaholic—whenever she exercised on a stationary bike, for example, she'd place a laptop in front of her and reply to emails. That kind of dedication was common among the most effective people at AHF. I asked Campos, who was fifty-one years old, what inspired it.

"I believe the reason is because the work in HIV and AIDS is like the life of the salmon," she replied. "All the time, all the minutes, we need to go up, opposing to the river. If we stop, the river will return us many kilometers down."

It was easy to understand why Campos's staff was devoted to her.

"She's a strong person and smart," said Jess Dector, the national rapid-test program coordinator. "It's not possible to corrupt Dr. Campos. She's clear about her mission and what she wants to do."

Campos's commitment to the battle against AIDS was ignited in 1986. Her first husband, the father of her two sons and daughter, was infected with HIV through a blood transfusion. "At this time," she explained, "we only had the drug AZT." She saw firsthand the

devastation of the disease and dealt with a sense of powerlessness as her husband slowly, and agonizingly, wasted away. He died from AIDS, and the experience would always inform Campos's work.

"The most power is inside of the people," Campos told me. "I wanted to work with the people to find this power. When all the other persons said that AIDS was a mortal disease, I wanted to go the other way and help people find the hope to be alive."

So much so that she was fired from her job as the HIV/AIDS program director in Jalisco for making a somewhat risqué video for gay men about how to use a condom. Since she planned to have the video shown at gay bars and nightclubs, she wanted it to be informative, largely uncensored, and attention-grabbing. With a kind of mischievous pride, she brought out a copy and showed it to me.

"Everyone said that people should use condoms," she said, "but no one said how they should use them correctly."

The video didn't seem too outlandish to me, but local government officials, who are conventional by nature, were shocked by it—and sent Campos on her way. She called Jessie Gruttadauria, who had partnered with her for numerous projects. Within a month, Michael Weinstein brought the doctor on board.

At the time we met, Campos was keeping tabs on AHF's Latin America programs in eight countries, where, in 2013, AHF performed 105,039 HIV tests and distributed 520,769 condoms. As part of that work, she and her team were often fighting battles against plodding bureaucracies, outdated governmental policies, and societal stigmas. The doctor also started a new program in Jamaica with Kahane, and she was fine-tuning and expanding AHF's work in Mexico, where poor patient care, governmental corruption, and finding people who are HIV positive but don't know their status were regular problems that needed constant attention.

"Mobile testing is important because we go and look for the people," Campos said, "the people that always find barriers to the health system and don't have access to the testing."

The doctor was particularly proud of a mass mobile testing program in which AHF and its partners set up tents in public, conducted rapid HIV tests, and offered counseling and education. Some bureaucrats insisted that people wouldn't want to lose their confidentiality and therefore wouldn't participate. They were proven wrong.

In 2013, AHF tested 68,571 people in Mexico, 1,086 of whom were reactive for HIV—a remarkable capture rate of 1.6 percent, eight times the country's HIV rate of 0.2 percent. In addition, Campos believed that AHF was changing minds—since people saw others get tested for HIV, their fear of being stigmatized by getting tested decreased, and the disease itself was becoming less of a social sin.

"We remove the fears," she said.

At a mobile testing site at Nezahualcoyotl, a poor, crime-ridden city about an hour east of Zona Rosa, AHF employees set up tents in a dusty parking lot just off a congested thoroughfare. Around 150 people quickly formed a long line. An old man—bald, tan, and wrinkled—walked over and stopped to look at the hubbub. He then approached Jess Dector, AHF's rapid-test coordinator. After he was gone, I asked what the man said. "He wanted to learn more," Dector replied, "so he can tell his family and invite them to come."

—

WITH AHF OPERATING IN more countries, Weinstein and his senior managers realized that the organization's hard-driving, patient-centered culture in the US needed to be firmly established in other parts of the world. AHF, after all, was trying to build an effective global movement. So, Weinstein came up with AHF's five core values: patient centered, respect for diversity, value employees, nimble, and fight for what is right.

"We're a business, and we're a bureaucracy, but we're not going to give up fighting for what is right," Weinstein told me at one point.

A few years later, Weinstein wrote AHF's simple, six-point "management philosophy." Anywhere in the AHF universe, one's

leadership style should include these traits: mission driven, fairness, learning, hands-on, accountability, tenacity.

"Fairness is probably the most important management value," he explained. "First of all, when you have corporate propaganda, which every organization does, the more of it that you have, the more obligation you have to live up to it. Nothing demoralizes people more, or gets them ticked off, than when you have all these banners and you don't do it. People will deal with a lot of adversity and give a lot when they think they're being treated fairly."

He added, "We think management should get their hands dirty and be on the front lines."

In Mexico City, just like her colleagues in South Florida, Campos clearly embraced AHF's core values and management philosophy. She was hardworking, mission driven, and so willing to get her hands dirty that she was planning for a trip into the Amazon rainforest to help people there. Others I talked with—Dr. Galileo Vargas, Jess Dector, and Impulse Group president Alejandro Reyes—were full of fight, tenacity, and nimbleness. And, like Dr. Schumann, they were consumed with figuring out ways to best serve patients.

"We need more change," said Galileo Vargas, a senior medical advisor for the Latin America Bureau, "and we need to improve the health systems, improve the laws, eliminate stigma and discrimination. Every day if you go to the hospitals, you can learn about a complaint against a doctor or a nurse with stigma and discriminatory behavior."

For the 20×20 campaign, Vargas wanted AHF to be a leader in both training doctors and HIV testers in Latin American countries and moving patients into treatment more quickly. Unlike the US, many countries only offer free access to HIV drugs until a person's CD4 count, or T-cell count, falls below 350. Other countries, in accordance with World Health Organization (WHO) guidelines, have a lower threshold of 500. Either way, an individual who's not taking antiretroviral therapy is still infectious, even if his or her own

health isn't in immediate jeopardy. When I was visiting Mexico, the CD4 threshold was 500. Months later, however, AHF played a key role in getting the Mexican government to eliminate that threshold completely—people could receive free antiretroviral therapy as soon as they tested HIV positive.

The decision by governments to not immediately put an HIV-positive person into treatment is purely economical and shortsighted. For one person in a low- to middle-income country, according to the WHO, "first-line" ART costs $115 annually—and the patient must take that medication for the rest of his or her life. If a person doesn't respond well to that treatment, he or she needs to take "second-line" or "third-line" ART, which costs around $330 and $1,500, respectively, per year. AHF and other AIDS organizations argue that if people continue to spread HIV because they don't immediately take antiretroviral therapy due to the threshold, that will increase the number of people who will be infected—and who will need HIV drugs. It will cost much more money in the long run.

Jess Dector was another person who walked the walk at AHF. In fact, she got emotional when I asked her about working for the organization. "Many people want to make a difference," she told me, "but few have the resources to do that. AHF has given me this opportunity to have the resources to make a difference. We want to help you, and you help us, and we work together. You give us this, and we give you that. That is an important opportunity."

Dector, who was twenty-nine years old, had a quiet intensity. One could sense that nothing was going to stop her from doing her job—not even Mexico's infamous drug cartels. Around the time of my visit, the cartels were making international news for their cruel, deep reach into Mexican business, politics, and society. The danger was real, and AHF tested near a cartel stronghold. Dector was wisely cautious but not intimidated. "We're going to work slowly to get to work there," she said, "because they don't know that we're there. We've been told to be careful because if they notice that we have a

presence, they'll ask for money. That's a problem we haven't had yet, but we need to be careful it doesn't start."

Alejandro Reyes, a thirty-two-year-old who had cofounded a gay magazine, was eager to make his contribution to the AHF cause by expanding Impulse Group in Mexico. "When we talk to young people," Reyes told me, "they don't even know this information about HIV and AIDS. They have computers and the internet, and they go to school, but they don't care and ignore it—they think it's a joke."

Impulse Group was Weinstein's brainchild, launched in Los Angeles to infiltrate gay culture's fast lane of partying and sex and to connect with young gay and bisexual men, who are still getting infected with HIV at high rates. According to the CDC, the greatest number of new HIV infections in the US is among men aged thirteen to thirty-four who have sex with men.

Weinstein is an avid reader of Malcolm Gladwell, particularly his book *The Tipping Point*. In it, Gladwell explains that one way an idea, product, or social behavior becomes widely embraced is when a handful of opinion leaders and trendsetters support it. Weinstein used that concept when creating Impulse Group, which is made up of younger gay men who are well connected in the gay nightlife scene but promote safer sex.

Impulse Group members are not AHF employees but volunteers. Their work is to enlist new members and host special events, perhaps a nightclub party or a panel discussion at a comedy club, where condom usage and other sexual health issues are talked about and promoted—and where free condoms are handed out. Other than receiving money and guidance from AHF, Impulse Group is largely autonomous. There are chapters in Los Angeles, San Diego, and San Francisco in California; South Florida; Orlando and Tampa Bay in Florida; Delhi, India; Beijing, China; Phnom Penh, Cambodia; Bangkok, Thailand; Washington, DC; Dallas, Texas; Atlanta, Georgia; New York City; Guadalajara, Mexico; and Mexico City, whose chapter was established in 2013.

As the Impulse Group president in Mexico City, Alejandro Reyes, who turned into an AIDS activist after his two best friends tested positive, wanted to reach out to all of gay society in Mexico—poor, middle class, and wealthy. "It's our main goal," he told me, "and I think we can do it."

In Zona Rosa, at night, Reyes saw dozens of young male sex workers on the street, willing to have unprotected sex if a man handed over a few more pesos. Just like other places in the world, including California, the government routinely ignored the plight of sex workers. Reyes, though, wanted to connect.

"We have to come up with a strategy for the young people," he said, "and we're doing that, but we need to get them to know the Impulse Group. Then we can do that better."

On the plane back to LA, I thought about the dusty parking lot in Nezahualcoyotl and what Jess Dector told me: "It's the perfect work for a dreamer. You can see that you're doing something that works." She was speaking about her experience at AHF, but, for me, there was a larger ring of truth to it, something that described the very essence of the organization. The invaluable work I'd seen in Florida and Mexico had originated from a dream, a vision, a fearless, innovative thought.

Chapter 5

February 2014 Continued—Las Vegas & Los Angeles

AIDS Is a Civil Rights Issue town hall in Los Angeles

IN 2009, MICHAEL WEINSTEIN decided he would establish, of all things, a global holiday. Dubbed "International Condom Day," it would take place in February, the day before Valentine's Day. It would promote safer sex, and it would be observed in every country that AHF operated in. The organization would also hand out millions of free condoms.

Not coincidentally, 2009 was also the year that AHF got into the condom business. Since then, it has distributed two brands for free worldwide: Love condoms, a regular size that comes in shiny red packaging, and Icon condoms, a large size that comes in shiny gold packaging. Getting more people to practice safer sex was important,

but there were additional motivations to break into condom production and distribution.

First, Weinstein came up with the idea that AHF could sell low-priced condoms at supermarkets and pharmacies, as well as distribute them for free. If they sold well, the thinking went, major manufacturers such as Trojan and Durex might be forced to reduce their prices to stay competitive. And if overall prices dropped, that would make condoms more accessible, especially among cash-poor young people. AHF has yet to carry out that experiment, but, over the next five years, it has given away nearly 117 million free condoms. In 2009, AHF distributed 6.1 million condoms around the world; in 2010, 10.8 million; in 2011, 8.1 million; in 2012, 15.4 million; in 2013, 33.8 million; and in 2014, 42.6 million.

AHF also saw that many developing countries weren't providing condoms or were giving away condoms that didn't fit well or smelled bad because they'd expired. People, as a result, didn't use them. So AHF provided what governments couldn't: a quality condom.

"Love condoms were created at a roundtable discussion," Herb Fisher, the fifty-nine-year-old director of AHF Global Advocacy Operations, who handles the worldwide distribution of condoms, told me, "and the topic was, why can't we have our own condoms and import them around the world? We shouldn't rely on governments that run out of condoms or won't buy them."

In 2009, AHF started working with Unidus, one of the largest condom manufacturers in the world and headquartered in Seoul, South Korea.

"They made it cost-effective to get started," said Fisher, who worked as a banker in a previous life, "and they've been with us every step of the way. When we had a problem, they fixed it. When they made a mistake, they fixed it. They were just amazing people to work with."

AHF now deals with two other manufacturers, in Malaysia and India, and ships condoms to twenty-six countries at an average total cost of 4.2 cents each.

Condoms, which range in price from AHF's free ones to Trojan's twelve-pack at $12, continue to be the most effective, cheapest way to prevent HIV and other sexually transmitted diseases. By comparison, Truvada, the HIV prevention drug also known as PrEP, costs between $11,000 and $14,000 annually, or between $30 and $38 per pill—and it doesn't guard against other STDs.

On February 13, 2014, the sixth annual International Condom Day took place in twenty-nine countries with the theme "Love is the best protection." AHF donated six million condoms to departments of public health in Texas and North Carolina and gave away 4.5 million condoms to community programs around the world. There were also many public events geared toward younger people.

In Ethiopia, for example, AHF set up a flash dance. In Nigeria, a "love ride." In Delhi, India, flash mobs and mobile HIV testing. In Mexico, flash dances, condom distribution, and HIV testing. In Beijing, China, a flash mob and condom distribution. In the US, "hug-and-kiss" photo booths, flash mobs, and nationwide condom giveaways.

Even at the 2014 Winter Olympics in Sochi, Russia, which took place in February, AHF made a deal with Olympic organizers and distributed a hundred thousand Love condoms to athletes from eighty-eight nations.

The cumulative result of International Condom Day, in 2014, was a global safer-sex promotion that no other AIDS organization, including UNAIDS, had ever pulled off in a twenty-four-hour period.

—

A WEEK AFTER INTERNATIONAL Condom Day, AHF was giving out more free condoms in Las Vegas, where I went to drop in on the Condom Nation tour. Launched in 2012, Condom Nation, which purposefully played off the word "condemnation," sought to widen AHF's condom distribution in the US. "We wanted to generate enthusiasm here," Herb Fisher told me, "and it worked."

Americans' use of condoms takes dips in popularity from time to time, resulting in higher STD rates. In January 2014, a CDC report found that rates for chlamydia, syphilis, and gonorrhea were all on the upswing, indicating that condom usage was probably on the downswing.

Rather than quietly ship boxes of condoms to clinics and partner organizations, AHF wanted to stir up more public awareness about safer sex. It bought an eighteen-wheeler and slapped "Condom Nation" on both sides of it. Stuffed with boxes of condoms, the tractor-trailer traveled all over America as the Condom Nation team handed out the merchandise at stops in New York and Texas and dozens of other states. The truck turned heads, caused some nervous laughter, and caught the attention of countless people who took pictures with their smartphones and posted them on social media. Perhaps millions of Americans, if only for a brief moment, were reminded about safer sex.

Pat Ruiz, an amiable, no-nonsense female trucker, drove the eighteen-wheeler. Marco Benjamin, Condom Nation's program manager, drove a van to accompany Ruiz. They hit the road for weeks at a time, handing out free condoms and making connections with local AIDS organizations, which ordered and distributed more free condoms from AHF. By 2014, the Condom Nation team had attracted wide media coverage, posted a steady stream of dispatches and photographs on social media, and had given out more than 1.5 million condoms.

"Your life was about condoms and Condom Nation," Benjamin told me. "You kept going to help that next person."

Ruiz said, "The one thing that touched me was when the mothers would come, even at a truck stop where I was fueling up. They'd see the truck, and they'd ask me about Condom Nation. And I'd say, 'Yeah, I'm carrying condoms for safe sex.' Then they'd bring over a son so I could let him know about safer sex and hand him some condoms."

During my visit to Las Vegas, I could see that the work hadn't changed. Anthony Marshall, Condom Nation's new program manager at the time, handed out condoms to a line of homeless men; carried cases of condoms into two gay sex clubs in a strip mall; gave away buckets of condoms at the Sin Sity Sisters of Perpetual Indulgence's Red Dress party, an annual AIDS fundraiser that AHF was cosponsoring; and offered free condoms outside Charlie's, a gay country-western bar.

At Charlie's, one night, a slender young man with bleached-blond hair approached Lori Mizuno, a friendly, thirty-three-year-old director of AHF's Public Health Division. She'd flown out from LA to see how Marshall was faring and now stood near the Condom Nation van where condoms in big red buckets were ready for the taking. He sheepishly confided in her that he was a porn star and needed condoms for work. For a moment, Mizuno's mind flashed to the Condoms in Porn bill that AHF was pushing in California, then she told him to take as many as he wanted. He quickly grabbed a fistful of gold-packaged Icons.

—

In Clark County, Nevada, home to Las Vegas and the vast majority of Nevadans, 2013 data from the Nevada Division of Public and Behavioral Health showed that young people aged thirteen to thirty-four made up 58 percent of new HIV infections. Whites accounted for 39 percent, African Americans 23 percent, and Latinos 30 percent. Once again, African Americans were disproportionately impacted—they made up only 11.5 percent of the county population.

Yet the local government's approach to combating AIDS had been troublesome. A few gay men walked up to the Condom Nation van at Charlie's and told Mizuno that employees at the public health department had asked odd, judgmental questions when they took HIV tests. "They almost make it like they don't want you to get tested," said one man.

AHF had recently opened two clinics in Las Vegas and was also having a problem. Dale Gluth, the regional director in Northern California who also supervised Nevada, told me that local restrictions essentially banned mobile HIV testing. "The testing regulations here are very old school," Gluth said, "so we can't test in the van." It was something that boggled the mind; no other major metropolis in the entire country had such a prohibition.

Adam Ouderkirk, AHF's senior director of program and business development, who was in Las Vegas for the Red Dress party, told me that AHF would fight the ban. In the meantime, they had to play it safe: Marshall and Mizuno handed out free home HIV testing kits rather than perform on-site mobile tests.

Days later, Weinstein learned about the situation. He wasn't happy. In short order, AHF charged into Las Vegas and started performing mobile tests, aggressively defying local health officials. Carrying out its hard-hitting brand of advocacy, AHF had shifted into full-battle mode.

—

ON FEBRUARY 23, AHF hosted an AIDS Is a Civil Rights Issue town hall at Holman United Methodist Church, a well-known African American institution in South Los Angeles. It featured the Reverend Al Sharpton and LA Mayor Eric Garcetti at a Sunday service and a public discussion afterward with Sharpton, AHF's Samantha Granberry, AIDS activist Gabriel Maldonado, and leading African American ministers Cecil "Chip" Murray and James Lawson Jr. In The Meantime Men's Group, Inc., a support group for Black gay and bisexual men that was founded by activist Jeffrey King, cosponsored the event.

Going into the day, Weinstein wasn't sure how the AIDS Is a Civil Rights Issue campaign would be received, although he didn't have to worry about AHF's credibility in the Black community. In a pioneering effort in South LA, in 1992, it opened a hospice that served African Americans dying from AIDS—and many Black community

leaders never forgot that. AHF's lifesaving work in Africa was also held in high regard.

But Weinstein knew the Holman event was going to be something different. While African Americans were disproportionately impacted by HIV, the disease was still negatively associated with homosexuality in some parts of the Black community, especially among influential ministers. Even in 2014, homosexuality and AIDS were considered dirty secrets unsuitable for discussion in much of South LA. That awkward, even lethal silence was about to be broken at Holman, and no one could predict what the reaction would be.

At eleven in the morning, Holman congregants and guests sat shoulder-to-shoulder inside the packed, white-walled sanctuary. Weinstein sat in the front row with Garcetti, AHF medical provider and longtime friend Mary Adair, and former LA city councilman Bill Rosendahl, who was a consultant to AHF. Senior vice president Peter Reis and global advocacy chief Terri Ford took seats in the second row. Near the pulpit, Sharpton sat with Holman senior pastor Kelvin Sauls, who was born and raised in Johannesburg, South Africa, a country devastated by AIDS. A huge wooden cross hung on the wall behind them.

At one point during the service, a choir sang lyrics that seemed appropriate for an AHF fight song. "I'm gonna stay on the battlefield," they belted out. "I'm gonna stay on the battlefield / "I'm gonna stay on the battlefield / Till I die!" Reis and Ford sang along with the choir. Weinstein, wearing a navy blue suit and a blue-striped tie, watched and listened with a grin.

"We will stay on the battlefield," Reverend Sauls said moments later. "We will stay on bended knee. We will pray with our eyes open, with our hands open as we welcome, oh God, all those who continue to be marginalized, stigmatized. Affirming, oh God, their dignity and their humanity."

After an impassioned rendition of "We Shall Overcome," Weinstein stood at the pulpit and gave a brief speech. It was vintage

Weinstein—he pledged solidarity, but he also called out failings within both the gay and African American communities.

"In the 1970s," he said, "I marched to integrate the largest gay bar in Los Angeles, Studio One, which asked for three IDs from African Americans. The gay community remains discriminatory to this day, and people of color have faced high levels of prejudice. At the same time, the homophobia within the African American community has prevented Black gay men from being accepted in their own community. AHF has teamed up with Jeffrey King and the In the Meantime organization to empower and serve these men.

"To me, the current sky-high rates of HIV among Black men is a direct result of the devaluing of their lives by both the gay and Black communities. In addition to coping with all of the issues of poverty and lack of opportunity, they're treated as outcasts. They have no place to truly call home. Black women represent the most cases of HIV among women in our country by far, and they have less access to prevention, testing, and care than their white counterparts.

"AHF has embarked on the campaign of AIDS Is a Civil Rights Issue with Reverend Al Sharpton to underline that the social determinants of disease are the reason that HIV is having such a terrible impact on the African American community. I, as the leader of the largest AIDS organization, have a moral obligation to do everything I possibly can to fix it.

"I know that if we make the commitment today to control the epidemic of AIDS in Black America, we will succeed. And I pledge to you my undying support for that effort."

The crowd showered him with applause.

Mayor Garcetti, known as a cautious politician, followed. He talked about inequalities, said little about AIDS or gay Black men, and never mentioned AHF, which certain LA officials have long regarded as too controversial and antagonistic. But Garcetti curiously raved about Sharpton, who was close to President Barack Obama and a

political heavyweight within the African American community. Sharpton then took the podium.

Sharpton, a rousing preacher, showed himself to be the perfect spokesman for the AIDS Is a Civil Rights Issue campaign, which had taken him to cities around the nation. In contrast to Garcetti, Sharpton wasted no time in mentioning AHF and its leader, describing Weinstein as "unselfish" and "visionary." He then launched into his sermon.

"We are somehow confused into believing that civil rights are for some of us rather than all of us," he said, then mentioned that a friend in the civil rights movement told him that he had problems with the idea that AIDS was, in fact, a civil rights issue.

"I said, 'Well, that's interesting. I have problems with how we don't deal with AIDS.' He said, 'What do you mean?' I said, 'Because at the base of our lack of involvement is a real and live homophobia in our community and in our churches. And if we are honest, many of us that have had to fight against bias act as though it gives us the right to harbor bias ourselves.'"

An approving murmur sounded from the pews. Sharpton continued, and the crowd egged him on with applause and knowing laughter.

"What we hide behind is the scriptures, just like those that segregated and enslaved us—get behind the scriptures to justify racism, slavery, and Jim Crow!"

The crowd roared. Someone yelled, "Amen!"

"The reason I fight for immigrants is I want to be like Jesus. The reason I fight for the rights of gays and lesbians is I want to be like Jesus. The reason I stand for the poor and afflicted—I want to be like Jesus! Jesus didn't have requirements. He said, 'Come ye that love the Lord, and let your joy be known!'…

"The disproportionate amount of Blacks who have HIV/AIDS in this country, in this city, ought to mean we should be at the head of the line and not hold our own biases, to suspend our commitment

to rights and civil rights. That's why this is important! That's why this is mandatory!"

At the end of Sharpton's sermon, the sanctuary reverberated as if a small earthquake had just hit.

Days later, the *Los Angeles Sentinel*, one of the oldest and most influential African American newspapers in the US, noted that the audience was "captivated" by the reverend's "powerful message." With the *Sentinel* weighing in, AIDS was losing its status as a dirty secret. That boded well for the change that Sharpton and AHF sought, and a movement was now rising up. It started with an AHF marketing campaign.

—

ON THE LAST DAY of February, I met with Weinstein at his office. I wanted to catch up with him before I left for Washington, DC, where AHF was planning to drop a bill in the House of Representatives that would change the way federal funding was distributed to HIV/AIDS programs through the Ryan White CARE Act. We sat at the conference table with the wall-size world map to his right.

Weinstein, who's usually very measured, was still excited about the town hall at Holman. A few days earlier, at the start of a marketing meeting, he'd declared, "It was a high-water mark of raising consciousness in the African American community about HIV and AIDS. There was a palpable sense of history being made." I now asked why he thought that.

"Because of where it was. Holman is a really important institution. Also because of who it was: the standing-room only congregation, Pastor Sauls, Sharpton, the mayor, the LA County supervisors, the state senator, and me. And the honesty of the discussion. The fact that homophobia in the Black community was being called out from the pulpit in this most elite of Black churches, and people were being called to action about the fact that homophobia in the Black community was contributing to the spread of HIV, and it was hurting

the community. It is possible that that message has been delivered with that many power brokers in one room, but I'm not aware of it."

He added, "AHF now has had Cornel West, Tavis Smiley, Julian Bond, Andrew Young, and Al Sharpton—these esteemed thought leaders who not only endorsed AHF but also endorsed this cause. That means something."

Weinstein's mobile phone then rang. He was expecting a call from a *Washington Post* reporter, who wanted his thoughts on the drug Sovaldi, Gilead Sciences' breakthrough medication that cures most people who have hepatitis C. Weeks after AHF sounded the alarm, more insurance companies and patient advocates were starting to denounce Sovaldi's $84,000 price tag.

AHF had been strongly advocating for lower drug prices for years, even though that advocacy could hurt AHF Pharmacy's ability to generate major revenue. Weinstein, in fact, was probably the most vocal critic of Gilead in the US, and he was about to let it rip with the *Washington Post*.

"This is the poster child for pharma greed," Weinstein said to the reporter. "If you put this together with [the other drug that] Sovaldi has to be used with, it has broken the six-figure price barrier."

The reporter asked a question, and Weinstein replied, "This [price] was not a result of research. This is a result of Gilead buying Pharmasset at $11 billion—$11 billion, all of which came from overcharging for AIDS drugs, bought overwhelmingly by the US government. So, basically, the US government subsidized Gilead's purchase of hep-C medication, which Gilead is now charging $84,000 for, which they will sell back to the US government."

He continued, "They have the twenty-ninth largest market capitalization in the country. [Gilead CEO] John Martin will make over $100 million this year. He will be the eighth-highest-paid CEO in the country. They have market caps far in excess of GM and Ford and McDonald's and Target and all these other companies. It is a new level of insanity."

Weinstein went on, "There are 170 million people in the world with hep C. Based upon what they are charging for it, only two or three percent of the people in the world who will need this drug will get it—because [the rest]can't afford it. Is the government of Malawi going to pay $84,000? Or even if it is brought down to $2,000? If the individual income in a country is $600 a year, and a drug costs $2,000, how is anyone going to get access to it? This is the AIDS drug scandal all over again."

After another question or two, Weinstein wrapped up: "This is the government saying that because this is so valuable to people's health, we're going to allow Gilead to monopolize this, and we are going to prevent any competition. When it comes to co-pays and deductibles, there are people who are deciding between medicine and food in the richest country in the world because John Martin has to make $100 million."

The interview ended, and Weinstein apologized for taking the call. "If it wasn't the *Washington Post*, I would have said I was busy."

Our talk then veered toward the fact that AHF was working in many dangerous hotspots, especially in Ukraine, where a bloody revolution had just taken place in Kiev and resulted in the ousting of the country's president, Viktor Yanukovych. The Ukrainian leader had declined a much-needed economic deal with the European Union, instead taking a multibillion-dollar loan from Russia. He was deemed its puppet. Things got so tense and violent that two foreign-born AHF employees, one of them Russian, had to flee Kiev.

"We're having these discussions," Weinstein said, "and very sober conversations within AHF on how to protect our people and how we could respond or not respond. We are on high alert."

The senior management team and board were also discussing if AHF needed to pull out of certain countries due to problematic policies. It was an option that Weinstein understood and seriously considered but made him uncomfortable—a lot of ordinary people who had nothing to do with war and politicians counted on AHF.

Weinstein's mind, however, kept looping back to the town hall at Holman, an event that had cemented his notion that creating change through culture was key to making gains in controlling AIDS.

"I've really always been a political junkie," he said, "and I've focused a lot on politics, but I've really come to the belief that culture is where it is at. What I mean is, first of all, people are not really focused on politics or policy. But when you're talking about [openly gay football player] Michael Sam or the Rose Parade or all sorts of things that impact the culture, whether it's race or class or gender or orientation—those are things that get people talking and thinking.

"When we were focused on needing to get money to treat people, or needing to get certain rules changed so people wouldn't be discriminated against, that was one thing. But now we're more in the realm of, 'How do we deal with Black homophobia in order to create a more wholesome environment?'—like in that speech I gave at Holman, but I also talked about the racism in the gay community and how bad that was for the identity of Black gay men."

He added, "Think about Impulse Group and what we're doing there. You can't come at a twenty-five-year-old gay guy with the whole political platform. It isn't going to work. Last night, we had a little thing at my house with the leadership of Impulse here in LA, and I said I thought we ought to think about expanding the agenda beyond just prevention or health and wellness in the community. I think part of what's contributing to people not looking out for themselves is just the fact that gay culture isn't very nourishing— the gay community doesn't provide a very nourishing, supportive environment.

"I said that when you compare the gay community to ethnic minorities, like Jews or Italians or other groups that have fraternal societies that take care of people, there's a sense that they have to take care of their own and nurture their own culture. I don't see a lot of that in the gay experience. So I said we want to have a more nourishing community."

At the end of our talk, he mentioned an adage that he couldn't fully remember. "The quote," he said, "is basically to the effect that if you want to test somebody, see how he deals with power."

Having seen too many politicians in LA change for the worse once they got a little power, I agreed wholeheartedly. Later, I found the quote, attributed to President Abraham Lincoln. He said, "Nearly all men can stand adversity, but if you want to test a man's character, give him power."

That nugget of wisdom obviously weighed on Weinstein's mind, and it was probably something that guided his work at AHF. And by mentioning it to me, he was offering a way to measure him, which was unusual; as a journalist of seventeen years, I couldn't recall a single person who gave me a way to size him or her up. It begged a simple question: Who is this guy?

PART TWO

A Bold History

Chapter 6

The Weinsteins

The Weinstein family: Rose Ann, Samuel, Michael, and Gilda
at AHF's Chris Brownlie Hospice.

ONE SATURDAY MORNING, I drove to a senior citizens' home in Santa
Monica, a small, beachfront city next to Los Angeles, where Gilda
Weinstein lived. Rose Ann Weinstein would join us. I hoped Gilda,
Michael's mother, and Rose Ann, his older sister, could answer a few
things I wanted to know about Michael.

I met Gilda in her room, where she sat in a leather chair. She
was eighty-eight years old and had been dealing with memory loss
the past few years, but she was smiling and seemed happy about my
visit. Rose Ann, who's four years older than Michael, sat on the edge
of her mother's bed. Both women were upbeat and attentive and

had alert eyes. Rose Ann worked as a physical therapist and looked after Gilda. Michael usually visited his mother on Sundays. Samuel Weinstein, Michael's father, had passed away in 2005 when he was eighty-nine.

Behind Gilda, on the wall, were four rows of shelves lined with vases that Gilda had made herself. There were also many framed pictures, including one of Michael and Gilda, another of Michael and Gilda with Magic Johnson, and another of Michael with Whoopi Goldberg. And there was a photograph of a young Samuel Weinstein in his army uniform during World War II and another as an older, gray-haired man, sitting in a chair and laughing.

On another wall were colorful pieces of Gilda's more abstract ceramic art, the same kind of pieces that appear on the walls of AHF offices. For many years, Gilda earned a living as a ceramic artist by selling vases to high-end florists in Greenwich Village. Samuel ran his own business delivering potato chips and pretzels to movie theaters. Samuel and Gilda were both born in New York City and both to Jewish parents who had emigrated from Russia.

Michael was born on October 3, 1952, and raised in the Bensonhurst section of Brooklyn, a working- and middle-class neighborhood of Jewish and Italian Americans. On the day of his birth, the United Kingdom conducted its first test of an atomic bomb—a secret project called "Operation Hurricane," which AHF's critics and supporters alike may find fitting. Also, in 1952, the United States was in the middle of a serious public health crisis: a polio outbreak had claimed more than three thousand lives and sparked a nationwide panic. In that same year, Dr. Jonas Salk started testing what would become the first successful polio vaccine, which would turn him into a national hero. Weinstein's supporters may also find these connections fitting. Weinstein, himself, is very aware of Salk's legacy.

When I talked with Gilda and Rose Ann, they spoke proudly and openly about Michael. Both have been his trusted confidantes,

especially Gilda before her memory declined. Whenever he needed honest advice, he'd talk with his mother, who'd ask a number of questions before weighing in. Gilda, who's known for her unedited directness, had no problem saying he was wrong or should do something differently.

Gilda and Rose Ann told me that Michael was an intelligent, well-informed, politically-minded child who sometimes chose friends based on whether they read the *New York Times*. And from early on, he showed the kind of independent thought and spirit that would help him establish a hard-charging organization like AHF.

"This is sort of a benchmark," said Rose Ann, who was close to Michael when growing up. "Before he got involved in local politics, he thought it would be great to be a senate or congressional page. We knew nothing about this. He was eleven, and I was fifteen. And we decided that we needed to go to Washington, DC, to visit the congressmen and our senators to see how you would apply to be a page.

"This is going to sound kind of crazy, but my dad drove Michael and me to the airport. At that time, they had student fares, so if you showed up at the airport, you'd get a half-price ticket. So the two of us showed up in Washington and didn't know where to stay. We just picked a hotel where we could walk to Congress, and we didn't know that it was in a very bad neighborhood.

"The next day, we went to the congressional and senate office buildings and tried to talk to our representatives. We had no idea how political it was. They were pleasant to us, but they must've been a little shocked to see two kids. And they said that you should talk to your local people, or you have to be recommended by somebody."

Despite such gumption, Michael didn't get the page job. Knowing that her brother didn't accept defeat easily, I chuckled and said that must have upset him. Rose Ann looked at me for a moment.

"That wasn't an aspect of his personality when he was a kid," she said. "He wasn't like, 'It has to be this way or that way.' He'd never been like that."

"He was always out for a cause!" Gilda added.

Rose Ann nodded. "He wasn't out for himself," she said. "It was always about justice. He was always so motivated to make things right and to get people taken care of."

I understood what they were saying. Just like his critics, I had failed to make a key distinction about Michael's character: what had always driven him was a cause bigger than himself.

I brought up Michael's urge to tell the truth as he saw it, no matter the consequences. I asked Rose Ann and Gilda where that came from.

"This would be a funny example from our childhood," Rose Ann said. "We were forced to take piano lessons because we had this piano. All of my mother's brothers and sisters had played on this piano growing up. Michael was a terrible pianist."

"He had no sense of music," Gilda added.

"I was eight when my mom started working part-time for a doctor's office," Rose Ann continued, "and so we were supposed to practice when we got home from school, and then my mom would get home and ask if we'd practiced. I'd put out the music on the music stand beforehand and say, 'Well, what does it look like?' And Michael would honestly say, 'I didn't practice.' He was never one to needle around."

Michael was also a youngster with a very active mind, and I mentioned a story that Miki Jackson, Michael's good friend, had shared with me. She said that Rose Ann had told her brother that just because he had good ideas didn't mean he had to act on every single one.

"I'm famous at AHF with that quote, apparently," Rose Ann said with a laugh, then switched to the voice of a vexed AHF employee. "'So why don't you listen to your sister?!'" She added quickly, "But it's a good thing he didn't listen to me—he wouldn't have done all those things!"

As one might suspect, the Weinstein children didn't grow up in an ordinary, blue-collar household. While Gilda was the disciplinarian and more traditional parent, Samuel was a nonmaterialistic left-winger

who deplored US Senator Joseph McCarthy's red-baiting policies during the first half of the 1950s; who adored Eleanor Roosevelt; who fully embraced the civil rights and anti–Vietnam War movements; who read avidly and closely followed politics; and who always challenged conventional wisdom and mainstream values. Samuel was very different from many of his peers and family members.

In addition, he loved sports and movies and had a deep knowledge of both subjects—Michael is also an avid moviegoer. Samuel was funny and smart. "He could do the *New York Times* Sunday crossword puzzle in ink," Rose Ann boasted. (For many New Yorkers, that feat holds more weight than a high IQ.) And her father was loyal to his parents, which was why Samuel was delivering potato chips and pretzels. It was a family business that his parents counted on for income.

That loyalty sometimes confused his son, who thought Samuel could have done bigger things. Yet Michael would later tell me that his father—not a famous activist or artist—was the person who most informed his iconoclastic ways at AHF.

Samuel deeply loved his children. He'd bring them to movies and Broadway plays, listen attentively to their thoughts about current affairs at the dinner table, support all of their interests, and drive Michael to protests in the 1960s. But Michael wanted his parents to do more than discuss politics—he wanted them to actively engage in the struggle of the civil rights and anti-war movements.

"He resented us a little bit because we would talk about these things, but we wouldn't do anything," Gilda said. "So he got us involved."

"He pushed my parents pretty hard," Rose Ann added.

I asked why it was important for Michael to get Samuel and Gilda involved in his causes. Many teenagers, after all, want to do their own thing without their parents. "He wanted people to be proactive," said Rose Anne.

"Don't just talk the talk," Gilda added.

Michael was certainly a doer.

In 1966, at the age of thirteen, he joined his first political campaign, working for anti-war Democratic candidate Mel Dubin, who was running for a US congressional seat in Brooklyn. Dubin lost by a handful of votes, but Michael loved the battle and fighting for a cause he believed in. He subsequently threw himself into the civil rights and anti-war movements, taking part in sit-ins and demonstrations. Sometimes he got his parents to join him. Gilda and Rose Ann were baffled about where Michael got the drive to actually do something about social injustice.

"The important thing was to right these wrongs," said Rose Ann, "and take care of the problem. But that's just him, and no one else in our family is like that."

"I don't know where Michael got the genes for doing things," Gilda said.

Rose Ann remembered watching the TV news with their father when they were kids in the 1950s. One big event was when Senator Joseph McCarthy, who would eventually be censured by his fellow senators, was dividing the nation and wrecking lives with his anti-communist witch hunt. Another was when the Arkansas National Guard, armed with rifles and taking orders from Governor Orval Faubus, stopped nine Black teenagers from integrating Little Rock Central High School. For the Weinstein children, who saw Samuel watch the news with unmuffled outrage, it all seemed crazy and unjust.

"We were all about the McCarthy hearings and all that sort of thing, and then the civil rights movement," Rose Ann recalled. "These groups were singled out and persecuted....I hadn't really synthesized it before talking to you, but that was such a powerful thing. I must have been nine, so Michael would have been five. The integration of the South and the persecution of the students who wanted to go to school—all of this was going on!"

In 1968, when he was fifteen years old, Michael worked on the campaign of anti-war presidential candidate Eugene McCarthy, a

maverick US senator from Minnesota. It was a rough, violent year in America. In April, Reverend Martin Luther King Jr., one of Michael's heroes, was assassinated in Memphis. Two months later, US senator and presidential candidate Robert F. Kennedy, another champion for the have-nots, was shot to death in LA. Two prominent men who gave voice to Michael's sense of social justice were viciously struck down. Then Michael took a trip with his twenty-one-year-old cousin, Mort Danziger, to Chicago.

Up to this point, Michael tried to work within the system to create change, and he went to Chicago, in August, to attend the Democratic National Convention to support Eugene McCarthy. On the third day of the convention, thousands of helmeted police officers charged young demonstrators in the streets, sprayed them with mace, whacked them bloody with billy clubs, and shot tear gas canisters into the crowds. Michael, who had joined the protestors, found himself in the middle of a riot, but dodged the police and avoided injury. By the time presidential nominee Hubert Humphrey gave his acceptance speech, Michael had come to a heady conclusion, which would forever inform his activism.

"I realized the system couldn't be changed from within," Michael would later tell me. "It felt like we were playing by the rules, but the fact that things were ending with a police riot and two leaders being assassinated led to a sense of defeat and hopelessness. How could you change anything if they could just gun people down and club people in the street?"

Only a few weeks before turning sixteen, Michael said, he had become "radicalized."

His father took a similar stand—Samuel vowed to not back Democratic candidate Hubert Humphrey. Instead, he was one of only 47,000 Americans who voted for Dick Gregory, an African American comedian, social critic, and civil rights activist who ran an unorthodox write-in campaign as a presidential candidate of the Freedom and Peace Party.

"He voted for the third-party candidate based on his conscience," Rose Ann said, "rather than worrying about the politics. We'd tell him that that's like throwing away your vote. But my dad didn't feel that way. He went on his principles."

I couldn't help but think that Michael had conducted himself the same way years later at AHF.

In addition to activism and school, Michael worked for his father and his maternal grandfather, a self-made man named David Lazar who was a risk-taker and inventor. Lazar once designed and manufactured small, personal vending machines for movie theater seats so people would not miss a second of a film if they got hungry. He later built up a small chain of homemade chocolate candy shops in Manhattan where Michael worked. A line of people often stretched out the door. While Samuel influenced his son's worldview, Michael would tell me, his grandfather showed him that he could strike out on his own and make something of himself.

I asked Rose Ann and Gilda if Michael had been a good kid.

"Yes," Rose Ann said. "Because all the things that he was involved in were good things. It wasn't like he was in a gang or something."

But, she added, "We always had ants in our pants. Michael is an ants-in-the-pants kind of person. He always had to be doing things. Like, I was a good reader. So if my mom said, go to your room, I thought, great, I can now read. But Michael wasn't like that. In school, he had problems with things, and he was restless. The teachers would say that he was always jumping out of his seat."

Michael made friends, Rose Ann said, but it wasn't always easy. "It was hard to find other children who were informed. I don't think it was too common."

Once you became his friend, he was dedicated to you—almost to a fault. "He's very loyal," said Rose Ann, "until a person pushes him to a point."

Sometimes Gilda took heat from other adults who thought Michael and Rose Ann, who started Cornell University when she

was sixteen, were too independent. They especially thought Michael needed reining in.

"They couldn't believe that we let them do the things we did," Gilda said. "But I said, 'Well, you don't know Michael.'"

Michael, however, wasn't without plans and considered being an architect—he and Rose Ann admired Frank Lloyd Wright's work. He was admitted to the High School of Art and Design, a selective public school in Manhattan. But he dropped out to start his own high school with a group of friends. That didn't last long either. Since he wanted to attend college, he took and passed the GED.

(Weinstein's artistic sensibilities and architectural interests have never left him. He gets a noticeable pleasure from creating AHF marketing campaigns, and he's very involved in the construction or renovation of the organization's clinics and offices. He even chooses the carpeting and interior colors. When I once asked what he wanted to come back as in another life, he said, without hesitation, "a fine artist.")

In the early 1970s, Michael wrote an important letter to Samuel and Gilda, who had moved to Manhattan. Rose Ann was living in upstate New York and received a copy in the mail. When Michael was fifteen years old, he had realized he liked other boys. He'd also felt panic and tried to banish any homosexual thoughts from his mind—he even lived with an older woman when he was eighteen. Now, in the letter, he was coming out to his family as a gay man.

It was not an accepting time for gays and lesbians. The modern gay rights movement had only started a few years earlier with the Stonewall Riots in New York City; the American Psychiatric Association had just removed homosexuality from its list of mental illnesses; and people continued to be fired from their jobs for being gay. But Samuel and Gilda were not hypocrites.

"My parents, their principles, they accepted it on principle," Rose Ann recalled, "but they thought that his life was going to be tough, so my parents were protective. But my parents knew a lot of

gay people because they lived in Greenwich Village. My mom sold pottery to the florists there. It is a cliché, but most of them were gay. So she was in that environment, but, at first, she didn't want to see him being affectionate. My dad was more accepting than my mom was at first. That was an interesting thing."

By this point in our conversation, Gilda had left for lunch, and Rose Ann and I talked a bit more. I wanted to know if Michael's feelings ever got hurt when he took certain public stands, which were sometimes aggressively criticized by people in the AIDS movement. "After all," I said, "he's human."

"I would think so," Rose Ann said, "but if he's hurt by things, he doesn't share it. If I'm talking on the phone and I hear something in his voice, I'll say something. And he'll say, 'Oh, something happened,' and then he'll move on. He doesn't dwell on those things."

She added, "There are so many things happening at AHF that there isn't time to dwell on it. It boggles my mind how he runs this thing. It is incomprehensible to me."

Rose Ann continued, "For me, I just think that people mischaracterize him. But they have their own agendas, and they think that AHF's work takes away from them. There's always been that conflict with AIDS Project Los Angeles and AHF. They've really been pretty negative over the years. AHF gets attention because they do things that are out of the box, and people go, 'Oh, what are those guys doing?!'"

I asked if Michael could help himself by being more diplomatic.

"I don't know if he's capable of doing that because then you're sort of lying," Rose Ann replied. "His problem is that maybe he's too honest."

When Gilda returned from lunch, Rose Ann and I prepared to go. Before we left, as a female nurse helped Gilda get situated in her room, Rose Ann spotted dust on her mother's framed pictures. It reminded me of Michael at one of the marketing meetings, noting that the font size of a billboard looked too big. Also like Michael, Rose Ann didn't worry about coming off as fussy. She firmly, yet respectfully told the nurse that her mother's room needed a dusting.

Chapter 7

Feisty Activists Meet

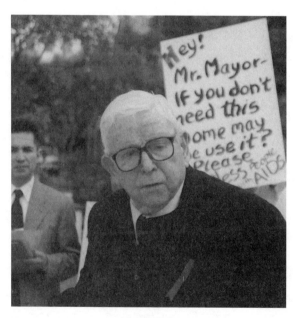

Morris Kight

By 1972, WEINSTEIN WAS searching for a calling in his life. He was still living in New York City and worked as a nineteen-year-old grassroots activist for a social justice organization called Centers for Change. One of his assignments was to travel around the US and build up a network of community activists. Weinstein decided to visit the Gay Community Services Center in Los Angeles, which was cofounded by gay-rights activists Morris Kight, John Platania, and

Don Kilhefner. It was one of the first LGBT centers in the nation, if not the world.

Los Angeles had always been a hotbed of gay-rights activity, which the book *Gay LA: A History of Sexual Outlaws, Power Politics, and Lipstick Lesbians* by Lillian Faderman and Stuart Timmons capably lays out. In 1950, for example, the Mattachine Society, one of the first modern gay-rights organizations in the US, was established in LA by gay-rights icon Harry Hay. *ONE* magazine, the first national publication for gays and lesbians, and the *Advocate*, the nation's largest and oldest LGBT newsmagazine, were also started in Los Angeles. And the Municipal Elections Committee of Los Angeles (MECLA), the country's first openly gay political action committee, was founded in the city. There were also such groups as the Gay Liberation Front and Gay Women's Liberation.

The Gay Community Services Center, which opened in 1971, was located in an old, beaten-up Victorian house on Wilshire Boulevard. It offered legal services, support groups, and a free venereal disease clinic, where gay men could get treated without fear of judgment. Years later, the Gay Community Services Center would change its name to the LA Gay & Lesbian Center, which changed its name again to the Los Angeles LGBT Center.

"It was a very specific idea: for gay people, by gay people," Mary Ann Cherry, Kight's biographer, told me. "People went into that place scared because they knew once they entered that their lives were going to be changed. They came out not only empowered but happy. There was a reckoning of self that happened in that house and also a coming to terms of broken individuals who were creating a community."

When Weinstein arrived at the center, he found a bustling hangout for political types, do-gooders, and nonconformists.

"It was a very vibrant time," Weinstein told me, "and that specific place, the center, was on the vanguard of gay rights. There was something constantly going on or some kind of demonstration."

Through the center, Weinstein met Kight, a high-profile member of the Gay Liberation Front and a prominent figure in gay Los Angeles. Born in Comanche County, Texas, in 1919, Kight was brainy, creative, tenacious, outrageous, and well educated. He sometimes clashed with other gay-rights activists and practiced an activism that was decidedly community-based. He would become a mentor to Weinstein—a portrait of Kight, who died in 2003, hangs on a wall near Weinstein's office at Sunset Media Center.

"They were very close," Cherry said. "Michael confided in Morris about a lot of things. Morris gave him a lot of ground to stand on, encouraged him to be bold, and to draw outside the lines, so to speak."

Miki Jackson, who had worked closely with Kight since the late 1960s and had been a consultant and confidante for Weinstein since the mid-1990s, told me about Weinstein and Kight: "It was a storied relationship in a way—mentor, teacher, and sometimes opponent. There were times they disagreed. There were times when they agreed and worked together. Michael always felt there was much he could learn from Morris. Morris would say that out of all the people who came to him and learned something and participated, Michael was by far the one who had done the most good. That didn't mean that Michael did it the way Morris did it. Michael did it his own way. But there were things that Morris taught us all, and he was a great mentor. He taught us to be unselfish in our work and to really work for a goal and to make sacrifices."

At the Gay Community Services Center, Weinstein also befriended Mina Meyer and Sharon Raphael—the lesbian couple who rode on AHF's 2014 Rose Parade float. In 1972, Meyer and Raphael, both of whom are intellectual, sassy, and opinionated, were already trailblazing activists. They once ran the Gay Women's Services Center, one of the first programs in the nation that was designed specifically for lesbians and provided legal services, support groups, and temporary housing. When that center closed, Meyer and Raphael were recruited to work for the Gay Community

Services Center, where Meyer created the country's first medical clinic for lesbians. Today, the couple, who have been together for more than forty years, live in Long Beach, California.

Meyer and Raphael were ten years older than Weinstein and found the teenager endearing. He had a winning personality, according to Meyer, and the right kind of politics—and he was already showing strong leadership skills.

"There was something unique about him," Raphael, a longtime sociology professor at Cal State University, Dominguez Hills, told me.

Weinstein also met Chris Brownlie and Mary Adair at the Victorian house on Wilshire Boulevard. Brownlie was twenty-two years old and brainy and an aspiring writer from Farmington, New York. Mary Adair was nineteen years old and bright and an aspiring opera singer from Portsmouth, Virginia. Brownlie and Adair were tight friends, and they attended support groups at the center.

"We'd go to those groups and talk about coming out and what it was like and how our parents relate to it and falling in love for the first time," Adair told me.

They would all come together—Weinstein, Kight, Meyer, Raphael, Brownlie, and Adair—fifteen years later to create AHF. A few other friends would also make important contributions. Without the Gay Community Services Center, which was a magnet for the kind of dynamic, tough-minded people needed to get results during the early years of the AIDS crisis, the activists might have never found each other.

—

WEINSTEIN ENJOYED LA IMMENSELY. The Mediterranean climate, of course, was terrific, and one could live well in the city without going broke. Los Angeles was also wide open to anyone with a pioneering spirit, which was in evidence with the start-up of the many gay and lesbian services. Weinstein went back to New York for a time, and then moved to a little house in West Hollywood with his first serious

boyfriend, who was an actor. Chris Brownlie, who needed a place to stay and some looking after, joined them.

"Before HIV or anything," Weinstein said, "Chris always seemed to be sick—he was always fragile. So he stayed with us in the little two-bedroom house."

When Weinstein's relationship ended, the actor left the house, and Weinstein and Brownlie grew closer. They were both smart and shared similar values and, like many young activists, enjoyed talking about ways to change the world. But Brownlie, whose mother had died years earlier, was a little different from the unorthodox Weinstein.

"Chris was sort of a dichotomy," Weinstein said. "In one respect, he was kind of conventional. He wasn't fashionable in his dress. He was an avid sports fan. He could amuse himself with crossword puzzles endlessly. He and my father got along very well because of those things. But this other side of him was radical."

Their personalities were also different. Friends described Brownlie to me as "loving," "emotional," "sweet," "caring," and "precious." Brownlie, in other words, displayed his emotions openly. Weinstein was more composed and cerebral.

"Michael and Chris were this yin-yang kind of thing," said Adair, who's now director of AHF's task shifting programs. "Chris was very well spoken, and he was that type of very warm, hugging kind of person. Michael was more political and get out there and get the work done."

Brownlie was also more inclined to be a peacemaker and try to win people over.

"It was a lot easier for me to write somebody off and say they're a jerk and I don't want to talk to them," Weinstein explained. "We used to have these really bitter debates because he believed that you could reach everyone, and I would say that's bullshit. I tended to think that there was inherent evil in a lot of people. We used to also have quite heated arguments about how I was more a believer in the ends justified the means, and he was less on that spectrum. I thought you

had to use the weapons of your opponents to defeat them, and he didn't really go along with that. He was very militant in his own way."

Years later, when they founded AHF, Weinstein said, he and Brownlie successfully modified each other.

"His willingness to go and talk to other activists was good," said Weinstein. "He was able to reach some of them, and there were people who weren't as hopeless as I thought they were. It worked out well."

In 1976, the year of America's Bicentennial, Weinstein attended a gay liberation dance with Chris Brownlie at Larchmont Hall, a red brick community center in LA's Larchmont neighborhood. As a deejay played songs by Wild Cherry and KC and the Sunshine Band, Weinstein spotted a handsome, twenty-five-year-old Mexican American named Albert Ruiz. Weinstein was instantly smitten. So was Brownlie.

"Chris really had a crush on me," Ruiz told me, "and my roommate had a crush on Michael. So Chris and I went out a number of times, but it never really went too far. But Michael had a really bad crush on me. I later found that out, and we got together."

Weinstein and Ruiz moved into an apartment in Hollywood and would remain a couple for more than twenty years. Ruiz, a kind, good-humored native of Montebello, California, would be one of Weinstein's most important confidantes. Today, Weinstein still considers Ruiz, who works for AHF as a director of wellness center programs, his "closest friend." Rose Ann Weinstein described them as "brothers."

"I trust him completely," Michael said.

Not long after the dance, Weinstein and Ruiz, along with Brownlie, joined the Lavender and Red Union, a left-wing gay liberation group that was founded in Los Angeles. At the time, many left-wing organizations were either lukewarm to the gay rights movement or outright homophobic. The Lavender and Red Union, perhaps ironically in Weinstein's case, worked to create change from within left-

wing political circles. It also battled racism in the gay community, which other gay groups regularly ignored—a little-discussed reality that Weinstein would always be mindful of during his work at AHF.

In 1977, however, Weinstein's political work with the Lavender and Red Union took him back to New York, where racial tensions were high, the serial killer Son of Sam had put New Yorkers on edge, and a massive blackout had plunged the city into chaos. Ruiz, who went with Weinstein, landed a job at AT&T. Weinstein attended City College of New York and studied architecture. To make money, Weinstein briefly worked as a waiter at Windows on the World, a popular restaurant at the top of the World Trade Center in Lower Manhattan. It didn't suit him.

"He was a terrible waiter," Rose Ann said. "He just wasn't waiter material. You have to act to be a good waiter, which is maybe why so many actors have wait jobs. They act like a great waiter."

That same year, Weinstein met Paul Coleman, a member of the left-wing Spartacist League, which had merged with the Lavender and Red Union. Coleman was a UC Berkeley graduate and native San Franciscan, whose parents, as he described them, were "intellectual radicals." He was two years older than Weinstein and had the same kind of spunk and intellectual might, although Coleman was perhaps more militant.

"We were the first generation that said we're not going to be in the closet anymore," Coleman said, "and we don't care what anyone thinks. And if you have a problem, then fuck you—it's your problem. That was the attitude from day one. It was that generation."

The two instantly bonded.

"We were like a tsunami washing over you," said Coleman. "Together, we were formidable, to say the least."

—

BY THE LATE 1970S, Weinstein had been an activist for more than a decade, but he was starting to reassess everything. The internecine

battles of the left-wing and gay-rights movements, in his mind, impeded progress, and the gay political establishment dismayed him.

"It was a very insular thing," Weinstein said. "It was as though groups defined themselves on who they excluded. Also, it was a very narrow agenda or point of view on the world, and it was a turnoff."

Political ideology was now less attractive to him. He felt it didn't give him room to think for himself.

"I always had this practical aspect about how to get things done in the real world," Weinstein said, "but I was also caught up in these abstract ideological things that wasted a lot of time and energy."

In 1980, the year that Ronald Reagan defeated President Jimmy Carter, sparking the rise of modern-day conservatism, Weinstein left activism to concentrate exclusively on architecture.

"I really wanted to advance and make something of myself professionally," he said.

But Weinstein wasn't looking to be a run-of-the-mill architect. Like his hero, Frank Lloyd Wright, Weinstein wanted to do work that brought joy and serenity to people's everyday living.

"It wasn't just about building a building," he said. "It was about creating a social, humanistic environment."

Not long after Reagan's inauguration, in 1981, a gay neighbor who was a doctor told Weinstein and Ruiz that gay men in New York City were mysteriously falling ill. That same year, the Centers for Disease Control published a scary, groundbreaking report by Dr. Michael Gottlieb, who specialized in immunology at UCLA. He found that five gay men in Los Angeles had inexplicably come down with Pneumocystis carinii pneumonia, and they all appeared to be suffering from immune system disorders. It was later recognized as the first official documentation of AIDS cases in the US. A year later, the term "Acquired Immune Deficiency Syndrome" was conceived.

Weinstein remained focused on his career, and he and Ruiz left for London in 1982. Weinstein had won a scholarship to study at the prestigious Architectural Association School of Architecture.

Ruiz attended Le Cordon Bleu, a culinary arts school. When they weren't studying, Weinstein and Ruiz traveled throughout Europe, including the Soviet Union. Upon their return to New York City, in 1983, Weinstein and Ruiz concluded it was time to move back to California.

"I had enough of New York," Ruiz told me. "Also, my mother at the time was transitioning—she had breast cancer, and my brother had been taking care of her for a number of years. So I wanted to be with her and closer to home."

The plan was for Weinstein to study architecture at California Polytechnic State University in San Luis Obispo, a coastal town midway between Los Angeles and San Francisco. But he had been thinking for a while that architecture might not suit him—he thought there'd be little demand for his humanistic approach, and he'd have to work on projects that wouldn't interest him. Also, Ruiz's fifty-eight-year-old mother, Julie, was taking a turn for the worse. After a few weeks of school, Weinstein decided that architecture wasn't his calling, and Ruiz and he moved to Montebello and stayed with Julie.

"She didn't want to be in a hospital," Ruiz recalled, "and we didn't want to put her in a hospital. She really wanted to die at home."

Mina Meyer and Sharon Raphael, who had kept in touch with Weinstein and Ruiz, suggested hospice care for Ruiz's mother. It was an innovative approach not widely used in the US, which attended to the physical pain and emotional needs of a seriously ill patient. As gerontologists, Meyer and Raphael were strong advocates of hospice care for ailing gay and lesbian seniors. With their expertise, they helped Ruiz and Weinstein set things up. Months later, in 1983, Ruiz's mother passed away at home—with dignity and surrounded by family. Weinstein took note.

As more and more people died from AIDS, Meyer, Raphael, and Weinstein started discussing hospice care for terminally ill AIDS patients. In 1983, 2,304 people died from AIDS-related illnesses in the US. The year before, 853 people had died from AIDS. Nobody

understood what was to come, yet at the same time, there were no signs that the epidemic was slowing down, and certain measures needed to be taken.

"We were thinking that they'll find a cure," Meyer recalled, "but, in the meantime, it seemed like hospice would fit, that it would be a good thing to have."

New York writer Larry Kramer, who cofounded the Gay Men's Health Crisis in 1982, was not as optimistic about a cure. In March 1983, Kramer sounded the alarm with his explosive, impassioned essay "1,112 and Counting." First published in the *New York Native*, a biweekly gay newspaper, Kramer's piece made its way into the hands of gay men across the country.

"If this article doesn't scare the shit out of you," Kramer wrote, "we're in real trouble. If this article doesn't rouse you to anger, fury, rage, and action, gay men have no future on this earth. Our continued existence depends on just how angry you can get."

Later in the essay, Kramer described what thousands of people were facing in New York, Los Angeles, and other American cities and towns.

"Many serious victims of AIDS have been unable to qualify for welfare or disability or social security benefits," Kramer wrote. "There are increasing numbers of men unable to work and unable to claim welfare because AIDS is not on the list of qualifying disability illnesses. (Immune deficiency is an acceptable determining factor for welfare among children but not adults. Figure that one out.) There are also increasing numbers of men unable to pay their rent, men thrown out on the street with nowhere to live and no money to live with, and men who have been asked by roommates to leave because of their illnesses. And men with serious AIDS are being fired from certain jobs.

"I am angry and frustrated almost beyond the bounds my skin and bones and body and brain can encompass. My sleep is tormented by nightmares and visions of lost friends, and my days are flooded by the tears of funerals and memorial services and seeing my sick friends. How many of us must die before all of us living fight back?"

Around the same time, Mary Adair was working at USC Kenneth Norris Jr. Cancer Hospital, near downtown Los Angeles. Among her duties, Adair was drawing the blood of young gay men who looked beyond death. She called Brownlie and Weinstein.

"It was just horrid," Adair told me. "I would see them lined up in these long hallways, on the hard benches, covered in [Kaposi's sarcoma] lesions....I said, 'Guys, we've got to get involved here. You guys are political. You've got to do this!' I said, 'Call the *LA Times*. This is Dante's *Inferno* here. Call them!'"

Weinstein was deeply concerned, and, like many others, he was outraged by the federal government's slow, unsympathetic response to AIDS. Kramer's essay was stuck in his mind as well.

"Larry Kramer was the person most responsible for the birth of AIDS activism," Weinstein said. "Set aside Kramer's noise and drama and performance art—he got the gay community angry enough to do something and not just be lambs to the slaughter."

But in his thirties and unsure about a career, Weinstein was hesitant to throw himself into AIDS activism.

"You have to come to terms at that age that if you're going to have any success or higher standard, then you better get busy," Weinstein said. "It's not that you're old, but if you haven't started something by thirty-five and aren't attracted to anything by forty, there's a good chance you're not going to wind up anywhere at all."

In 1984, Weinstein returned to his roots in a way. That year, the Summer Olympics was held in Los Angeles, where Angelenos and fanny-packed tourists were giddy with Olympic fever. Inspired by his grandfather, Weinstein started up a candy company with Ruiz called Gold Medal Chocolates. Gilda and Samuel Weinstein didn't approve and sounded a note similar to Adair's.

"My parents didn't like the idea of me being involved in business," Michael said. "They were really into, especially my father, making a contribution."

The company was profitable. But once the Olympics were over, there was little demand for chocolate gold medals. Ruiz saw that they were headed for trouble. Weinstein was determined to make a go of it.

"We had no chance," Ruiz recalled with a chuckle. "There was no way. But you know Michael. It's hard to keep him down." He added, "We lost our asses off in the candy business, but Michael learned from that—how to deal with money better."

Gold Medal Chocolates went out of business in 1986, and Weinstein was broke and somewhat rudderless. Then Lyndon LaRouche Jr. came onto the California political scene.

—

LaRouche, a cult-like figure, and his followers had formed a group called "PANIC," or "Prevent AIDS Now Initiative Committee," which had successfully placed an initiative known as Proposition 64 on California's November 1986 ballot. PANIC sought to put AIDS on the state's communicable diseases list, which would allow public health officials to isolate or quarantine people with AIDS. Also, if people with AIDS worked at a job in which they came into contact with a large number of people, they could be fired.

Medical experts decried the ballot measure as unscientific, harmful, and overkill, particularly the idea of quarantine. They feared that if Proposition 64 became law, and quarantines were imposed, people would not get tested and the spread of AIDS would worsen. During the summer of 1986, though, polls showed that a majority of California voters backed the initiative. An op-ed writer in the *New York Times* deemed Proposition 64 "the biggest referendum yet on AIDS policy in the United States."

For gays and lesbians in California, where thousands of gay men had died from AIDS, where the majority of a scared public favored quarantines, and where gay Californians felt under attack, Proposition 64 was barbaric and homophobic. It was also the final straw.

"It was like the perfect storm," Ruiz explained. "You were getting this ballot initiative, and you have friends dying every month. The only way to deal with it was to fight back."

Mary Adair said, "We thought it was going to be like every other oppressive law toward gays and lesbians."

Paul Coleman told me, "After five years of grief and everyone dying, here comes LaRouche saying that we're going to put you in concentration camps. It was like, what the fuck? That's not going to happen."

Weinstein, however, continued to be wary of AIDS activism, especially if it meant working with California's gay political establishment.

"I was looking for something different in my life," he told me candidly. "It wasn't something that I sought out. Chris and Mary were guilt-tripping me into it."

After attending a No on 64 campaign meeting in West Hollywood with Brownlie, Weinstein finally gave in but told Chris he needed to work outside the gay establishment. He recalled, "I said, 'Look, I'm willing to help, but not as a part of this. I can't go to these meetings or deal with these establishment people. First of all, it's not urgent enough, particularly in the face of LaRouche and the concentration camps. Second of all, there are going to be endless meetings, and nothing is going to get done.'"

Similar to starting up his own high school or candy company, Weinstein proposed launching their own political group, the name of which was direct and unequivocal and somewhat menacing: Stop the AIDS Quarantine Committee.

Chapter 8

Stop the AIDS Quarantine Committee & Los Angeles AIDS Hospice Committee

URGENT COMMUNITY MEETING
STOP AIDS
CONCENTRATION
CAMPS
THURSDAY, JULY 24th AT 7:30
• Silverlake Recreation Center •
1850 W. Silver Lake Blvd., Los Angeles
South End of Reservoir

There is an initiative on the November ballot which would mandate the quarantine and detention of any person with AIDS or with antibodies to the virus. The specter of AIDS concentration camps, along with a host of other repressive measures, defies all medical common sense and preys upon public fears.

This initiative is promoted by a group called PANIC which is affiliated with the right wing fanatic Lyndon LaRouche.

Join with the STOP AIDS QUARANTINE COMMITTEE to defeat this vicious attack. If you value your freedom you must get involved now—after November will be too late.

- -

☐ I cannot attend the meeting but I am interested in contributing $_____ .

☐ I cannot attend the meeting but I am interested in volunteering.

Name _____ Address _____

Phone _____

STOP THE AIDS QUARANTINE COMMITTEE
(213) 661-1664, (818) 241-8757
4010 Santa Monica Blvd., Los Angeles, CA 90029

Signing for the
Hearing Impaired

Labor Donated
Type donated by TradeMark Type

Stop the AIDS Quarantine Committee flyer

118

SOCIAL MEDIA DID NOT exist in 1986. Neither did email nor texting nor the World Wide Web. To spread the word about Stop the AIDS Quarantine Committee's first public meeting, Weinstein, Brownlie, and their friends stood outside shopping centers and gay bars for hours at a time, handing out hundreds of flyers. When a person read the leaflet, he or she was probably jolted by its subject matter and directness.

"URGENT COMMUNITY MEETING," the top of the flyer read in bold, black letters. "STOP AIDS CONCENTRATION CAMPS."

It went on: "There is an initiative on the November ballot which would mandate the quarantine and detention of any person with AIDS or with antibodies to the virus. The specter of AIDS concentration camps, along with a host of other repressive measures, defies all medical common sense and preys upon public fears.

"This initiative is promoted by a group called PANIC, which is affiliated with the right-wing fanatic Lyndon LaRouche.

"Join with the STOP [THE] AIDS QUARANTINE COMMITTEE to defeat this vicious attack. If you value your freedom, you must get involved now—after November will be too late."

Weinstein, who helped write the flyer, had been away from serious activism for six years. Now, confronting LaRouche and PANIC, he was back in the thick of the fight.

The nucleus of the quarantine committee was comprised of friends from the days of the Gay Community Services Center and Spartacist League: Weinstein and Ruiz; Mina Meyer and Sharon Raphael; Mary Adair; Chris Brownlie and his boyfriend, Phill Wilson; and Paul Coleman and his boyfriend, Mark Gallardo. The committee, which was small and underfunded, planned to battle the LaRouche campaign in a crucial battleground: Los Angeles County. For statewide races in California, whoever won LA County—the most populous county in the state—often won the election.

The Proposition 64 fight also had national ramifications. If AIDS quarantines were set up in politically progressive/libertarian California, it was easy to think that other states would do something

similar. "As California goes," according to the old maxim, "so goes the nation."

Weinstein's instincts were correct, however, that a leap into AIDS activism would involve a tense tango with California's gay political establishment, which was mostly composed of politically connected, affluent, white men. The No on 64 campaign, which spearheaded the official effort to defeat the ballot measure, was largely funded by gay establishment money and headed by gay-rights leaders who took orders from that establishment. It wanted things done a certain way.

Over the years, the gay establishment had cultivated alliances with gay-friendly politicians in the California Democratic Party. For the gay rights movement to be successful, the common wisdom went, it needed powerful friends in high places. It was a strategy that worked at times. But it also involved playing by the rules of the politicians, which meant a middle-of-the-road, go-along-to-get-along approach that didn't risk offending voters, especially when an issue was linked to homosexuality. No on 64, as a result, ran a polite campaign against a belligerent opponent in PANIC. There was little, if any, mention of quarantines.

"This tamer opposition to Proposition 64 wasn't delivering the message of what a dangerous idea the quarantines were," Miki Jackson explained.

Stop the AIDS Quarantine Committee, on the other hand, was organizing an urgent, grassroots campaign. It focused on empowering the LGBTQ+ community and educating LA County voters with blunt, straightforward messaging. Talking about AIDS concentration camps was considered too militant by the gay elite.

"The gay establishment did not like that," Paul Coleman told me with a laugh. "'Don't say that! It's going to shock people too much!' We were saying, 'No, we're going to call it what it is.' They didn't like that right off the bat."

The mention of "concentration camps" wasn't out of order for those who knew their history. During the Nazi regime in Germany,

for example, an estimated five thousand to fifteen thousand gays were sent to concentration camps between 1933 and 1945 under a criminal code known as Paragraph 175. Proposition 64 was wickedly similar.

Coleman further explained, "It's always the same old thing: 'Don't yell too loud, you're going to upset people, and don't push too hard.' That's what the establishment says to every movement that comes along. 'You're going to alienate people, and you're going to make them react.' Whether it's the Black movement, gay movement, Latino movement, or whatever movement."

The brash yet seasoned activists of the quarantine committee were not a welcomed addition to the Proposition 64 fight.

"We weren't part of the establishment," said Sharon Raphael. "We were trying to make certain changes, and they were concerned about control and power."

Catching flak from the political and gay establishments—risk-averse politicians, mainstream gay-rights and AIDS organizations, and the wealthy gay men and women who funded those politicians and organizations—would repeat itself throughout AHF's history.

Weinstein said, "In fairness to that group, rubbing elbows and that kind of thing did a lot of good. They got people like Ted Kennedy and Jerry Brown, but it was so ill-suited to what was happening in 1986. We obviously had to have a knockdown fight because of the way we were being treated. People were dropping like flies. There was no time for rubbing elbows."

Many ordinary people who were not political insiders agreed—something that would also happen time and again in AHF's history. On July 24, nearly a hundred men and women showed up at the Silver Lake Recreation Center to hear about Stop the AIDS Quarantine Committee's campaign strategy. The committee had set up its headquarters nearby in a small, fluorescent-lit office above a rundown storefront in Silver Lake, a diverse, working- and middle-class neighborhood five miles northwest of downtown LA.

What the quarantine committee proposed at the meeting was electrifying, and, to some, outrageous. In about seven weeks, on September 15, Stop the AIDS Quarantine Committee wanted to confront PANIC on its home turf with a "torchlight march." Not a solemn "candlelight" march but one with actual torches.

"We did that intentionally," said Coleman. "Was it threatening? It was, and we meant it to be threatening."

First, the quarantine committee would hold a public rally at Friendship Auditorium near the Los Angeles River. After a few speeches, everyone would march with their torches to LaRouche's headquarters a mile away in the LA neighborhood of Atwater Village. The quarantine committee, Coleman said, wanted "to intimidate the hell out of the LaRouche camp."

It was a bold, possibly dangerous strategy.

LaRouche and his followers were no pushovers. They had been routinely accused of using intimidation tactics—picketing offices, making harassing phone calls, sending threatening notes—against perceived enemies, who included labor leaders, politicians, and journalists. During the petition drive to put LaRouche's initiative on the 1986 ballot, California Secretary of State March Fong Eu, whose office supervised elections, reprimanded the LaRouche campaign, demanding that it stop "harassing" people. Facing such an opponent, Stop the AIDS Quarantine Committee planned to use LaRouche's own weapons to defeat him.

But when word spread about the torchlight march, LA's gay establishment was appalled and attempted to shut down the event.

"The gay establishment worked overtime to tell people, 'Don't go,'" said Paul Coleman. "So we said, 'Okay, we don't know what's going to happen,' and we worked overtime."

During the weeks leading up to the torchlight march, committee members rigorously promoted the event while also raising awareness about Proposition 64. They fanned out across Los Angeles County and handed out more than sixty-five thousand flyers in such places as West Hollywood, Long Beach, the San Fernando Valley, Hollywood,

and Silver Lake. The leaflets, which were given to all kinds of people, once again warned of "AIDS concentration camps."

For another widely distributed flyer leading up to Election Day, the quarantine committee hit upon a theme that would become a lifelong mantra for Weinstein and continues to guide AHF's work. In large, black letters at the top of the leaflet, it read, "PROTECT THE PUBLIC HEALTH." The flyer described Proposition 64 as a "serious threat to the public health" that "defies medical common sense and preys on fears. America's #1 health problem deserves a more responsible and educated approach."

"This was our main thing," Coleman told me, "to protect the public health!"

Pushing such a reasoned message, the quarantine committee secured mainstream endorsements for the march, including actress Patty Duke, the president of the Screen Actors Guild; Jackie Goldberg, a Los Angeles Unified School District board member; and Wayne Johnson, president of United Teachers Los Angeles, a powerful labor union. And the committee sought the expertise of other LA-based activists. One of them was John Brown, a go-getting, third-generation Californian, who would become one of AHF's first board members.

Born in 1950, Brown grew up in Whittier, a middle-class town twenty miles southeast of downtown Los Angeles. Brown moved from that quiet suburb to LA in 1978 and was among the first of many gay men to settle in Silver Lake. But they didn't want the neighborhood to turn into another West Hollywood—meaning, to them, heavily white and gay and male.

"We wanted it to remain diverse," Brown told me, "and be careful about the mix of people."

To ease growing tensions between the gay and Latino communities—gay men, at times, were physically attacked by some Latinos—Brown and other activists threw a street party on Sunset Boulevard so that Silver Lake residents could get to know each other. Started in 1980, the Sunset Junction Street Fair was an instant

success, and Brown became widely known and well-connected. In 1982, he was a steering committee member for the founding of AIDS Project Los Angeles, the preeminent AIDS organization in LA, which held the world's first AIDS Walk in 1985. The gay establishment enthusiastically supported APLA with money and set it up with political and showbiz connections. In the mid-1980s, as the executive director of the LA Gay & Lesbian Center, Brown helped establish the first HIV/AIDS clinic in Los Angeles.

Brown, though, was not another cautious member of the gay elite. He liked the quarantine committee's fighting spirit and knew about crowd control from his work on the Sunset Junction Street Fair. When Weinstein and Coleman asked for help, Brown eagerly signed on. He quickly felt an affinity for Weinstein that would continue for decades.

"He was great to work with," Brown said. "I would love when he'd get excited and start talking about things; he was filled with this passion."

Weinstein's attention, though, was not limited to Proposition 64. As the quarantine committee members met with other activists, Weinstein, Brownlie, Meyer, and the others kept learning more about LA County government's scandalous response to AIDS.

LA County was one of the worst AIDS epicenters in the US with nearly 3,000 cases by the end of 1986—only San Francisco and New York City had more. But the mostly conservative board of supervisors, a five-member governing body that presided over a $7.1 billion annual budget that included a public health department, seemed uncomfortable with homosexuality and uninformed about AIDS prevention and treatment.

Five years after Dr. Michael Gottlieb published his ground-breaking report about gay men in LA with immune-system disorders, LA County had yet to develop a long-term, coordinated plan for AIDS prevention and treatment. And there was only one county-sponsored outpatient AIDS clinic and only one county-sponsored HIV testing program in a region with 8.3 million people. The

county's AIDS program had not even launched a robust prevention effort. According to a damning *Los Angeles Times* editorial in March 1987, San Francisco officials spent ten times more on AIDS than LA's supervisors, which prompted the newspaper to note that the county's AIDS response was "conspicuous for its inadequacy."

It just so happened that all this was unfolding under the watch of APLA, the darling of LA's gay political establishment. That did not go unnoticed by *LA Weekly*, which reported extensively on the AIDS crisis. "Los Angeles is the sort of city where most gay politics is moneyed and polite," the alternative paper noted disapprovingly. "It's the home of ME-CLA, which prefers discreet lobbying to displays of anger, and of AIDS Project LA, which dislikes boat-rocking so much it hasn't confronted the LA County Board of Supervisors on its knee-jerk homophobia."

But certain battles needed to be fought first. On September 15, hours before the torchlight march, Weinstein, Brownlie, Coleman, and their friends readied themselves. Friendship Auditorium had been rented and prepared, more than a hundred torches were ready to be lit, and the LA media had been alerted. Both Weinstein and Coleman would give speeches. But no one knew how many people would actually show up.

By seven thirty that evening, the auditorium, which seated five hundred people, was filled beyond capacity, with another large crowd waiting outside to march. The *Los Angeles Times* conservatively estimated "over two thousand" people attended the event. Quarantine committee members believed the figure was closer to five thousand.

"We were surprised by the turnout," Weinstein told me.

Miki Jackson, who shuttled people to Friendship Auditorium, wasn't so astonished. The rally and march, she thought, were destined to attract people.

"It really struck a chord because there was a fear of the quarantines," Jackson explained. "It was a very strange and frightening time—people were sick and dying all over the place. Things were still new, and there were no treatments, and people died rapidly and horribly."

Before the torchlight march kicked off, Coleman told a pumped-up crowd that, in a matter of weeks, voters could defeat Proposition 64 and prevent the same kind of internment camps in California that Japanese-American citizens were forced into during World War II.

"I got louder applause for that than any other thing I said," Coleman recalled. "The roof came down."

Thousands of men and women then poured into the streets, marching and chanting and thrusting tiki torches into the sky. When they stopped in front of LaRouche's headquarters in Atwater Village, many people hoisted placards that read, "LaRouche: Public Health Enemy #1." That evening, the march led all the local TV news broadcasts. In the following days, numerous newspapers reported about what took place. PANIC had been put on notice, the voters had been informed, and activists and the LGBT community felt empowered.

"We were a movement at that point," said Sharon Raphael.

The LaRouche camp tried to spin the march as a "terrorist incident," according to the *LA Times*, but the quarantine committee didn't back down. In October, it organized a car caravan with two other anti–Proposition 64 groups. Hundreds of people drove all over LA County with signs that read, "Vote No on Proposition 64/Stop AIDS."

On November 4, 1986, Proposition 64 lost in the crucial battleground of LA County and was defeated in every other county in California—more than five million people, or 71 percent of the electorate, voted against it. Far from harming the movement to stop Proposition 64, the quarantine committee helped turn the once-close election into a blowout. The experience—from the skirmishes with the gay establishment to the public's embrace of the committee—was an eye-opener for Weinstein.

"I thought that the organized gay community was kind of unified behind this A-list crowd," said Weinstein, "but it wasn't. It turned out that a lot of people felt very alienated from that, and they were cheering on what we were doing."

He added, "I also learned that people recognized that what was going on with AIDS was something different. It was a terrible crisis, and there was more support for the militancy that we represented than I'd realized. People were really like, 'Go for it.'"

With Proposition 64 soundly quashed, Weinstein, Chris Brownlie, Paul Coleman, Mina Meyer, Sharon Raphael, John Brown, and their friends were only starting a ride on a tricky, yet momentous wave.

—

AFTER THE NOVEMBER ELECTION, the quarantine committee members found themselves with considerable street credibility—and leading an emergent grassroots movement. That cachet and momentum, they believed, couldn't be wasted. With the county government's AIDS infrastructure just one level above nothing, people were inexcusably suffering.

"We had to get the county supervisors to pay attention," Mina Meyer told me.

By that time, Meyer, Raphael, and Weinstein were seriously talking about the need for a dedicated hospice facility for terminally ill AIDS patients. Hospice was far more cost-effective than hospital care, and, most importantly, a hospice facility could offer attentive care to an extremely sick person in a humane setting. AIDS patients suffered, among many other things, dramatic weight loss, neurological problems, Kaposi's sarcoma, severe diarrhea, blindness, and constant fatigue. At hospitals, AIDS patients often received shockingly inadequate services and were sometimes treated as lepers by fearful doctors and nurses.

San Francisco activists had already set up a hospice for AIDS patients. But aside from a few nonmedical hospices, which were more like hostels for people dying from AIDS, LA County offered nothing. Rather than storm the streets, the members of Stop the AIDS Quarantine Committee decided to be calculating.

At the end of 1986, Weinstein hosted a meeting at his apartment in Los Feliz, where he lived with Ruiz. Paul Coleman, Mina Meyer, Sharon Raphael, Chris Brownlie, Phill Wilson, Mary Adair, Albert Ruiz, and activist Richard Starr showed up. After hours of discussion, they decided to establish an activist group that would advocate on behalf of AIDS patients, push for hospice care, and force the LA County supervisors into action. It was dubbed Los Angeles AIDS Hospice Committee.

Weinstein was now a principal player in the formation of two aggressive, media-savvy AIDS advocacy groups. They were founded months before Larry Kramer and other New York City AIDS activists started, in March 1987, AIDS Coalition to Unleash Power (ACT UP), another pioneering advocacy group. Despite Peter Staley's 2014 comment that Weinstein "is not an AIDS activist," Weinstein, Brownlie, and their friends, who lived in the nation's second-largest city, were clearly on the cutting edge of AIDS activism in the US.

At the meeting in his apartment, Weinstein was chosen to lead the committee, and his friends voted unanimously to give him a salary, but that wasn't done only out of a sense of fairness. They believed Weinstein was a one-of-a-kind activist, and they wanted him to focus solely on battling the county.

"We decided that he should get paid so he could make a living," Meyer said, "and work full time on this issue."

At thirty-four years old, Weinstein, who earned a meager $250 per week, was now committing himself to the AIDS movement. "I just thought that there was this emergency," said Weinstein, "and this need."

He wasn't thinking, in 1986, that it would become his life's work.

"If we were going to just be an advocacy organization," Weinstein said, "it wasn't clear what would perpetuate us indefinitely. I think the general atmosphere around AIDS was the hope that there would be a magic bullet. There was talk of a cure—because people didn't

know what the hell they were talking about. But it wasn't the idea that AIDS would go on for generations."

Weinstein, with help from Coleman and Brownlie, first created an advisory board comprised of numerous AIDS and gay-rights activists—Morris Kight, Meyer and Raphael, John Brown, Phill Wilson, Reverend Troy Perry of Metropolitan Community Church, and Reverend Carl Bean of the Minority AIDS Project, among others. Then, on Meyer and Kight's suggestion, the hospice committee organized a public hearing—county supervisors had yet to convene an official commission to inform them about local AIDS issues. The hearing was ingenious. The committee planned to document, in detail, all the problems facing AIDS patients in the county, and then publicly sock the board of supervisors with a long list of indisputable facts and needs.

"One of the things we learned from the movement is that you just go ahead and do what you think needs to be done," Raphael said. "If it isn't done by others, just go ahead and do it, and then it becomes the norm."

On February 16, 1987, Los Angeles AIDS Hospice Committee sponsored a daylong hearing inside a community center at Plummer Park in West Hollywood. Speakers included the noted UCLA immunologist Dr. Michael Gottlieb, George Sonsel of APLA, Joyce Green of the AIDS Interfaith Council, Rob Saltzman of the county's AIDS program, Suzann Gage of Women's AIDS Project, Michael Hedderman of LA County+USC Medical Center, and others.

"It was an important event because for the first time it got all the Los Angeles AIDS people together in a single place," said Paul Coleman. "These were all the heavy hitters—this was the A-team. It was like telling the county, 'We're coming for you.'"

To prevent critics from questioning the legitimacy of the hearing, Weinstein and Coleman cleverly adopted the language of government. They created a "blue-ribbon panel," which was made up of "commissioners."

"We just said, 'Isn't that something that the government does?'" Weinstein explained. "So what's somebody going to say; that it isn't official?"

Weinstein chaired the hearing. With him on the dais were Morris Kight; Los Angeles Community College Trustee Wallace Albertson, an activist and wife of actor Jack Albertson, who would become an AHF board member; Rabbi Allen Freehling, a widely respected religious leader; LA school district board member Jackie Goldberg, who would later become an LA city councilwoman; California State Assemblyman Richard Polanco; Dr. Laud Humphreys, a prominent sociologist and author; West Hollywood Mayor Steve Schulte; and American Civil Liberties Union attorney Susan McGreivy.

In front of a crush of TV news cameras, speakers gave a seven-hour stream of testimony—some of it horrifying. AIDS activist Ron Rose, for example, talked about the awful conditions at the LA County+USC Medical Center, one of the nation's largest public hospitals.

"You see patients weighing ninety pounds sitting on a wooden bench for three to four hours," he said. "This is not humane to me. You see people suffer. You walk the wards, and you see rooms with eight or nine people in them." He later noted, "Anyone who has AIDS is more willing to die at home than die at USC."

Others explained that families and friends of AIDS sufferers were incapable of dealing with the opportunistic infections that attacked patients, that people living with HIV/AIDS were worried about getting evicted by bigoted landlords, and that people needed assistance with cooking, bathing, and routine chores.

The consensus was that county politicians had turned their backs on people. During his testimony, Paul Coleman was more than willing to explain why. "I think the reason is very simple," he said. "It's homophobic bigotry. It needs to be said, people. These people don't care because gay people are dying—IV drug users are dying or, in some cases, it's Black people who are dying. And the government

does not care, and this permeates on all levels of government. I'm talking federal, state, and city."

Coleman wasn't off the mark. In the fall of 1987, journalist Randy Shilts, who died from AIDS in 1994, released an explosive book titled *And the Band Played On: Politics, People, and the AIDS Epidemic.* It detailed the US government's disastrous response to AIDS and the heroic work of activists, researchers, and doctors. The book also explained the missteps and infighting of the gay male community, in which many people disapproved of hard-charging activism, feared losing sexual freedoms, and refused to change unsafe sexual practices—with tragic results. Those attitudes would never go away in the fight against AIDS, and AHF would have to navigate them for decades.

In the book's prologue, Shilts hits upon issues that are still relevant—not just in the United States but also around the world. In fact, they can be applied beyond gay men to all types of underserved people impacted by HIV/AIDS, whether it's the poor, women, transgender people, communities of color, or intravenous drug users.

Shilts wrote: "In those early years, the federal government viewed AIDS as a budget problem, local public health officials saw it as a political problem, gay leaders considered AIDS a public relations problem, and the news media regarded it as a homosexual problem that wouldn't interest anybody else. Consequently, few confronted AIDS for what it was, a profoundly threatening medical crisis.

"Fighting against this institutional indifference were a handful of heroes from disparate callings. Isolated teams of scientists in research centers in America and Europe risked their reputations and often their jobs to pioneer early research on AIDS. There were doctors and nurses who went far beyond the call of duty to care for its victims. Some public health officials struggled valiantly to have the epidemic addressed in earnest. A handful of gay leaders withstood vilification to argue forcefully for a sane community response to the epidemic and to lobby for the funds that provided the first breakthroughs in

research. And there were many victims of the epidemic who fought rejection, fear, isolation, and their own deadly prognoses to make people understand and to make people care."

The public hearing held by LA AIDS Hospice Committee was a standout example of activists fighting institutional indifference and making people care about AIDS sufferers. Since the event received wide media attention, the LA County supervisors' shameful handling of AIDS was no longer a secret. The *LA Times*, in fact, published a sympathetic article headlined "Increase Urged in Government AIDS Efforts." It listed demands directed at the county read during the hearing—from prohibiting evictions of people with AIDS to requiring resistant nursing and convalescent homes to accept AIDS patients.

To further drive things home, the hospice committee sent a hard-hitting white paper to media outlets, county supervisors, and LA City Council members. Written by Sharon Raphael and Paul Coleman, it compiled the hearing's testimony and not only highlighted the serious problems in LA County, but also offered solutions, including the need for a "residential" hospice facility.

"Home healthcare can only work in a home environment where a significant support structure exists," they wrote. "One of the cruelties of AIDS is that it turns the majority of its sufferers into paupers prior to death." They also noted, "Freestanding hospices are especially necessary for those who have no home or do not choose to live out their lives at home."

The hearing increased the momentum and credibility that the grassroots activists had first earned with Stop the AIDS Quarantine Committee.

"All of a sudden," Meyer said, "everyone was taking notice."

But Brownlie, who had fought through numerous illnesses during the Proposition 64 battle, could not attend the public hearing. On the day of the event, Brownlie checked himself into LA

County+USC Medical Center, which largely serves the uninsured. He was diagnosed with AIDS.

The ordeal he underwent there mirrored what Ron Rose was testifying about ten miles away in West Hollywood. For the next three days, Brownlie, frail and ill and gaunt, was left on a gurney in the hospital's bustling emergency room. At one point, a nurse rolled Brownlie into the hallway and left him there for hours. As if caught up in a Third World nightmare, he received no medical attention.

"He lay there sick as a dog and couldn't breathe," Mary Adair, Brownlie's close friend, recalled.

Over those three days, Brownlie saw firsthand that poor care for AIDS patients at LA County+USC was the norm, not an anomaly.

Weinstein, who had been swamped at the public hearing, finally got news of what was happening to Brownlie. He immediately went straight to the top, calling powerful LA County Supervisor Ed Edelman, a solid supporter of AIDS causes whom Weinstein had gotten to know.

"Ten minutes later," Adair said, "Chris had a bed."

Brownlie and Weinstein were furious. Aside from Brownlie's ordeal, it was obvious that underserved people, who didn't have political connections, were horribly mistreated by the county government. If things didn't change, people living with AIDS would continue to endure archaic, even life-threatening conditions.

"Then they really started advocating for hospice," said Adair.

Chapter 9

AIDS Hospice Foundation & the Death of an AIDS Crusader

Chris Brownlie

AFTER HIS DIAGNOSIS, SOMETHING inside Brownlie seemed to click, as if he was determined to become everything he wanted to be, if not more. He became more philosophical—facing death prompted him to explore the deeper life lessons of his illness. And although a talented writer, Brownlie had been plagued by a lack of confidence. He now pushed that aside and composed thoughtful, nakedly honest newspaper columns and poems about AIDS. And while many people tried to hide their illness because of intense stigma, Brownlie made

a point of speaking at public events and introducing himself as a "Person with AIDS," or "PWA." He wasn't going to hide from anyone.

"Chris was really an amazing guy," recalled John Brown, who got to know Brownlie through the quarantine committee, "with a great sense of humor that he never lost. He never stopped seeing the irony with what was going on with him personally. He truly believed that what was keeping him alive was the work."

Brown added, "He was absolutely the spiritual visionary of that whole movement. He wrote prolifically during that period of time. It was what set him apart....He became the voice for so many people living with the disease."

A poem by Brownlie titled "AIDS" was particularly strong. It was turned into a framed poster and placed on a wall at AHF's Public Health Division building in Hollywood. For one passage, he wrote this:

It is a whimper and a scream.
It is the brush of a branch on the screen of your window, a rustle, a rattle.
It is being in your center and being so far from your center
That you don't know if you'll ever find your way back.
It is relentless. It is daunting, a great mountain which you must climb.

It is the caring for your friends in ways you never have.
Intimate ways, horrible ways,
Ways that take more of your love that you never knew you had.
It is being there when the coma comes.
It is begging in your heart for some little piece of mercy.
It is going to the church, or the park or the beach to say:
"Farewell and Godspeed, beloved one."

It is the fighting back.
It is the building of places to care for the living and the dying.
It is courage, it is honor, it is integrity.
It is people joining forces in a time of great need.

It is hope, it is sharing the burden.

It is people caring for their own and finding love.

It is surviving and believing in the future.

Even when we are hurting more than we have ever hurt before.

It is a wail.

It is a howl.

It is beyond our grasp.

It is awful.

It is awesome.

It is AIDS.

As a writer and speaker, Brownlie was invaluable for the hospice committee's advocacy work. Sharon Raphael considered him to be "a spearhead in the AIDS movement for us." But he was constantly sick. Weinstein, with help from Coleman, ended up doing much of the committee's legwork, such as organizing protests, writing press releases, speaking at meetings, and raising money to keep everything running. At public gatherings, Weinstein was often seen holding a tin coffee can, soliciting donations.

"He was a very determined activist," Miki Jackson said.

Weinstein was now a leader in LA's AIDS movement, but he purposefully avoided the pitfalls of power: he continued to be aggressive; he didn't play nice just to be accepted; and he continued to think outside the box. Weinstein was so feisty and independent that even Morris Kight, who frequently ran into trouble with other gay activists because of his nonconforming ways, worried about him.

Jackson recalled, "Morris would say, 'Oh, he walks close to the edge—right on a razor. I get so frightened for him sometimes.'"

Whenever necessary, Weinstein and Coleman played hardball.

"If you had Michael and me coming for you," Coleman explained, "you were in some deep shit. Politicians would say, 'Oh God, those two together are going to make my life so miserable.' And both of us could switch it off, so we'd be like, 'Are you the bad cop today or am I the bad cop?' We'd make them scared like cockroaches."

Weinstein came up with an irreverent, spot-on advocacy campaign in which the hospice committee inducted President Ronald Reagan, California Governor George Deukmejian, and LA County Supervisors Pete Schabarum, Deane Dana, Mike Antonovich, and Kenneth Hahn into the "AIDS Hall of Shame"—county supervisor Ed Edelman was exempted, receiving the "Heart of Gold Award." Reporters ran with the controversial inductions, which further turned up the heat on the politicians. The hospice committee also organized candlelight marches on the homes of Deukmejian and Antonovich, although they were more like funeral processions—in front of the politicians' private residences, Weinstein, Coleman, and a crew of activists laid a black coffin.

Antonovich, a Republican who once said gays could avoid AIDS by simply becoming heterosexuals, seemed deliberately clueless about government's responsibility to protect the public's health. At a March 1987 press conference, he told reporters, "The responsibility for the AIDS epidemic does not belong to the board of supervisors. It belongs to the heterosexuals and the homosexuals who are drug users and engaging in promiscuous sexual behavior." Weinstein told the *Los Angeles Herald-Examiner* that Antonovich was the "most callous and indifferent" of all the county supervisors.

LA Weekly loved Weinstein's pluck. In the paper's annual "Best of LA" issue, he was anointed Best Young Activist and hailed as "a young visionary who somehow got it in his head that you don't get what you want unless you fight for it."

What Weinstein and his fellow activists wanted was a county-operated hospice. In public, the supervisors welcomed the idea. Then they dragged their feet and said they didn't have the money. In response, the activists took their work to another level. On June 10, 1987, LA AIDS Hospice Committee became AIDS Hospice Foundation (AHF), a nonprofit that, according to a press release, would "guide, fund, and monitor AIDS hospice programs." The foundation members, however, were still not thinking of actually operating a hospice. That changed in the fall of 1987.

ONE AFTERNOON, DAVID KESSLER, a home care expert who had been following AHF's battles with the county, called Weinstein. He told him that Barlow Respiratory Hospital, which specialized in treating respiratory diseases, was considering an expansion into AIDS care on its twenty-six-acre campus in LA's Elysian Park. Barlow, Kessler said, might be interested in working with AHF to create a freestanding hospice for terminally ill AIDS patients.

In no time, Weinstein met with Barlow officials and toured the proposed facility—a two-story, former dormitory for nurses. It sat on top of a hill, just down the street from Dodger Stadium, and was surrounded by tall, leafy trees with a view of downtown Los Angeles. The location was serene and beautiful and perhaps a bit mystical—the perfect place for one to spend his or her last days. Weinstein realized underserved people could finally get a full-service hospice, but AHF would have to run it.

To make that happen, AHF had to raise $700,000 to renovate the building and another $400,000 for operations. It also needed to pass state legislation that would allow hospices to be officially licensed, making AHF eligible for government reimbursement—a crucial stream of revenue that would keep it afloat.

Guided by AHF's new motto, "Fight for the living and care for the dying," Weinstein, Brownlie, and John Brown went to work and hired Joyce Green, a knowledgeable hospice expert, to help develop a first-class facility at Barlow. "She was by my side all the time," Weinstein said. "She set up a system of care. We were partners." Paul Coleman, the militant activist, amicably left the organization. "I wasn't good with institutions," he told me.

For the legislation, Weinstein got California State Assemblyman Richard Polanco of Los Angeles, who sat on the hospice committee's "blue-ribbon" panel, to push forward a bill. Weinstein and Mina Meyer then moved into negotiations with Barlow. For the money to

renovate and operate the hospice, AHF could get funding from local and state governments, but it first needed a private donor to provide a stake; this would assure politicians and bureaucrats that everything was well funded and legitimate. Weinstein called John Brown, who had risen from working with Stop the AIDS Quarantine Committee to chairing the AHF board of directors. They needed someone who was wealthy and politically connected. Brown rang up his close friend, Gene La Pietra.

Born and raised in Providence, Rhode Island, La Pietra was the shrewd, plainspoken owner of Circus Disco, a popular gay nightclub in Hollywood. He was surrounded by gay men, constantly seeing the ravages of AIDS. If employees got sick from the disease, he'd keep them on payroll so they could have an income and pay for food and rent. For close friends, La Pietra would put them on his medical insurance policy.

"Nobody knew what to do," he told me. "There were no real rules. It's like anything else—you're grappling in the dark until something happens and then you start to get a grip on it. In the early years, it was all about dying. I knew people that got diagnosed and died in days."

Over the years, like many nightclub owners, La Pietra became a power player in gay Los Angeles and once sat on the board of directors at the LA Gay & Lesbian Center, where Brown got to know him.

"Being an owner of a nightclub," La Pietra explained, "there was a certain responsibility that went with that privilege. You funded what needed to be funded because there was no money out there doing it. It meant that you listened to everyone and that you did what you could to make whatever difference you could."

La Pietra also had political connections at LA City Hall, but he was a maverick within the gay establishment. Interested only in results, he was open to anything that could bring relief to LA's badly impacted gay community. When Brown came calling about an AIDS hospice, La Pietra didn't hesitate to meet with Weinstein.

"We had to take a chance," La Pietra explained, "because nothing else was working. If you ever went to the hospital to visit a friend with AIDS, it was so inhumane."

On the day of the meeting, only weeks after the phone call with Kessler, Weinstein waited for La Pietra and Brown at his makeshift office in a somewhat decrepit building on the Barlow campus. Brown, meanwhile, drove over to Barlow with La Pietra. They talked about AHF's project and the history of the hospital.

"My head was swirling around the tuberculosis thing," said La Pietra, "and looking at all these buildings and thinking, 'Oh, my God, it's like Amityville or something. What's going on here? How can all these buildings be locked up and boarded up?' It's like the set of a horror movie."

When Brown and La Pietra walked into Weinstein's office, they saw a man who appeared to be haunted himself.

"He looked completely down," said La Pietra, "as down as a person can be. There was complete hopelessness surrounding him."

Brown said, "He looked like somebody who had the weight of the world on his shoulders."

Weinstein, in fact, was dealing with exactly that. In addition to raising more than $1 million as quickly as possible, executing and overseeing a massive renovation project at Barlow, and helping steer a bill through the fickle California legislature, he was getting pushback from small operators in LA who didn't want state regulations placed on their hospices.

"People just wanted to open up places and put people in them," Weinstein recalled. "We argued that the care wouldn't be good enough that way."

He added, "What we were proposing to do was much more costly. People were really sick. They couldn't be unattended. You couldn't have six people in a three-bedroom house without care. Not just nursing care—you needed medical care, too."

At the same time, a group affiliated with LA's gay establishment realized that hospice care, which was first promoted by LA AIDS Hospice Committee, was the up-and-coming cause in California's gay and political worlds. In the eyes of Weinstein and others, certain people within the gay establishment decided they needed to own the issue or else run the risk of being left out. They went public with plans to build their own hospice—without extensive medical services—and lobby for a large chunk of the government funding that was inevitably coming.

"It was definitely stealing our thunder and our hope," Weinstein said.

Sharon Raphael said more bluntly, "We felt like they didn't know shit about hospice, and they were trying to take hospice away and make it their issue. They knew nothing." She added, "You don't know how many times these people have pulled this on stuff we've done."

Further burdening Weinstein, some AIDS activists flat-out opposed hospice care.

"People were saying that we were consigning people to death," Weinstein explained.

Despite all that, Weinstein pulled himself together. He walked La Pietra and Brown around the dusty, ramshackle dormitory and laid out his vision.

"He did a very good job of making a case for it," said Brown.

A few weeks after the meeting, with additional lobbying from Brown, La Pietra agreed to give $200,000. The generous donation shocked the gay establishment.

"I knew everyone in West Hollywood," La Pietra said, "and they all said, 'Are you crazy? You just blew $200,000!' I said, 'No, I didn't.' These people just weren't on board. So be it. You can't have kumbaya all the time, and you're going to have different ideas, especially when nobody knows what is right. Nobody had a plan, and nobody knew what to do. Michael came in and said, 'I have a plan. I don't know how to cure [AIDS], and I don't intend to cure it, but I intend to provide a place for people to come and die with dignity, and not at a

hospital.' Cedars Sinai, Kaiser Permanente, and other places offered horrendous service. Horrendous."

Local politicians, who had long worked with La Pietra, were now more responsive. In December 1987, the LA County Board of Supervisors committed to allocating $400,000 for AHF's hospice at Barlow and to deliver a total of $2 million for hospice care in the entire county. It was a stunning victory for the AIDS movement in LA—and proof that Weinstein's dynamic advocacy worked.

"I said to Chris that they knew not what they did," Weinstein recalled, "because they would never be able to stop us again."

Taking a cue from the county, the city of Los Angeles gave AHF $250,000, and the state of California kicked in $325,000. Assemblyman Richard Polanco also successfully ushered through the state legislation that AHF needed. In September 1988, *LA Weekly* again singled out Weinstein and AHF in its "Best of LA" issue. This time, the organization was recognized for "Best Hospice," although the facility wouldn't open for another three months.

LA Weekly reporter Doug Sadownick wrote: "Mainstream organizations like AIDS Project LA get bogged down in Westside fundraising parties, slowly deprioritizing the dying clients for whom their organization was founded. A notable exception to the corporate AIDS style is AHF. Michael Weinstein, PWA Chris Brownlie, Joyce Green, and John Brown have consistently stuck their necks out lambasting the conservative Board of Supervisors, fighting for bills in Sacramento, and becoming outspoken leaders in the AIDS community, while also building a hospice designed to serve PWAs who might otherwise be dying on friends' couches, on gurneys in County Hospital, or on the streets."

There was good reason to be impressed by Brownlie, Brown, Weinstein, and their fellow activists. Between the fall of 1986 and the winter of 1988, they had spearheaded or played important roles in the defeat of Proposition 64, the creation of a county AIDS commission weeks after the blue-ribbon public hearing, the supervisors'

commitment of $2 million for hospice care, the supervisors' approval of a specialized AIDS ward at LA County+USC Medical Center, the decision by Los Angeles Mayor Tom Bradley to appoint a full-time AIDS coordinator and to commit $1 million in housing assistance to people with AIDS, and the December 1988 opening of the AHF hospice. Using a mix of wit, sophistication, tenacity, and provocation, they were activists par excellence.

—

BEFORE THE HOSPICE OPENED, Weinstein visited La Pietra at Circus Disco, where they sat inside a cramped, somewhat disheveled office. Weinstein proposed naming the facility after La Pietra, who, after all, was an all-important rainmaker for AHF. The nightclub owner was taken aback.

"I said, 'Are you freaking crazy!?'" La Pietra recalled. "'You have to name it after someone who suffered, who people can really relate to.' [Weinstein] said, 'What about Chris Brownlie?' I said, 'Perfect. Chris Brownlie.' And that took all of thirty seconds."

Brownlie accepted the honor but was a little rattled.

"It was a weird thing for him," said Mary Adair. "I don't think he ever thought of something being named for him, and actually being there and dying there. I think he didn't know how to deal with it."

On December 26, 1988, Chris Brownlie Hospice opened. A sign on the front door read, "Gay, Lesbian, Bisexual, Straight, Women, Men, Black, Brown, White, Yellow, Red, Young and Old. All Are Welcome Here." It was LA's first full-service hospice for AIDS patients, with twenty-five beds, a large common area with a fireplace, and a patio with views of downtown Los Angeles. The rooms were sizable and comfortable with large windows, and guests received twenty-four-hour medical attention. When a person passed away, family or friends could plant a tree on the grounds in his or her honor.

At the opening ceremony, Brownlie, who was sick and battling cryptococcal meningitis, told the *LA Times*, "Of course, I've always

hoped that I would not die, that I would live forever. But on another level, I actually get a sense of well-being about this experience. Sometimes it becomes very profound in a religious sense at the edges of my consciousness. And this is what the hospice program is about—it will help others accept the fact that death, too, is part of the life experience."

Around 1,200 people would pass away at the hospice between 1988 and 1996, when the facility closed with the advent of the AIDS cocktail. It was later turned into an AHF office building, but the spirit of the old hospice was always present. For years, employees saw apparitions or heard strange noises. One evening, a staffer heard what sounded like a young man repeating the same word over and over. "Help," the voice said. "Help. Help. Help…"

But during the nonstop work to open the hospice, Albert Ruiz, Weinstein's longtime partner, didn't feel right and took an HIV test at the LA Gay & Lesbian Center. Unlike today with the one-minute rapid test, he waited two agonizing weeks for the result. He was HIV positive.

"When I found out about myself," Ruiz told me, "it was really the compounding of so many people dying, plus now finding out the possibility of myself dying that way. The only way to describe it, I guess, is sort of like a trauma."

Weinstein was devastated.

"It was like the bottom fell out," he said.

The only thing that kept Weinstein sane and moving forward was his activism. "Work was actually a saving grace for me," he said. "It was a refuge. I was so submerged in everything that it distracted me."

While Weinstein and Ruiz remained a couple, Mary Adair and Ruiz legally wed, something that was done often in the 1980s and 1990s between gay men living with HIV/AIDS and their female friends.

"We got married so that he would be covered under my health insurance," Adair explained. "He couldn't be covered under Michael's because there was no domestic partnership or gay marriage." Because

The 2018 World AIDS Day Celebration in New York City, honoring AHF's achievement of one million lives in care.

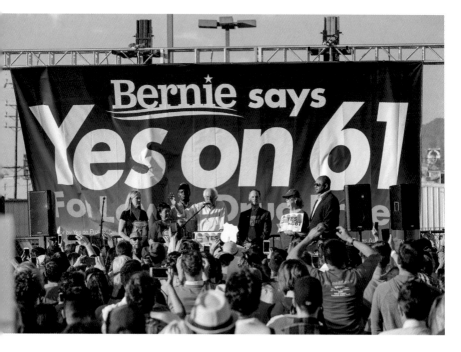

Bernie Sanders at a 2016 rally in Downtown Los Angeles to support Proposition 61, a drug pricing state ballot measure sponsored by AIDS Healthcare Foundation.

International Women's Day in Argentina in 2017. AHF staff carry a banner that says "Keep the Promise to Women."

A 2020 ribbon cutting and dedication of AHF's Valley Haven Hotel, which provides lower-income homeless housing in LA. The hotel is managed by AHF's Healthy Housing Foundation.

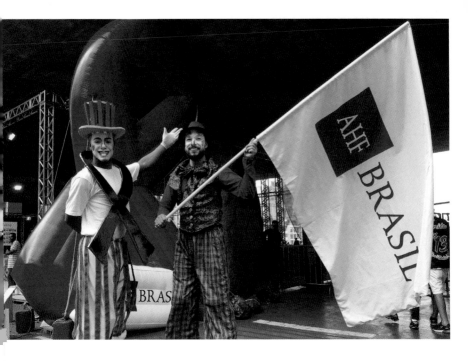

AHF's World AIDS Day Celebration in São Paulo, Brazil, in 2018.

In 2021, AHF and partner organizations hold a protest and "die in" in front of the world headquarters of COVID-19 vaccine maker Johnson & Johnson in New Jersey as part of AHF's "Vaccinate Our World" campaign.

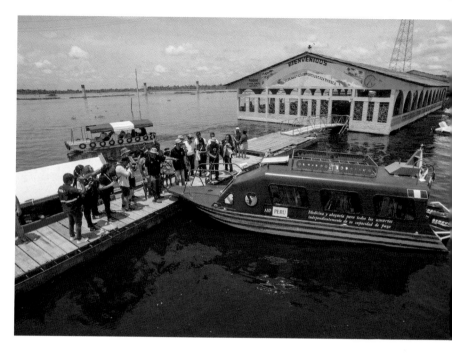

AHF Peru Testing Boat, which reaches remote communities along the Amazon River to provide HIV testing.

AHF Malawi's 2019 ribbon-cutting launch and commission of the Ngabu Rural Hospital.

A 2019 World AIDS Day testing event in Peru.

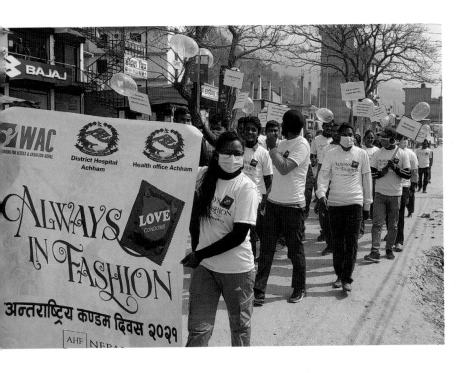

AHF's International Condom Day parade in Nepal in 2021.

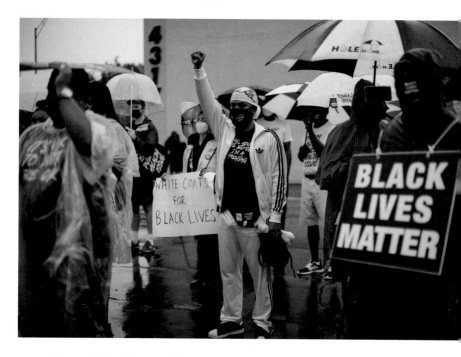

The 2020 "Get Off Our Necks" march in Cleveland, where AHF protested against racism in law enforcement across the United States.

The 2017 World AIDS Day celebration in The Netherlands with a human-made AIDS ribbon created with red umbrellas.

of their technical marriage, Adair said, "If Albert got sick, which we were expecting within the next couple of years, he would end up at a nicer hospital than LA County. Basically, so he would get good healthcare."

Luckily, Ruiz remained healthy, but Brownlie continued to decline. He still lived with his boyfriend, Phill Wilson, but opportunistic infections were battering him. At one point, Brownlie briefly went blind. Adair was always driving him to the hospital.

"There was a lot of going back and forth and just the craziness of being so afraid that your friend was going to die," Adair said. "When Chris would go through these bouts he would be given a lot of sedatives, and he would just say all these incredibly loving things to us, and we'd all be crying and hugging each other. It was just like a scene out of a movie."

Brownlie desperately wanted to live and hoped he could somehow cheat death. Despite his pain and sickness, he continued to write his newspaper column, "Liberation Politics," for the *News*, a local gay publication. In one column, Brownlie wrote:

"I have learned many lessons from the experience of the last few years. One lesson is that we will never be given something unless we ask for it. Another is that we have to make it clear that we will fight back when we are denied. Or to put it another way, that we are willing to stand up for ourselves. They can't treat us like a bunch of sissies. But perhaps the biggest and most astonishing lesson is that if we fight, we can win."

By November 1989, at the age of thirty-nine, Brownlie knew the end was coming. Weak and sometimes delirious, he agreed to take a bed at the hospice named after him, where friends held him and kissed him and tried to comfort him. Robert Brownlie, Chris's father, came for an emotional visit.

"That was heavy," Adair said. "Chris really loved his father."

Brownlie drifted in and out of consciousness. Then, on Monday, November 27, he snapped awake and asked to be moved back to his

apartment. Wilson and Weinstein obliged. As Brownlie faded away in his bedroom, Wilson, Weinstein, Adair, and Ruiz kept a vigil, taking turns sleeping on the floor near him. On Tuesday, November 28, a nurse woke everyone up. They huddled around their dear friend, who was breathing irregularly.

"We were all very quiet," Adair said. "And then all of a sudden, he just breathed out and breathed out. Very peaceful. And he was gone."

Standing at Brownlie's side, Weinstein became unraveled.

Adair recalled, "Michael was always the one who was steadfast and just pushed through. I have never seen him cry like that before or since. He was like this little boy, like this little eight-year-old boy who'd lost his best friend. He cried and cried and cried and sobbed like this little boy, just standing there."

For months, although he never talked about it, Weinstein had been deeply upset about the constant pain Brownlie had to endure. All that pent-up emotion came pouring out.

"The suffering was over," Weinstein said. "He had a very ugly last period of time in his life. It was an ugly death. How many more insults could a person's body take? It was horrible. It was painful to watch what he was going through, let alone go through it."

And, like Brownlie, Weinstein had been hoping that his best friend could somehow rally and defy death. Now, with Brownlie lifeless in his bed, Weinstein was confronted by a harsh reality.

"The idea of not having him here made me feel very alone," Weinstein said. "The finality that he wasn't going to be here anymore."

For his obituary, the *LA Times* headline read, "Chris Brownlie; Crusader for AIDS Care, Hospices." The world had lost another funny, loving, talented, compassionate human being to AIDS.

Chapter 10

AIDS Healthcare Foundation—The Early Years

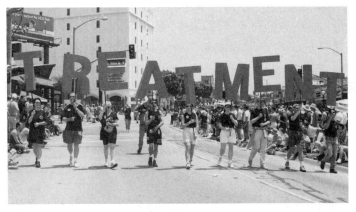

AHF makes a statement at the LA Gay Pride Parade

THE ACTIVISTS OF STOP the AIDS Quarantine Committee, LA AIDS Hospice Committee, and AIDS Hospice Foundation carried out a type of work that wasn't complicated. In fact, it largely boiled down to one concept: fulfill a public need.

When the gay political establishment didn't aggressively confront the possibility of AIDS quarantines, Weinstein, Brownlie, Coleman, Meyer, Raphael, and the others organized a vibrant campaign that helped to smack down a dangerous ballot measure. When LA County supervisors were failing the underserved during a public health emergency, Weinstein and his friends established LA AIDS Hospice Committee and forced the politicians into action. When LA

County didn't operate a top-notch hospice for terminally ill AIDS patients, the activists opened Chris Brownlie Hospice.

Figure out the need and then fulfill it. That's what AHF would continue to do throughout the 1990s and into the 2000s, even if that meant courting economic disaster.

"I don't want to overstate it," Peter Reis, AHF's senior vice president, told me, "but it was fairly dramatic. The financial realities of this organization flying into the side of a mountain were absolutely there."

Between 1990 and 1996, Weinstein continued to operate with the same sense of urgency as he had in the late 1980s. Jerry Baughman, the one-time AHF finance director and an amiable Iowa native four years older than Weinstein, was among the first of many employees who felt as if he were strapped into a roller coaster.

"I was trying to figure out how to make the payroll every week," Baughman told me, "and Michael was thinking way beyond that." He added, "Michael wanted AHF to be a political player in California, in the nation, and internationally. We joked that we'd be the first AIDS group in space."

In 1990, as a sign of the much broader scope Weinstein intended for AHF, AIDS Hospice Foundation changed its name to "AIDS Healthcare Foundation." It also opened, in October 1990, the first of many Out of the Closet stores, which was managed by Marc Neighbor, a former manager of a Salvation Army thrift shop. AHF, at this point, had its offices in a tinted-glass-and-steel building on Yucca Street and Argyle Avenue in Hollywood, only yards away from the 101 Freeway.

"Michael walked into the office one morning," recalled Jessie Gruttadauria, who started with AHF as a receptionist, "and he blurted out that we were going to open a thrift store. I said, 'Okay.' And he said, 'We're going to call it Out of the Closet!'"

Gruttadauria wasn't impressed by the idea, even thinking that Weinstein was out of his mind. She wouldn't be the only AHF staffer

to have such a thought or to later have an epiphany that Weinstein might actually be quite brilliant.

"I thought that this small office was going to be filled with second-hand stuff and that we had to find a place, and we had to finance it," she said. "I was doubtful. And then it was successful. Immediately, we started making money."

Out of the Closet sold clothing, furniture, and knickknacks donated by the public, with the revenue helping to fund AHF's work. It was Weinstein's first social enterprise business as president of AHF—and it was done out of necessity. Weinstein, who kept up with the newest developments in HIV/AIDS treatment, thought AHF needed to do more than just provide hospice care.

"If people take ten years to progress to AIDS," Weinstein told me, "and then they take three years to die, and we were covering hospice for the last six months of a person's life, then we weren't really addressing the need that people had throughout the entire spectrum. It seemed clear that there would be life extension, and how you provide that life extension to the most people would be the most important thing."

Weinstein wanted AHF to undertake a vast expansion. Life-saving treatment for HIV/AIDS did not exist in 1990, but AHF could deliver something that LA County lacked: a safe, well-organized clinic that handled the opportunistic infections of underserved people. Opening a treatment clinic would also help AHF's clients in the long run—as medical care for HIV and AIDS improved, Weinstein figured, AHF would be well-positioned to offer those vital services. Weinstein wanted to open a number of clinics in targeted locales throughout LA County. For all that, it needed money, and a constant flow of it. He started up the Out of the Closet chain.

"There wasn't a month Michael wasn't trying to open a thrift store," said Baughman with a chuckle.

Beyond the revenue, there were other benefits from quickly expanding Out of the Closet—the stores offered people easy,

nonclinical access to HIV testing and promoted AHF's work to the general public.

"Most people don't come into contact with our clinics," Weinstein said, "and only a subset of the public use our testing services. But anybody can donate and anybody can shop. As a brand, Out of the Closet helped make us more famous."

Only months after the grand opening of Out of the Closet, AHF started its first healthcare center, in January 1991, at the Hollywood Presbyterian Medical Center. Assemblyman Richard Polanco, the good friend of AHF, got the state funding to operate the clinic. Weinstein initially wanted it to be located above the thrift store to set up a kind of "one-stop shop"—a model that would be established years later. But it ran into unresolvable zoning issues. Nevertheless, the clinic instantly attracted a large clientele—and continues to be AHF's busiest healthcare center in LA.

The clinics also came with an extra benefit. By opening centers in different communities, AHF became a more effective advocate.

"If we went to the board of supervisors or state legislators or city council members on behalf of patients," Weinstein said, "and we had facilities in their districts, it built up political support. That was very helpful."

After the openings of the thrift store and clinics, AHF kept rolling. The organization opened Carl Bean House, in 1992, to serve residents in South Los Angeles, an LA neighborhood with a large African American and Latino population that was greatly underserved and ravaged by HIV/AIDS. In Los Angeles, Black and Latino AIDS activists often found themselves lacking financial resources and battling politically connected gay organizations for federal AIDS funding, which was distributed by the county government.

"For years," Cynthia Davis, a veteran African American AIDS activist, told me, "providers from South LA had concerns about disproportionate amounts of money going to the gay community—for example, AIDS Project Los Angeles and the LA Gay & Lesbian

Center—and not sufficient amounts of these federal resources coming south of the Santa Monica Freeway. We talked about this for years with the county's AIDS program."

She added, "It was a fight because we felt that a lot of decisions were being made behind closed doors—we would show up at a meeting and the decision had already been made."

Reverend Carl Bean, founder of the Minority AIDS Project and the trailblazing Unity Fellowship Church, which served gay and bisexual African Americans, found much of the same thing.

"The white gay boys weren't so excited about someone else getting the money," Bean told me.

In fact, some of LA's most prominent AIDS groups were perplexed about why Bean couldn't get frail, horribly sick African Americans to use their services in West Hollywood or Hollywood—an hour-long bus ride away, if not longer, from South LA. Bean told them that Blacks should be able to access services in their own neighborhoods, just like white gay males did.

"It was as if I was speaking a foreign language to them," the reverend said. "I decided I didn't have enough time for that."

Bean was born and raised in Baltimore and moved to New York City in 1960 when he was sixteen to pursue a professional singing career. He eventually landed a job with the famous gospel group Alex Bradford & the Bradford Singers. In 1972—the same year Weinstein showed up in LA—Bean took a bus to Los Angeles to break out as a pop singer. Signed by Motown Records, Bean had a disco hit in 1977 titled "I Was Born This Way," a gay anthem that came out thirty-four years before Lady Gaga's wildly popular "Born This Way." (The catchy chorus went, "I'm happy / I'm carefree / And I'm gay / I was born this way!") By 1982, Bean, an openly gay man, watched friends and associates from the music industry, especially African American men from his gospel days, become deathly sick with AIDS.

"I wasn't going to do nothing and allow these guys to be thrown under the bus," he explained. "They had done so much for the church."

Bean left the music industry and dedicated his life to AIDS work, hoping to use his fame as a way to get people to take up his cause. A deeply spiritual man who came from a Progressive Christianity background, Bean also decided to become an ordained minister to better carry out his mission.

"I knew I needed to be ordained to go against the clergy who would come at me with hate," he said.

By 1985, Bean had founded the Unity Fellowship Church and the Minority AIDS Project in South Los Angeles. "I wanted to unify people spiritually," said Bean. Not long after, Bean met Weinstein at an LA County Board of Supervisors' meeting. Sharing a passion for social justice, they became fast friends. "We fit like hand in glove," said Bean.

The reverend had also connected with Chris Brownlie, a self-described atheist. Brownlie started attending Bean's church services and found himself delving deeper and deeper into his own spirituality.

"He said he didn't know what I was doing to him," Bean recalled with a chuckle. "That I was throwing some kind of mojo on him. I said, 'I'm just saying that God is love. That's it.'"

But the African American community in South LA didn't know Weinstein or AHF—and they were received hesitantly. Weinstein sought the help of Cynthia Davis, who was widely respected in South LA and would become a longtime AHF board member, and Bean, who was also highly regarded. Over the course of a year, Davis and Bean were indefatigable, holding community meetings and talking one-on-one with African American leaders.

"I had to explain to them that Michael was different," Bean explained. "That he would have walked with us in Selma and over the bridge."

Black community leaders finally signed off, and AHF opened Carl Bean House. The name was as much a tribute to the reverend as a clever political move. "I was the name that was associated with AIDS in South Los Angeles," said Bean. "Michael was smart."

The reverend was ecstatic about the new facility. For years, African Americans with AIDS were suffering through the same shoddy, dehumanizing service in LA hospitals as white gays, but Blacks had far fewer alternatives for care outside of those hospitals. AHF and Carl Bean House brought indispensable relief.

"All that ugliness went away with the hospice," said Bean. "This would really be a safe space for people, and that had me jumping for joy."

In 1996, AHF opened what would become its last hospice, Linn House, in West Hollywood. It had been mired in red tape and construction problems until Terri Ford took over and successfully pushed things through.

The year before, AHF had launched Positive Healthcare, the nation's first capitated (meaning paid per subscriber, whether or not they had treatment) managed care program for people living with AIDS. Donna Stidham, the one-time nurse, oversaw the new venture.

"It's something that really treats patients and helps them navigate," Stidham, now chief of managed care at AHF, told me. "It makes sure they are cared for appropriately."

Positive Healthcare was another social enterprise business. It fit the AHF model of the more people helped, the more money it could earn to remain sustainable—and help more people. But Positive Healthcare came with greater risks than a chain of thrift stores. Peter Reis was hired in 1995 as a financial analyst for the business.

"Michael was nervous about it," said Reis, "because if the patient racked up more dollars in costs than we received, we could have gone under, and Michael was hoping to make some money. And, in fact, we did make money for quite a number of years. In the early days, it wasn't a lot, but then it turned into a lot."

By the mid-1990s, Weinstein was well underway in turning AHF into an AIDS healthcare provider. But he knew that he didn't have the expertise to create systems within AHF to bring about medical service improvements. He wanted a reputable person in charge to make things happen.

"Michael was looking for somebody to put us on the map," Reis said, "and to give us some credibility—medically."

Weinstein boldly approached Dr. Charles Farthing, a global star in the AIDS movement. Born in Christchurch, New Zealand, in 1953, Farthing was talented, passionate, charismatic, and highly intelligent. He started one of the first AIDS wards in England, headed up a distinguished AIDS program at New York City's Bellevue Hospital, and was widely respected among prominent AIDS researchers and doctors. But taking a job at AHF, which was located outside of New York and Washington, DC, could have seemed like a backward career move for Farthing.

"Charles was trying to figure out why this was a good spot for him," said Reis, who became a close friend of Farthing's, "and Michael said that we're going to grow, and you can make it your own, and you can do what you want."

Weinstein also appealed to Farthing's attraction to something new and exciting.

"The way that I hooked Charles," Weinstein explained, "was by asking him, 'Haven't you always been an adventurer? AHF would be an adventure.'"

In 1994, Farthing became AHF's first chief of medicine. He lived up to Weinstein's high expectations. "He set up structure and processes, established a research program, and recruited new doctors," said Weinstein. "We were running MASH [Mobile Army Surgical Hospital] units and doing the best we could, but he professionalized it."

Farthing, who passed away in 2014, was a perfect fit for AHF's patient-centered ways.

"He was really a clinician," said Weinstein, "and had a passion for treating patients. He would go to great lengths to get patients to follow treatment protocol or to try something different."

Farthing, who could be impatient with anything that he perceived as staff incompetence, had an enormous impact.

"Besides Michael," said Reis, "I don't think there is anybody, arguably, who has put a bigger stamp on AHF than Charles.... Charles helped get AHF into a different league."

Ged Kenslea, AHF's longtime communications director, said, "Charles—and Michael will tell you this as well—was really responsible for creating a lot of the medical template that allowed AHF to grow."

Farthing badly wanted to keep people alive. He constantly educated himself and AHF medical staff about the newest HIV drugs, and he kept close tabs on AIDS research. AHF patients, in fact, were taking part in clinical drug trials, and, little by little, Farthing and Weinstein could see that something big was coming down the road. Together, they would make a decision that would save hundreds of lives in Los Angeles. It would also spark a coup to oust Weinstein.

—

1995 WAS A GOOD year for AHF—and for its clients. The California Medical Assistance Program signed a $26-million contract with Positive Healthcare, giving hundreds of low-income people the kind of quality HIV/AIDS care that was normally reserved for the affluent. Under the AIDS Drug Assistance Program, AHF became the largest provider of medications in LA County, which meant that lower-income people were getting better access to HIV/AIDS drugs. And AHF, which increased revenues to a new high of $21.4 million, recorded twenty-six thousand patient visits at its five clinics. But while AHF was expanding, AIDS was still raging.

By the end of 1995, 513,486 Americans had contracted HIV/AIDS, and a total of 319,849 people had died from AIDS, which was then the leading cause of death among individuals between the ages of twenty-two and forty-four. Nearly 2,000 of those AIDS victims passed away at AHF's Chris Brownlie and Carl Bean hospices. Then, in July 1996, Dr. David Ho, a top AIDS researcher who would become *Time* magazine's Man of the Year, made an extraordinary announcement.

At the International AIDS Conference in Vancouver, Ho explained that he and his research team had found that combination drug therapy reduced the viral loads of people living with HIV/AIDS to undetectable levels. AIDS patients, in other words, no longer faced an almost-certain death sentence. The breakthrough treatment—called the "AIDS cocktail"—was hailed around the world.

Weinstein, who attended the conference, wasn't surprised by the incredible news. Months before Ho took the stage in Vancouver, many terminally ill patients at AHF had been receiving combination drug therapy free of charge. Weinstein and Farthing saw nearly all of them make an amazing turnaround.

"The dementia and all the different manifestations of HIV reversed to a large degree," Weinstein recalled. "People who were considered to be within weeks of dying got better and left."

Ho's findings only confirmed Weinstein and Farthing's belief that the AIDS cocktail actually worked.

As Weinstein flew back to LA, his thoughts turned to a close friend, Connie Norman, who had recently moved into Chris Brownlie Hospice. Norman was a pioneering transgender advocate, a leading member of ACT UP's Los Angeles chapter, and one of the most respected AIDS activists in LA.

"Connie was the conscience of the AIDS movement," Weinstein told me. "She couldn't be bullied. If she had a position, she was going to stand for it regardless."

Weinstein hoped she could stay alive and start the AIDS cocktail. But the day after he returned, the "AIDS Diva," as Norman called herself, passed away. The world had lost another passionate, soulful AIDS crusader. In her *LA Times* obituary, Weinstein said, "Her outspokenness frequently made people uncomfortable, but she said things that needed to be said. Her efforts on behalf of gay and lesbian youth, the transgender community, and people living with HIV and AIDS were extraordinary." She was only forty-seven years old.

—

AFTER THE INITIAL ELATION over Ho's announcement, Weinstein and AHF had to face some hard facts. The AIDS cocktail was expensive—a year's worth of treatment cost around $12,000—and government was slow to set up reimbursement systems for providers such as AHF that paid for combination drug therapy for the poor and uninsured. If AHF wanted to save more patients, it had to dip into its own financial reserves. In addition, by bringing people back to life, AHF was directly contributing to the demise of its own hospices, which brought in essential revenue.

"We'd just opened our third hospice," said Reis, referring to Linn House in West Hollywood. "We had mortgages, and it was a lot of money to shell out."

Within AHF, some employees didn't want to put the organization in financial jeopardy by paying for the AIDS cocktail without reimbursement. Others believed that AHF shouldn't stray from its core mission of providing hospice care. Weinstein disagreed with both camps.

"Whether to give the hospice patients drugs was, to me, a very clear-cut moral issue," said Weinstein. "I'd be damned that we now have a life preserver and that people aren't going to get it. It seemed to me that we didn't really have a choice. On the cost-benefit scale, what if we had survived but continued to be a hospice organization and allowed those people to die? Morally, it would be reprehensible."

He added, "I couldn't get why people would want to stay in death mode when they could switch to life mode. That was just weird."

In pure business terms, Weinstein thought that sticking with hospice care was actually suicidal for AHF. With the coming of combination drug therapy, the future of AIDS healthcare had been undeniably altered, and hospice would soon become obsolete. In Weinstein's mind, AHF had to adjust, especially if it was serious about providing the best care to its largely underprivileged clientele.

The turmoil within AHF closely matched a larger schism that was developing in the national AIDS movement, which was detailed in a 1996 *Wall Street Journal* story titled "Powerful Treatments Create Growing Rift Among AIDS Groups." In essence, one group wanted the federal government to aggressively expand access to the lifesaving AIDS cocktail while another group wanted to protect the government funding that paid for social services, such as precooked meals, housing, and psychological counseling. The latter group was largely composed of social service providers who believed their work was still valuable to people with AIDS and didn't want to go out of business.

When interviewed by a *Wall Street Journal* reporter, Weinstein held the opinion that the bulk of AIDS funding should be directed toward medical treatment. While he applauded the important work of social service groups, Weinstein also told the paper, "A whole industry has developed around this [disease], and as much as people said they wanted pink slips, now that the time is upon us, most aren't willing to downsize." Weinstein was referring to the often-repeated sentiment of many AIDS organizations that they hoped a cure would someday force them to shut their doors.

Weinstein's critics didn't take kindly to his frankness and shot back in the article that he was making a power grab for money. Perhaps so, but an AHF patient, who was also interviewed for the story and was already taking the AIDS cocktail, unknowingly explained why. "Without these things," he said about the drugs, "I die."

Regardless of what his critics were saying, Weinstein wasn't waiting around for a government payday. Instead, he decided that AHF would risk bankruptcy, pay for the AIDS cocktail, and put hundreds of AHF patients on drug therapy as quickly as possible. Dr. Charles Farthing backed Weinstein's decision. AHF Chief Financial Officer Craig Thompson was opposed.

"He thought we were going under," said Weinstein, "and there was good reason to believe that. He thought that I was reckless."

(Thompson, who's now the chief executive officer of AIDS Project Los Angeles, the longtime AIDS services organization, declined to be interviewed for this book.)

As expected, AHF soon got hit with a double whammy. First, since people were getting well, the number of hospice patients plummeted by 50 percent, which caused AHF to lose around $200,000 per month in government funding. On top of that, the bill for drug therapy was skyrocketing into the hundreds of thousands.

"We basically screwed ourselves in-house," Reis said matter-of-factly. "It was a dangerous position to be in."

Weinstein freely admitted, "We were teetering on the edge of bankruptcy. There was no turning back. We had said, 'Okay, if we go down, then we go down. But this is what we're doing.' You could say that was a reckless thing, but the line between visionary and fool is a very narrow one."

Miki Jackson said, "The mission was to do all we could to save people's lives in any opportunity we had, no matter what it cost us. And we did that."

For an advocacy campaign, and as a counterargument directed at critics, Weinstein came up with another motto: "Treatment = Life." It made clear that Weinstein believed drug therapy, not social services, ultimately kept people alive. It was also a life-affirming spin on ACT UP's famous slogan: "Silence = Death."

The internal pushback at AHF continued to be intense, especially when, in 1996, Weinstein closed Chris Brownlie Hospice, which, of course, held sentimental value for him. Some staffers lost their jobs and others were moved into different positions, but nearly all of them were angry. For years, they had attended to every need of the dying and put significant emotional investment into their work. "They felt betrayed," said Jerry Baughman, who acted as a referee and conciliator between Weinstein and the agitated employees. Then, with AHF's financial health still in serious question, Craig Thompson decided to take matters into his own hands.

In the winter of 1996, Thompson quietly approached several members of AHF's board of directors with an idea to oust Weinstein and take over himself. The plan didn't stay a secret for long. Even John Brown, who had left AHF's board, got wind of the situation.

"I talked with a couple of board members, and I made my support for Michael known," said Brown. "Craig was delusional."

Jessie Gruttadauria also heard about Thompson's intentions.

"It was very, very shocking," she said.

Gene La Pietra recalled, "I told people who were passionately wanting to get rid of him that if you replace Michael at the helm of AHF, this organization, like so many others, will be slowed, and it won't go anywhere."

And, of course, Weinstein was tipped off—two employees showed up at his home one evening and told him what was happening. Weinstein quickly reached out to his allies on the board.

Over the next few weeks, Thompson and a few board members insisted that Weinstein should resign. Weinstein refused, with a majority of the board backing him. He could have turned the tables on Thompson and demanded his resignation but chose not to.

"I thought it was funny that Michael didn't get mad," said Cynthia Davis, a board member who watched the attempted coup implode, "because other people would have."

Gruttadauria observed something similar.

"Michael kept his chin up," she said, "and it was very admirable that he didn't let this person take him down. He was the bigger person."

But Weinstein took the high road for a very pragmatic reason. Further internal strife could have seriously harmed AHF, and that would have impacted its patients.

"I reassigned him, and he decided to leave," Weinstein explained of Thompson. "You always have to be careful about the collateral damage from coming down on someone, even if it is justified."

With government systems finally in place to reimburse AHF for purchasing the AIDS cocktail, the organization survived—and

changed completely and forever. Rather than comfort the dying, AHF was now giving life as a provider of HIV treatment.

"It tested our mettle," said Weinstein. "We went from hospice care in one city to eventually treatment for the world. So it shaped our ambitions and our agenda. It falls under the category of whatever doesn't kill you makes you stronger. It was kind of a crucible—and it weeded out people."

In 1997, Thompson left AHF to run APLA, where he has stayed to this day. That organization has moved along sure and steady, focused on serving residents of Los Angeles County. If Thompson and his allies had been successful in their takeover, it would be reasonable to assume that AHF wouldn't be serving more than 350,000 clients around the world or operating forty-one clinics in thirteen states or managing 222 free HIV treatment clinics in more than thirty countries. Without Weinstein at AHF, the global fight against AIDS would have looked exceedingly, if not alarmingly, different.

Chapter 11

AHF Goes Global

AHF clinic in Masaka, Uganda, circa 2002

IT TOOK YEARS OF scrambling, but, by the end of 2000, AHF was no longer in the red—at least for the time being. Out of the Closet, in 2000, brought in a record $5.2 million in revenue. Positive Healthcare, which now operated in Florida as well as in California, had enrolled thousands of members and was making good money. And AHF continued to open new clinics that generated income. By the start of 2001, AHF reached a new high in total revenue: $35.1 million. While things had stabilized, Weinstein was still ready to spend money if that meant expanding and improving patient services.

"Michael had an agenda for any additional money we had," Jerry Baughman said, "whether it was opening thrift stores or buying condoms or something else."

In 2000, AHF distributed hundreds of thousands of condoms in LA County. It also served 8,150 clients, making it the largest nonprofit provider of HIV medical care in the US. And AHF conducted 6,161 free HIV tests with an exemplary positivity rate of 1.9 percent, bringing many of those people who tested positive into treatment. If it couldn't get reimbursed for something a patient needed, AHF continued to absorb the cost and provide it anyway. One time, two very sick clients approached Donna Stidham, requesting an expensive treatment called total parenteral nutrition, which fed a person intravenously.

"They couldn't eat," Stidham explained, "and they needed that to sustain them. I had tried all of my sources where I could get stuff for free, and I couldn't get anything. So I went to Michael, and I said, 'I've got two patients. They said that they really need this treatment.' He asked if they did, and I said yes. He said, 'Then get it for them, and we'll find the money somewhere.' I had never in my twenty-five years of nursing had a CEO or manager put a patient before cost."

In addition to the nuts-and-bolts work, AHF Research placed 460 patients in thirty-six studies that were developing more user-friendly HIV drugs. And it sponsored a successful bill in California that allowed individuals in HMOs to seek care from an HIV specialist. The *LA Times* heralded it as one of the most important healthcare laws of 2000, which other states used as a template for similar legislation.

AHF was making a difference in California and Florida, and combination drug therapy had substantially decreased AIDS-related deaths in the US. But AIDS was devastating sub-Saharan Africa, where 70 percent of the world's HIV/AIDS cases were located and more than five million children under the age of fifteen had lost their mother or father or both parents to AIDS. In that part of the world, in 2000, access to antiretroviral therapy was virtually nonexistent.

The problems in South Africa and in other African countries weighed heavily on the minds of key people in AHF.

In 1999, Terri Ford, who would soon become AHF's director of advocacy, went to the United States Conference on AIDS in Denver. During a panel discussion, a group of female African activists begged their American counterparts for help. When Ford returned to Los Angeles, she started pounding the drum at AHF.

"That conference changed me forever," recalled Ford. "I said, 'We have got to help Africa!'"

At the same time, Cynthia Davis, an AHF board member who was also a public health professor at LA's Charles Drew University of Medicine and Science, was keeping a close watch on Africa. In 1996, she had attended an AIDS conference in Uganda, the East African country that had been battling AIDS since the 1980s.

"In the 1990s," Davis told me, "as AHF was developing expertise in HIV clinical management, I religiously repeated to the board, 'You know what? We need to share our expertise with Africa, where people are dropping like flies!' I saw us growing as an organization, and I didn't understand why we weren't doing more for people outside of LA. All of my points fell on deaf ears. It was very, very frustrating for me because I saw us having the potential to go international, but people on the board were afraid to take that step."

Weinstein wasn't afraid but cautious and noncommittal. A global expansion, he knew, would be expensive and time-consuming, with countless lives on the line. He also thought that a treatment infrastructure would need to be built from scratch, and there would probably be no turning back once AHF arrived in a foreign country. There were many questions about Africa. One way to get answers was to go there, and the 2000 International AIDS Conference was set to take place in Durban, a coastal city in South Africa.

Weinstein, however, attended AIDS conferences sparingly. He thought the information shared at the meetings was rarely new or thought-provoking; he cringed at the sight of pharmaceutical

companies throwing money around; he believed grassroots activists were treated with little respect by organizers; and he was turned off by the general party atmosphere.

"I thought it was kind of gross," Weinstein said. "And there are endless, boring, ridiculous speeches….It is completely pointless."

He added, "I felt like it was a set piece. They had designated activists who would say something, but they weren't going to threaten anybody."

Charles Farthing and Mary Adair, however, were making the case that Weinstein should go to Durban. Farthing was another AHF insider who wanted to work in Africa.

"He was very passionate about care," Weinstein said. "When it came to issues like patients having access to antiretroviral therapy everywhere; he felt very, very strongly about that."

Adair was betting that once Weinstein arrived in Durban, it would be nearly impossible for him to turn his back on South Africa. Peter Reis was certain it would be a done deal.

"I knew that if Michael went to this place, the epicenter of the worst AIDS firestorm," Reis recalled, "he wouldn't come back and say that we should just let it burn itself out."

After more coaxing, Weinstein finally bought an economy seat for a daylong flight to South Africa.

—

PHARMACEUTICAL COMPANIES WERE MAJOR sponsors of the 2000 International AIDS Conference, which was held in July. Called "Big Pharma" in certain circles, the corporations were taking heat from AIDS activists for not lowering the prices of HIV treatment, which critics said restricted access to the lifesaving drugs in the developing world. The absence of antiretroviral therapy, critics further charged, brought about countless numbers of unnecessary deaths. Fair and reasonable drug pricing was an all-important issue for many, and one that AHF would soon take up.

During the AIDS conference, at a rally in Durban, Zackie Achmat, the legendary AIDS activist and founder of the South African Treatment Action Campaign (TAC), tore into Big Pharma. "AIDS is a holocaust against the poor and the responsibility lies with the drug companies who put their profits before their responsibilities," he said.

Tina Magongwa, a person who attended the protest, told the *Independent*, a British newspaper, "A lot of people do not know that drugs exist which can make you live longer. I hope this conference will spread the message to many people here. I think both the government and the pharmaceutical companies are to blame."

But the official theme of the AIDS conference did not take aim at Big Pharma. Instead, organizers came up with a different, yet still important focus: "Break the Silence." The theme hit upon the fact that a widespread, uniform hush-up about AIDS, sexuality, and stigmatization in South Africa and other developing countries by government officials was exacerbating the AIDS crisis. Nelson Mandela, for example, was largely mute about AIDS when he was president of South Africa—eventually, he turned into one of the world's great AIDS activists. His successor, Thabo Mbeki, was worse.

Before the start of the AIDS conference, Mbeki, a respected anti-apartheid leader who replaced Mandela in November 1999, insisted that HIV was not the sole cause of AIDS. Instead, the South African president said that poverty, malnourishment, and ill health led to a failing immune system. The cure, Mbeki said, was solving poverty and improving one's eating habits. The president saw little need for antiretroviral therapy. Later, in 2008, a Harvard University study estimated that Mbeki's stance caused 365,000 premature deaths in South Africa.

The outside world largely condemned Mbeki, but the president, who led the revered African National Congress party, came under little scrutiny in South Africa. Only beleaguered, cash-poor activists with TAC and other AIDS groups took a stand.

Mbeki, however, was invited to speak at the International AIDS Conference's opening ceremony at Kingsmead Stadium in Durban. Before that event, prominent AIDS researchers and doctors had signed and published the "Durban Declaration," a public rebuke of Mbeki's position. It stated that HIV unequivocally causes AIDS and any denial of that fact would worsen the epidemic. Some AIDS leaders hoped the declaration would force Mbeki to change his tune. In fact, if the president had been more politically astute, Mbeki could have bested Mandela and become a national hero in his own right by implementing a vigorous HIV treatment plan. Mbeki, though, wasn't about to reverse himself in front of the international community.

During his speech, Mbeki stuck with his usual line. "It seemed to me that we could not blame everything on a single virus," he said. The president also announced that the government was still studying the reliability of HIV tests and ways to better track the disease, even though an estimated 4.2 million South Africans had already been infected with HIV—the largest HIV population in one country in the entire world. His remarks didn't go over well; hundreds of conference attendees, including Weinstein, walked out of the stadium before Mbeki finished speaking.

After the walkout, Weinstein, who was joined by Charles Farthing, met up with AIDS activists at a bar at the Hilton in downtown Durban, where the conference attendees stayed. Weinstein had deep reservations about bringing HIV treatment to South Africa, which was nearly half a world away from Los Angeles. He repeatedly asked his colleagues the same question: Was South Africa hopeless with Mbeki at the helm? No one gave Weinstein a satisfactory answer.

The next day, at the convention center, Weinstein dutifully attended the conference's plenary sessions, which took up such issues as adherence to antiretroviral therapy and the science of HIV/AIDS. But Weinstein got antsy and went back to the Hilton for a break. As he approached his room, a bellman told him that people were looking

for him. "Who are they?" Weinstein asked. The bellman didn't know. When he entered his room, Weinstein found a letter in an envelope lying on the floor. It was from two South African AIDS activists.

"It said that they were waiting downstairs in the restaurant, and that seemed a little bit odd," Weinstein said.

Weinstein, though wary, turned around and went to the nearly empty restaurant. Off in a corner, he saw two women sitting at a table. One of them was Nomaswazi Mlaba, who reached out to Weinstein based on word of mouth from other AIDS activists at the conference. Mlaba had been waiting at the restaurant for hours, hoping Weinstein would show up. He introduced himself and took a seat.

Mlaba was actually representing a number of AIDS activists based in South Africa. One of them was Dr. Musa Gumede, who worked with the Networking HIV/AIDS Community of South Africa (NACOSA). That organization had been battling AIDS since 1991, and the conference was something of a godsend for his group and others. With or without Mbeki's approval, South African activists were determined to make connections within the international AIDS community and bring HIV treatment to their country.

"We decided that we were going to target people at the conference to fund us and our programs," Gumede told me, "and see if we could work with them."

Mlaba, Gumede, and their fellow activists specifically approached organizations that were providing HIV treatment—in addition to AHF, they were talking with AIDS groups from Europe and Australia. Yet Mlaba and her colleague didn't know that the challenges they faced in South Africa were eerily similar to those Weinstein and AHF had navigated in Los Angeles—from wrong-headed public health policy pushed by politicians to the public's fear and hostility that comes with an AIDS backlash. As the two women talked, Weinstein could relate to their horror stories.

"They were explaining the desperate situation," said Weinstein, "and how difficult it was to be an AIDS activist in that environment.

So I said, 'I'd like to see what is going on here locally, not at the conference, but in the community. So would you take me and show me?' We got a minivan the next day. We went into some pretty remote areas outside of the city. It was a really desperate situation."

With a small crew of activists, Weinstein spent part of his day in Umlazi, the third largest township in South Africa, fourteen miles south of Durban. With its windswept hillsides and brilliant blue sky, Umlazi was intrinsically beautiful. It also came with a shameful history. During apartheid, the white power structure instituted forced removals of millions of Black residents out of so-called white zones, sending men, women, and children to overpopulated, disease-ridden, extremely underserved relocation settlements. Umlazi was one of them, and it still had not recovered from the evils of apartheid. Shantytowns dotted the hillsides, and the poverty was appallingly apparent. Weinstein had never seen anything like it.

At another stop, in Durban North, Weinstein and the activists visited a community center that ran support groups for people living with HIV/AIDS. Weinstein talked with young men and women who were dangerously thin and obviously dying, but the center didn't have the funding to provide medical services. It further underscored why the activists needed help.

"The big thing that they wanted was treatment," Weinstein explained.

The next day, Weinstein skipped part of the conference and again met with Mlaba and other activists at the Hilton. He said he wasn't sure what he could do, but he was willing to work with them—only one other organization approached by Mlaba and her group had made such an offer. Weinstein invited them to Los Angeles, where they could see AHF's work and get a better idea of what could be done in South Africa. Four months later, on AHF's tab, Mlaba and a handful of others arrived in LA.

Never an organization to waste an opportunity, AHF held a demonstration at the South African consulate in Los Angeles, where

Mlaba and her colleagues delivered a letter demanding treatment. Weinstein, Terri Ford, and Peter Reis also talked details with the activists, determining what kind of operation was feasible in South Africa. By this point, Weinstein, who was already thinking that a clinic with a doctor and nurse would be needed, wasn't going to allow a lack of cash to be a deal breaker.

"We didn't have the money," he told me, "but that never really stopped us before."

While the South Africans were still in LA, Cynthia Davis just happened to meet Vincent Ssempijja, a gregarious, undaunted politician from Uganda's Masaka District, an agricultural center eighty miles south of the nation's capital in Kampala. Masaka was another AIDS hotspot in Africa. Ssempijja made the 9,400-mile journey to Los Angeles to attend a business conference, but his real mission was to find relief for his people, who were dying nearly every day from AIDS.

"I wanted to talk about it," Ssempijja told me. "I hoped to meet other people who knew what was going on and who might have an idea. Otherwise, we have no solution, and people are just suffering without any help."

The conference's organizers were sympathetic and allowed Ssempijja to deliver a special speech about AIDS in Uganda. Whether it was fate or luck, Davis, who had never met Ssempijja before, was sitting in the audience when the politician talked about the misery and devastation he witnessed—sometimes attending three funerals in one day. When Ssempijja finished, she approached him. He wasted no time in asking for assistance.

"He said he wanted AHF to come to Uganda to build a treatment clinic," Davis recalled. "I said I couldn't guarantee that, but that I could introduce him to Michael Weinstein, and he could present his proposal to him."

Weinstein and Ssempijja talked at length about the political situation in Uganda, which also lacked access to HIV drugs. Ssempijja,

in fact, didn't know about the AIDS cocktail—four years after its use began in the US—until Weinstein brought it up. By the end of their discussion, Weinstein promised to visit Ssempijja in 2001. At which time, he would seriously consider opening a free HIV treatment center in Masaka. Even though Ssempijja didn't get a firm commitment, he was impressed by Weinstein's willingness to move quickly.

"He made the decision then," Ssempijja recalled. "It was something I couldn't believe. But I heard it from his own mouth."

Weinstein was making another calculated move. He was nearly certain AHF should operate in Uganda, but he hoped to avoid another major showdown with a foreign government. AHF was already heading into an international duel with Mbeki in South Africa.

—

By 2001, AHF HAD created a new division: Global Immunity. The effort was led by Henry Chang, a well-regarded player in the AIDS world who had once worked at AHF Research. Chang visited Uganda and talked with numerous government officials. On his return, he recommended that AHF should win over Ugandan President Yoweri Museveni, who had established a robust AIDS policy in the late 1980s and was nearly the polar opposite of Mbeki.

In quick order, in September 2001, AHF's Global Immunity cosponsored the First African Great Lakes AIDS Conference at the Imperial Botanical Beach Hotel in Entebbe, Uganda. No one had to convince Weinstein to attend the event. It had been worked out that Museveni would receive, in person, a special accommodation from AHF for "distinguished leadership and excellence" in the fight against HIV/AIDS. The president, in return, would meet with Weinstein.

On the day of the ceremony, Museveni hosted Weinstein in one of the hotel's conference rooms. The president was surrounded by some fifteen advisors. Weinstein, who had a much smaller entourage, was suddenly struck by the immensity of what AHF was undertaking and that he was leading that global effort.

"Being in that position," Weinstein recalled, "there were voices in my head that said, 'Who the hell are you?!' And I would say to myself, 'No, shut up. I know what I'm doing.'"

Weinstein composed himself, somewhat. He asked Museveni for a modest financial commitment. It would help, Weinstein explained, AHF's lobbying efforts in Washington, DC, to secure monies for antiretroviral therapy in Uganda.

"This was unusual for me," Weinstein said, "but I said even a million shillings would be great, which at that time was around $700. Museveni looks at me, and says good-naturedly enough, 'We may be poor, but we aren't that poor.'"

Weinstein was embarrassed and apologized, but nearly everyone chuckled. By the end of the meeting, Museveni agreed to Weinstein's request and welcomed AHF to Uganda.

—

MEANWHILE, AHF DECIDED TO open its first global clinic in South Africa, in Umlazi, where a staggering one in three adults were infected with HIV. It would start as a pilot project, with one hundred patients receiving free antiretroviral treatment. Since AHF didn't have money for a larger program, and the South African government wasn't convinced that such an operation was necessary, starting small was the only way to go.

"You can't fight a huge government like that," Terri Ford told me. "You have to show it can be done; that people's lives can be saved, even if it's only a hundred patients."

AHF specifically chose Umlazi, in the province of KwaZulu-Natal, to prove a point to pundits and political leaders in the developed world. Among many experts in the early 2000s, there was a notion that poor Africans could not adhere to a strict antiretroviral therapy regimen and, therefore, giving them lifesaving drugs would be a waste of money and resources. AHF and the activists in Durban wanted to show that they were wrong.

"We wanted to prove that the poorest of the poor have the same need as a person who has money, and that they want to live," Diana Hoorzuk, an AIDS activist who worked with Weinstein and later joined the AHF board of directors, told me. "So we looked for the biggest sprawling township in the city of Durban, and that was Umlazi."

Weinstein was again taking a gamble, hoping that once AHF proved itself, the South African and US governments would pay for the costly HIV drugs. It would be a model of expansion that AHF would often utilize—known in AHF circles as the "build it, they will fund" approach.

It was an expensive bet. With no governmental funding, AHF had to pay for a doctor, a nurse, and the construction of a clinic. It also had to come up with $5,000 a year for each patient in the pilot program—a whopping total of $500,000 that AHF could not actually spare. The clinic, a joint venture with Nomaswazi Mlaba and her group NetCom SA, would be called Ithembalabantu. In Zulu, it meant "people's hope." Going into South Africa with little money, no international experience, and no blessing from a hostile South African government, that phrase applied to AHF's chancy venture as well.

Building the clinic was more difficult than anyone had anticipated. Weinstein turned to Terri Ford, who had managed the complex construction process of Linn House in West Hollywood.

"He called me on a Sunday and asked if I could go to South Africa and get this clinic going," Ford recalled.

US Congress members Barbara Lee and Diane Watson had agreed to lend political clout by attending, in person, the clinic's ribbon-cutting ceremony in late August 2001. That meant Ford had to immediately hop on a plane and complete her mission in three weeks. Henry Chang, the Global Immunity chief, would join her.

"I had never been to Africa," Ford said. "I didn't know what I was doing, but I knew I could figure it out."

For the site of the clinic, Ford and Chang chose a run-down, mouse-infested storefront located in a strip mall. On each side was a funeral home, which regularly served the grieving families of AIDS victims. A natural medicine store, which sold the kind of rudimentary treatment the South African government was advocating for HIV/AIDS, was also a neighbor.

"The thinking at that time in the public sector was that you could deal with this problem with normal eating, exercise, and other prevention," explained Dr. Gumede.

In spite of many obstacles, Ford and Chang quickly hired contractors, supervised a complete renovation, brought in medical equipment, and readied the clinic for a grand opening.

"We made something out of nothing," Ford said.

But there was more trouble to come.

When Weinstein, Cynthia Davis, and the congress members arrived in late August, it was made plain that AHF was not welcome. Mbeki and his associates were miffed that an American organization was coming into their country without an official invitation. They also believed there were more pressing problems in South Africa than AIDS, which, in their eyes, would be too complicated to treat.

"The government's main issue was that people were simply so disadvantaged," Hoorzuk explained. "People didn't have clean drinking water. People didn't have electricity. People didn't have houses. People didn't have land. So, they were saying, let's treat a person who has meningitis, that kind of thing, but going into the unknown, so to speak, on the antiretroviral issue for the masses?"

South African officials had another concern.

"The one thing that the government kept asking us was, 'What is your sustainability?'" Hoorzuk recalled. "'What happens if in three years you decide to walk out and leave us? Who will see those thousands of people that you were treating?' That was the biggest question everywhere we went, everywhere in the government."

Rather than listen to solutions for those questions, Mbeki and his crew contacted Congresswoman Lee and told her AHF was out of line. The South African minister of health, Manto Tshabalala-Msimang, then pulled a power move: she summoned Weinstein, Lee, and Watson for a sit-down but kept delaying the meeting. The AHF contingent waited for hours. When they threatened to leave, the minister still refused to see them and sent word that AHF should not open the clinic. Officials from the United States Agency for International Development told Weinstein that if he didn't back down, the government would probably expel him.

Weinstein, Watson, and Davis stood their ground, but Congresswoman Lee decided to not attend the ribbon-cutting ceremony. After visiting a number of AIDS wards in and around Durban, the three were only further resolved to defy Mbeki and the South African government.

Davis recalled, "It was a really tragic situation there. The people in these wards seemed so isolated. There was so much stigma around HIV and AIDS. You'd see a lot of women in the wards with babies who were born positive, and they were not being treated."

Weinstein said, "One of the most horrifying things I had ever seen was at the women's ward at King Edward Hospital in Durban—all of these young, totally hopeless women."

He added, "At all the places we went to, they said that they can treat people and keep them alive, but they don't have the drugs, and it really came down to that."

The AHF contingent weren't the only ones targeted by the South African government. Local AIDS activists were also enduring intense criticism from the political establishment.

"You were seen as not supporting your government," Hoorzuk said. "You were seen as rebellious and disrespectful."

Despite the heat from Mbeki and the South African government, Weinstein and the others didn't blink and went ahead with the ribbon-cutting ceremony. A few months later, in the winter of 2002,

after more skirmishes with South African officials, AHF opened Ithembalabantu Clinic, which included a data-gathering component so AHF could show that poor clients would adhere to treatment. The South African government, which had very reluctantly signed off on the clinic, would hold a long, deep-seated grudge.

"They were mad at us for a very long time—for years," said Terri Ford. "They basically punished us by making life for us hell for many years."

But Ithembalabantu Clinic was an overwhelming success. After the first year, one hundred men, women, and children had avoided certain death by receiving free antiretroviral therapy, and 99 percent of them adhered to their drug treatments.

"We had more and more people coming to the clinic wanting the medication," said Hoorzuk. "And because it was in their best interest, they adhered to the medication."

KwaZulu-Natal, one of the worst AIDS hotspots in the world, finally had its first free HIV treatment center.

—

THINGS WENT MORE SMOOTHLY in Uganda, where AHF opened an HIV treatment clinic in Masaka. AHF partnered with the Ugandan Ministry of Health, and Ugandan First Lady Janet Museveni attended the ribbon-cutting ceremony in December 2001. The pilot project would again serve one hundred people free of charge—and again AHF would be laying out hundreds of thousands of dollars for antiretroviral therapy and a two-person medical staff.

Weinstein wanted to give a special name to AHF's budding operation in Uganda, which honored the country's efforts to fight AIDS while also making politicians feel as if they had skin in the game. He got inspiration from the theme of the 2001 World AIDS Day, which put forward a question: "I care, do you?" As a kind of answer to the global community, Weinstein came up with the official name for AHF's work in the African country: "Uganda Cares."

But before the clinic opened in February 2002, Weinstein still needed a trusted hand to deal with bureaucratic delays and other key details. He sent his old friend, Mary Adair. She immediately cut through Uganda's red tape, trained personnel, and outfitted a cramped, five-room building on the campus of Masaka District Hospital.

"We worked sixteen-hour days," Adair recalled, "arranging the equipment, buying file cabinets, posters, benches, and water tanks, and getting HIV medications. We still didn't have the approval from the Ministry of Health, but we started anyway."

The first patients were two women, one of whom asked Adair if she would live to see her children grow up.

"I said I thought she would now that she had medications," Adair told me. "She smiled, but she was very ill. I went outside and sat on one of the steps of the clinic and cried and cried with joy and exhaustion."

That woman did survive.

As the program moved forward, Masaka native Hope Katete served as the clinic's first nurse, handling a steady stream of patients who were barely holding onto life.

"We never took breaks," she told me. "We really all worked together. The people we were caring for were really sick. It was a motivating factor to work and achieve more for the patients."

Yet AHF did receive some flak. Local AIDS organizations that specialized in social services were angry that AHF was providing antiretroviral therapy. It was the same kind of hostility that American AIDS groups directed at AHF in the 1990s.

"Treatment meant to some people that we were going to deny them jobs," Ssempijja explained to me. "These were the organizations for counseling and looking after patients....I had many meetings in Masaka, which was the center for all HIV and AIDS work. Most of the nongovernmental organizations are there. So, now I bring in this new organization, AHF, that is talking about treatment. People were not very happy with me."

The result of AHF's work, however, was immediate and long-lasting.

"Many of the people recruited in the first month are still living," said Ssempijja. "Most of them were brought in half dead. It started a revolution in the struggle against fighting HIV. We were fighting HIV going eastward, and now we turned the whole thing around and started going westward. It was a real revolution in saving lives."

And, for a second time, AHF proved the common wisdom wrong—the adherence rate at Masaka was an eye-popping 98 percent.

—

WHILE WEINSTEIN, FARTHING, AND others on the AHF team were flying back and forth between Los Angeles and Africa, the global AIDS crisis was finally attracting the world's attention. With its free clinics in South Africa and Uganda, its years of experience as a successful sponsor of legislation, and its years of knowledge as a healthcare provider, AHF was arguably the most qualified AIDS organization in the United States to contribute to a growing effort to control the global spread of HIV/AIDS.

AHF, in fact, was unique. In a Ford Foundation study titled "At the Crossroads," researcher Derek Hodel wrote that when "the global AIDS issue emerged, HIV organizations that were prepared, or who could get ready fast enough, participated in the debate. As a consequence, most domestic AIDS organizations [in the United States] were excluded." Hodel, though, noted that AHF wasn't in that group. Instead, it was one of only five American organizations that played an influential role in shaping global AIDS policy.

One major advance was the formation of the Global Fund to Fight AIDS, Tuberculosis and Malaria, which was founded in 2002. The other was the President's Emergency Plan for AIDS Relief (PEPFAR), which was championed by President George W. Bush in 2003. Through PEPFAR, the United States provided billions for antiretroviral therapy and other patient care in poor nations. AHF helped mold the landmark program.

During the creation of PEPFAR, AHF insisted that a majority of the funding go to antiretroviral therapy—a smart, sensible plan that would save millions of lives. But, according to the Ford Foundation report, it immediately stirred up controversy: certain AIDS advocates, once again, wanted more money for social services, not treatment. Federal officials weren't swayed and stuck with AHF's approach.

The Ford Foundation also noted that AHF was successful at "securing a requirement for an annual report on 'the number of new patients currently receiving treatment for AIDS in each country that receives assistance under this act.'" It was hugely important: foreign governments could be held accountable.

AHF's work on PEPFAR marked the beginning of a strong presence in Washington, DC. In 2004, Tom Myers, AHF's general counsel and chief of public affairs, moved there to set up a permanent office.

"We started having significant congressional influence with the creation of PEPFAR," Myers told me. "Since then, with the first PEPFAR reauthorization in 2008, we kept an emphasis on the bill on treatment and medical care, which was critical. And we got critical medical services into the Ryan White CARE Act. There have been some issues and changes around the Global Fund and the oversight of that program, and we've been able to have influence on them."

Myers's work is a great example of how things had changed rapidly at AHF. When he joined the organization in 1998, Myers spent much of his time on remedying the fiscal hangover that came with Weinstein's decision to buy the AIDS cocktail in 1996.

"Part of my job was defending lawsuits from creditors and collectors who claimed we haven't paid, and we may or may not have," he recalled, "but the point was that if we had the money, we were using it to buy drugs to save people's lives."

Five years later, Myers was no longer fending off bill collectors. Instead, he was working with the nation's top power brokers, creating PEPFAR and other vital policies that helped millions of people in the US and around the world.

—

PEPFAR WAS A GAME changer, but AHF didn't receive funding from the program to pay for the salaries of their global staff or the construction of new clinics. And, in 2002 and 2003, the organization had yet to secure monies from South Africa or Uganda to pay for HIV medications. Weinstein, though, kept "whipping the train forward," as Peter Reis described it to me—and AHF was again facing a financial crisis.

"Michael is a gambler when it comes to how we're going to pay for it," said Terri Ford. "Peter Reis was chief financial officer for three years, and I'm sure in those years he had a lot of sleepless nights."

Weinstein wasn't without his reasons. In his mind, clinics were imperative for providing long-term, quality care in developing countries. And, by constructing clinics, AHF was demonstrating to government officials an unwavering commitment to their country, which gave the organization political clout and wider global credibility—other government officials would see that AHF was in it for the long haul and would allow the organization to operate in their countries and save more people.

But AHF still wasn't bringing in the kind of money that was needed to pay for what Weinstein wanted to accomplish—AHF Pharmacy was not yet generating massive revenues. As a result, Reis was, indeed, sleepless with worry. What bothered him most was that AHF was repeating a nearly devastating pattern from the 1990s.

"We paid for our drugs once upon a time," Reis told me, "and it almost broke us, so maybe we should've learned."

Also, the stakes were even higher with AHF's growth in California and expansion into Florida, New York, South Africa, and Uganda.

"People's lives were held in the balance," Reis said.

To top it off, Weinstein was not acknowledging AHF's fiscal realities in a way that satisfied Reis.

"He sometimes pretends he doesn't see what the problem is," Reis explained.

The relationship between Reis and Weinstein had become thoroughly strained. But one evening after work, they grabbed a drink at The Well, a nearby bar in Hollywood. After a few minutes of small talk, Weinstein told Reis that he knew AHF could "flame out." The remark caught Reis by surprise, but he was relieved to hear it.

"I didn't know if he could see the matter I could see," Reis said.

Weinstein further said that he was willing to take the risk—whether or not Reis was on board. Reis asked what made him so sure that he could take such a chance. Weinstein replied with a touch of vulnerability.

"He said," Reis recalled, "'I'm not sure entirely, but I think I can see things other people don't necessarily see, and I feel that even under the circumstances, we have to do this.'"

Weinstein added that he wouldn't allow Reis to hold him back.

Reis had worked at AHF for eight years. He had watched it grow exponentially under Weinstein's leadership, and he believed Weinstein was the real thing—someone who truly lived the organization's mission, and who had dedicated his life to helping the vulnerable and underserved. Reis didn't think Weinstein was always right, but holding back such a person was the last thing he wanted to do. From then on, Reis toned down his objections. Weinstein, true to his word, kept whipping the train forward.

PART THREE

A Year of Fighting for What's Right Continues

Chapter 12

March 2014—Washington, DC, Las Vegas, & South Florida

AHF's Florida AIDS Walk

BY MARCH, AHF WAS taking another high-profile stand—to the intense irritation of certain insiders of the AIDS movement. At the center of the controversy was an HIV prevention drug called Truvada. A fierce, public battle would drag on for months, and AHF's critics would take dead aim at Weinstein.

More commonly referred to as PrEP, or Pre-Exposure Prophylaxis, Truvada protects an individual nearly 100 percent from HIV but adhering to a daily regimen is essential for it to work. And PrEP doesn't protect against other sexually transmitted diseases such as chlamydia, gonorrhea, or syphilis. The drug comes with

risks, including the fact that healthy people are ingesting a form of chemotherapy.

In the US, AHF was the only major AIDS organization that routinely brought up the problems with Truvada, and that thoroughly annoyed the biggest supporters of PrEP, most of whom were a vocal group of white gay men inside the AIDS movement and some gay journalists.

The first indication of trouble came in January with a *Slate* magazine article headlined, "There Is a Daily Pill That Prevents HIV. Gay Men Should Take It." The writer, Mark Joseph Stern, had singled out AHF for not fully endorsing PrEP, and then deemed Truvada a "miracle drug" that "every gay man with multiple sex partners should take."

Two months later, Gawker ran a think piece about PrEP. Writer Rich Juzwiak weighed the pros and cons of taking the pill himself and quoted AIDS Foundation of Chicago director of advocacy Jim Pickett, Harvard AIDS Institute researcher Iain MacLeod, a New York doctor named Stephen Dillon, and Michael Weinstein, among others. The article was jammed with opinions.

Pickett believed that too many gay men weren't using condoms, and, therefore, PrEP was a needed tool to add to the HIV prevention "toolbox"—an argument that was widely used by PrEP supporters. Dillon said the "medical community is still trying to figure out how to best implement" PrEP, which perhaps should have sounded an alarm for advocates like Mark Stern and Jim Pickett. MacLeod discussed the possible side effects, such as kidney damage.

But Weinstein pointed out that people had difficulty taking PrEP every day, so the pill wasn't, in fact, effective. One prominent analysis, known as the "iPrEx" study, showed a troubling efficacy rate of 42 percent.

"The theoretical possibilities for preventing infection based on people taking it every day is largely irrelevant if people don't take it," Weinstein told Juzwiak. "And the evidence is that they're not taking it.

So it doesn't work, from my point of view. There's no question...that people will stop using condoms if they're taking this medication, and they'll think they're protected when they're not. And their partners will think they're protected."

Weinstein was also concerned that PrEP threatened the very existence of the safer sex/condom strategy to prevent STDs and HIV, which had protected millions of people around the world for decades. If huge numbers stopped using condoms, that would almost certainly trigger another public health disaster, whether it was a syphilis outbreak or worse.

In addition, Truvada had the potential to be a boon for Gilead Sciences, the pharmaceutical giant that manufactured the drug. Gilead could now make billions in profits by providing HIV drugs to HIV-positive *and* HIV-negative gay men. Neither Juzwiak nor Stern wrote about the financial motivations underlying Gilead's Truvada push.

The Gawker piece made clear that the debate over PrEP was stirring up messy issues about safer sex, gay sexual freedoms, and the psyche of the sexually active gay male, which would give rise to a vicious showdown between those who championed PrEP and those who didn't.

But in March, AHF was still a few weeks away from a full-blown controversy, and it was busy with other important business.

AIDS Is a Civil Rights Issue was humming along with Reverend Al Sharpton speaking at town halls across the nation, and Mike Kahane's crew was preparing for the annual Florida AIDS Walk in Fort Lauderdale. AHF was also gearing up for a direct confrontation with health officials in Las Vegas over the mobile testing ban. And the organization was poised to introduce a bill in the House of Representatives against the wishes of the Obama administration, which was shaping up to be another hard-fought battle. During the second week of March, I flew to Washington, DC.

—

THE AMERICAN SOUTH, ACCORDING to the CDC, was in crisis. Of the top seven states with the worst rates of new HIV infections per 100,000 persons, six were in the South: Louisiana, Maryland, Florida, Georgia, Mississippi, and Texas. The CDC also found that the South accounted for 45 percent of new AIDS diagnoses in the United States, which dramatically outpaced all other regions—the Northeast was second with 24 percent. As a result, according to the most recent data, the South led the nation with 8,531 people dying from AIDS in 2009—a total of 17,774 Americans died from AIDS that year. The Northeast again ranked a distant second.

To put that in perspective, 4,492 American soldiers lost their lives in the Iraq War between 2003 and 2015. In 2009, 149 soldiers were killed. In that same year, 17,774 Americans died of AIDS.

Additionally, 62 percent of those AIDS diagnoses in the South involved African Americans, while 22 percent were white and 13 percent were Latino. Blacks also made-up 48 percent of the AIDS diagnoses in the Northeast and 52 percent in the Midwest. The data only underscored AHF's concern that African Americans were far and away disproportionately impacted by HIV/AIDS.

Even with those outrageous levels of deaths and infections occurring in the South, a federal AIDS program, known as the Ryan White CARE Act, wasn't directing enough money to fight the epidemic there. To correct that, AHF wanted to change the way Ryan White funds were distributed.

Yet AHF learned that the Obama administration was opposed to working on Ryan White and instead wanted to focus on the implementation of the Affordable Care Act, also known as Obamacare. AHF leaders, including general counsel Tom Myers, Southern Region chief Mike Kahane, and Weinstein, were deeply disturbed—the statistics showed that the American South was facing an escalating public health crisis that needed an urgent response. So, AHF moved forward, sending a group of mobilizers to congressional offices in hopes that key politicians would cosponsor the organization's reprioritization legislation.

On March 12, Tom Myers gathered a dozen mobilizers, nearly all of whom were African Americans from the South, for a strategy session at the headquarters of Parry, Romani, DeConcini & Symms—a lobbying firm that AHF had used since the late 1990s. Myers, a politically savvy sixteen-year veteran of AHF, had set up shop in the building, working in a windowless, basement office he proudly called "the bunker." Now, in a conference room, Myers gave the mobilizers the lay of the land.

"For these meetings," he told everyone, "you're going to be there for twenty minutes, and you will get someone who knows a little bit, and you'll have someone who knows a lot. That is why those charts are so handy."

Myers picked up a sheet of paper, pointing at statistics from the HIV Care Continuum. One disturbing fact was that only 40 percent of 1.2 million HIV-positive Americans were engaged in care.

"The problem here," he said, "is that there's not enough testing because people don't know they're positive. Since they aren't getting a diagnosis, they aren't going to the doctor. This is very simple stuff."

He explained that Medicaid and insurance companies didn't pay for certain services, but the Ryan White CARE Act covered such things as an HIV treatment adherence specialist, which helped to provide more comprehensive patient care. The mobilizers nodded.

Myers continued, "We have fifty thousand infections every year, and people who are getting more sick. Every new infection is $600,000 in medical costs. You know, why are we sitting around with our thumbs up our asses? But that, to my mind, is the whole point of this—this bill directly addresses these things....It's not reauthorization; it's just reprioritizing what we know based on the science and the facts. They're simple changes to help people right now."

Myers paused for a beat, then said with a dry, comedic touch, "Now that I have persuaded you, my work here is done."

The mobilizers chuckled, then grabbed the charts and headed to Capitol Hill.

Myers and I moved to his office. I wanted to know why several AIDS organizations were backing the Obama administration and not supporting AHF's effort to shift more funding to the South.

Tim Boyd, AHF's director of domestic policy, who was also headquartered in Washington, DC, had previously told me that the Obama administration was facing a public relations nightmare due to the shaky rollout of the Affordable Care Act, which Republicans had seized upon. Boyd believed the president's people didn't want to give Republicans more ammunition by bringing up the shortcomings of the Ryan White CARE Act, and Obama and his party were headed for a tough midterm election battle in November, hoping to keep a Democratic majority in the Senate. As a result, Boyd believed, AIDS groups had been enlisted by the administration to halt AHF's reprioritization plans until after the elections. Those groups took the public stance that more time was needed to see how the Affordable Care Act could best address HIV issues, despite the fact that thousands of Americans were still dying from AIDS every year. Carl Schmid of the AIDS Institute, for example, pushed a wait-and-see approach in a *Congressional Quarterly* article published the day before AHF mobilizers started lobbying in Washington, DC. The timing and publication didn't seem to be a coincidence—the *Congressional Quarterly* is widely read by politicians and their staffers.

So, Myers leaned back in his chair and gave me his take.

"The main groups that are pushing for a delay are either Beltway or insider groups who don't actually provide patient care. They're kind of creatures of DC. Perhaps they're trying to win favor with the administration because Obama would rather spend time on healthcare reform. This is all speculation, but any change to the status quo could be harmful to certain groups."

I asked if that meant some organizations worried about losing federal funding due to the money shuffle that came with reprioritizing the Ryan White CARE Act. He agreed and again pointed at the

HIV Care Continuum chart and its troubling statistics—168,000 Americans living with HIV don't know their status and only 30 percent are virally suppressed. "This is the status quo," Myers said. "And if we don't do anything, we have this, and people who are arguing that we shouldn't move from the status quo are essentially saying that the status quo is acceptable for them."

He added, "AHF just fundamentally disagrees with that."

AHF wasn't going it alone. It had lined up a long list of AIDS- and faith-based groups and local politicians to back its effort—from the Eastern Virginia AIDS Network in Norfolk to Mayor Chris Rey of Spring Lake, North Carolina, to the Gentle Spirit Church in Atlanta.

"People in the South know firsthand that the status quo isn't acceptable," said Myers, "and they know that change needs to happen now."

—

AFTER MY MEETING WITH Myers, I visited Romano Romani, one of the partners of Parry, Romani, DeConcini & Symms, at his office, which was spacious and sunlit and looked nothing like a bunker. He started his lobbying firm in 1984, and was once the legislative director for Senator Dennis DeConcini, a Democrat from Arizona.

Possibly one of the great inaccuracies with regard to the political response to AIDS in America is that Republicans have done little, a belief that stems from President Ronald Reagan's outrageously slow reaction to the epidemic in the 1980s. But his successor, President George H. W. Bush, had signed the Ryan White CARE Act into law. Years later, President George W. Bush pushed through PEPFAR, the President's Emergency Plan for AIDS Relief. Both are landmark pieces of AIDS legislation.

Knowing that, I was curious about the belief held by some AIDS groups that belt-tightening Republicans would drastically defund the Ryan White CARE Act if given the chance. That didn't jibe with the Republicans' record, especially since they had recently signed off on the PEPFAR reauthorization in 2013. I asked Romani what he thought.

"The Republicans have always taken a realistic attitude toward AIDS and AIDS treatment," said Romani. "They've been inclined to look at the medical side of things and not inclined to look at the social services side of things. And a lot of the AIDS groups provide a lot of social services. They could not have that much in common with Republicans."

It was an understandable position: the statistics in the HIV Care Continuum showed that medical services needed to be ramped up.

For Romani, the coziness between Democratic leaders and AIDS groups dated to the 1980s. Powerful Democrats from the East and West Coasts, the ground zeroes of the HIV/AIDS epidemic, pushed to get funding for social services, such as transportation to a doctor's appointment or prepared meals for a sick AIDS patient. But as the years went on, Romani said, Democrats found it politically expedient to be uncritical of AIDS groups, which resulted in poor decision-making on how to spend federal AIDS money.

"These elected leaders were likely to simply say, 'If the AIDS community wants it, that's what we're for,'" Romani told me.

AHF and Weinstein, of course, were ill-suited for this kind of go-along-to-get-along approach.

"Michael is a much different character," Romani said. "AHF is a group that has really, at one level at least, more in common with the sort of Republican mentality vis-à-vis AIDS than it does with the Democrats. Michael's attitude is: We want to get people in treatment, we want to find out who they are, and once they are in treatment, they aren't going to infect other people. So the keys here are the core medical services to get people on medications, keep them on medication, and make them productive citizens again."

(One of Romani's partners, former Senator Steve Symms, a Republican from Idaho, later told me, "Most organizations care about the organization, not the cause that they started out to fix. It's always the organization. AHF is still focused on testing and treatment.")

Romani, however, thought AHF's move to reprioritize the Ryan White CARE Act wasn't going anywhere in 2014. The Obama administration wasn't for it, and even some Republicans wanted more time to understand how the Affordable Care Act would impact the Ryan White program.

"But AHF is doing absolutely the right thing by trying to develop support," said Romani. "It sometimes takes a long time to develop that."

The next day, I met up with the mobilizers.

—

TIM BOYD, A QUIETLY confident twenty-nine-year-old, and I walked through an empty hallway of the Rayburn House Office Building. He was charged with collecting as many cosponsors as possible for the reprioritization bill by the time AHF introduced it on March 14, which was only a day away. There was no guarantee that the bill would receive a vote, but AHF had already lined up Congresswoman Renee Ellmers, a Republican from North Carolina, and Congressman Ted Deutch, a Democrat from Florida, to be the leading sponsors to show a spirit of bipartisanship.

"I want to create a coalition that people cannot ignore," Boyd told me.

But Boyd was hearing rumors that Deutch wanted to take his name off the bill.

Nearly twenty AHF mobilizers were sent to Capitol Hill to lobby Democrats and Republicans from southern states. The mobilizers initially ran into a wall of noncommitment, and Boyd learned that politicians were uncomfortable that AIDS organizations were not united behind AHF's bill. But he remained hopeful.

"Nobody wants to be first," he said, "and so once they realize that they're not the first, and that there's political cover, they may be more likely to sign on."

Boyd allowed me to attend several sit-downs with politicians. I heard mobilizers who knew the political subtleties of their home

states and provided a knowledgeable, boots-on-the-ground pitch for reprioritization that professional lobbyists and Beltway insiders could never deliver. They often knew more about HIV issues in their communities than the politician or staffer sitting across from them.

AHF mobilizers Elizabeth McLendon and Veronica Brisco, for example, had to navigate one Congress member's social conservatism—the politician talked about "strengthening" the family as the primary way to combat HIV and AIDS. Rather than get bent out of shape, the women explained the epidemiology of HIV. After that meeting, McLendon told me that the congressperson was "super conservative fiscally, so spending money wisely is really up [the congressperson's] alley." She believed AHF could win over Republicans with a checkbook argument: taxpayers will get better results for their money by spending existing Ryan White dollars on regions with the most need.

By the end of the day, Boyd told me he was "cautiously optimistic" that AHF could grab more cosponsors, but he heard that AIDS groups were telling Democratic politicians to not support reprioritization. Boyd stared down a long hallway at the Cannon House Office Building, and I could see a thousand thoughts churning in his mind. The bill's introduction was less than twenty hours away.

—

ON FRIDAY MORNING, BOYD's fears were realized at the last minute. Congressman Ted Deutch had pulled his name off the bill, even though AHF had strong political connections in Florida. In the end, Congresswoman Ellmers sponsored the bill and two Democratic African Americans from the South were cosponsors. It was not the awe-inspiring, bipartisan coalition AHF had sought, but Myers thought it was an important preemptive strike. AHF, he explained, had set the terms of the debate whenever the Ryan White CARE Act came up for reauthorization.

Boyd and advocate Garith Fulham pinned the politicians' hesitancy on what's known as AIDS Inc., the major AIDS organizations closely connected to Democrats. Fulham told me that more than once a politician or congressional staffer pulled him aside and said that AIDS Inc. was aggressively opposing the reprioritization bill. One senator told Fulham that AIDS organizations needed to "get their act together," figure out what was acceptable, and present the legislation with a "united front."

That senator was either naïve or unrealistic or disingenuous. A redistribution of government funding meant that many organizations would face a drop in federal funding, and that would never be welcomed by all AIDS groups.

AHF had no intention of following the senator's advice. During a conference call, Weinstein, who understood AIDS Inc.'s pushback and was generally pleased with how things went, told Boyd to stay focused on getting more cosponsors. "Once you get the critical mass of twenty," he said, "I think it'll be easy to get a hundred."

A few days later, when I was back in Los Angeles, Weinstein showed no signs of letting up. He told me that reprioritizing Ryan White and giving the South more funding would be "revolutionary" for fighting AIDS in the United States. If that was true, I thought, President Obama, who could speak so eloquently about the need to fix racial and economic inequities, all of which AHF's bill was addressing, was falling down on the job by opposing the reprioritization.

To add further insult to injury, a year later, in a presidential executive order, Obama claimed his administration "has been committed to reducing the HIV-related disparities experienced by certain populations," including "people in the Southern United States." Commitment, of course, meant nothing compared to action, and the executive order didn't bring up reauthorizing or reprioritizing the Ryan White CARE Act. At one point, Weinstein told me, "I'm so mad at Obama I could spit!"

—

WEINSTEIN WAS ALSO ANNOYED, and perhaps feeling a bit cantankerous, about the mobile HIV-testing ban in Las Vegas, especially after learning that AHF staffers didn't perform mobile HIV testing in late February. For Weinstein, it was the perfect opportunity to force the issue rather than play it safe.

"I was upset because I assumed that we were testing," he told me. "The idea that we were going to get arrested for testing was ludicrous." Weinstein added, "If you aren't going to get arrested, you should be testing and challenging that. The Las Vegas policy is so crazy and backward."

Other AHF managers wanted to delay a confrontation with Las Vegas health officials until after the organization had better established itself there with two new clinics.

Whitney Engeran-Cordova, the senior director of AHF's Public Health Division, told me, "AHF is a balance of hard and soft. The advocacy stuff breaks the rules, but the thing that gives us the moral authority to do so is the fact that we take care of so many people, and we do it well. So I've always worked under the premise that if I'm going to go in there and start beating the shit out of something, then I have to have the counterbalance. The counterbalance is that they have to know the good work that we do. So, I must admit that I played a little bit of a delay game because I wanted the service to get up so when we went in and started pounding on it that there was both the soft and the hard."

Engeran-Cordova joined AHF in 2006. He was smart and good-humored and once ran an AIDS organization in Long Beach, California. He helped grow AHF's Public Health Division from around twenty staff members in 2006 to nearly 175 employees in 2013. He was a key member of AHF's senior management team.

But by mid-March, Weinstein's patience was exhausted. He told Engeran-Cordova to send a mobile unit from Los Angeles to Las Vegas—about a four-hour drive—and start testing people on the streets in direct defiance of policy set by Southern Nevada Health District officials.

"Michael, in his typical fashion," explained Engeran-Cordova, "grew impatient and said, 'Just go do it.' So we said, 'Okay, we'll do it.'"

Adding to Weinstein's disgust was that Las Vegas officials charged up to $70 for an HIV test, which, along with the mobile unit ban, created another barrier to HIV testing, especially among low-income people. AHF's tests were free.

AHF's defiant approach in Las Vegas was not a covert operation. Every other weekend, it parked one of its big, colorful mobile units in a popular gay bar district called the "Fruit Loop," which attracted plenty of interest. During the first five weeks of working in Las Vegas, AHF had tested 221 people, and six of those individuals were positive for HIV.

"People were very responsive to it," said Engeran-Cordova.

AHF testers in LA, such as Jesus Martin and Alejandra Moratay, volunteered to drive to Las Vegas.

"We were backing up a righteous cause for testing services," Martin told me.

Engeran-Cordova nicknamed Martin the "Whisperer." He had an easy-going way of approaching people on the street and inevitably convincing them to take a test. It was the perfect touch for such a tricky mission in Las Vegas. This was particularly true when the AHF testers initially took heat from people who worked at the gay bars—they were worried that the mobile unit would scare off patrons.

"They were very reluctant to have testing there," Moratay explained to me.

Regardless, AHF kept pressing, and Engeran-Cordova waited nervously for something to pop.

—

DURING THE LAST WEEK in March, I traveled back to Fort Lauderdale for the Florida AIDS Walk. It was peak tourist season, and the weather was warm and clear and breezy. I expected to see Weinstein, and Southern Region chief Mike Kahane was holding the annual

bureau meeting where top AHF managers and Weinstein would talk about long-term strategy.

On the day of the AIDS Walk, at the beach, a stage was set up for a concert by the Go-Go's, a popular rock band from the 1980s, who would play after the walk. By 9:00 a.m., the place was jammed with a crowd of around two thousand people—women, men, and young people of different ages, races, and sexual orientations. Mark Martin, the director of the AIDS Walk, took the stage to charge them up.

Rather than stand with Martin, Weinstein quietly took a spot on the beach within the crowd. Not too far away, Dr. Patricia Campos from Mexico was standing with David Poole, director of legislative affairs for AHF's Southern Region. At the end of his pep talk, Martin asked the crowd to say in unison the name of the person who inspired them to walk. On the count of three, Weinstein said loudly, "Chris Brownlie!" It was time to hit the street.

At the front of the crowd, Kahane, Poole, Campos, Weinstein, and AHF board member Cynthia Davis held a wide Florida AIDS Walk banner. Weinstein stood in the middle—his customary place for such an event. Kahane and Campos flanked him. Whenever AHF holds a public event, employees use it as a way to gauge people's interest in AIDS and to see if AHF's advocacy and marketing are reaching people. This was on the mind of David Poole.

"I don't see apathy today," Poole told me as we walked past a group of cheering onlookers. "It's refreshing. It's exciting because it gives me hope."

Weinstein talked little, staring at the palm trees and the Atlantic Ocean and the people standing along the route waving and whooping and snapping pictures. When the AHF contingent completed the three-mile route, Weinstein walked over to the stage. Several people walked up to him and thanked him for his work and asked if they could take a picture with him. He happily obliged.

The AIDS Walk had raised about $800,000, which AHF would share with other AIDS organizations in South Florida. I asked

Weinstein what he was thinking during the walk. His answer surprised me.

"A lot of what I was thinking about was whether we can remain relevant to a younger generation," he said.

Weinstein paused.

"The gay community has a lot of ownership of the epidemic, which I understand," he said. "But sometimes I feel it's exclusionary, and I don't want anyone to feel excluded."

Weinstein looked around the crowd and smiled. He seemed happy with how things went. The next day, in a conference room at the Embassy Suites Hotel, Weinstein was all business at Kahane's management meeting.

"We have to show everyone that we will not accept that," he said, referring to a recent problem of retaining AHF patients. "We're not educating our staff enough and disciplining them enough. And retention and care are the hard core of controlling HIV."

But Weinstein made sure to give a nod to Kahane.

"I want to commend the leadership of the Southern Region," he said, "and Mike in particular. You have my sincere gratitude for making AHF look so good."

After the meeting, Weinstein told me that AHF should be more focused on improving than patting itself on the back.

"We can't get drunk on our success," he said. "That would be very dangerous."

Weinstein planned to stay in South Florida for another couple of days, visiting clinics and thrift stores and Dr. Esther Schumann. He wanted to listen, learn, and improve.

Chapter 13

April 2014—South Africa, Zambia, Uganda, India, Cambodia, & China

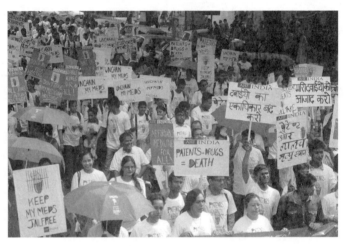

AHF-led protest in India

IN EARLY APRIL, A few days after AHF started providing free meningitis vaccines in response to a deadly outbreak in Los Angeles, I began a twenty-seven-day trip around the world. I would be constantly interviewing employees and meeting clients and jotting down pages and pages of notes. What I ended up with was a kind of journal, not only about the organization, but also the current state of the global AIDS crisis.

I first visited South Africa, then went north to Zambia and Uganda. From there, I headed east to India, Cambodia, and China, returning to LA from Beijing. I spent the majority of my time in poor,

underserved areas that were rarely, if ever, visited by tourists. These places desperately needed help, which was why AHF was there.

On the plane to South Africa, I read Nelson Mandela's autobiography, *Long Walk to Freedom*, and came upon this passage:

"When I walked out of prison, that was my mission, to liberate the oppressed and the oppressor both. Some say that has now been achieved. But I know that that is not the case. The truth is that we are not yet free; we have merely achieved the freedom to be free, the right not to be oppressed. We have not taken the final step of our journey, but the first step of a longer and even more difficult road. For to be free is not merely to cast off one's chains, but to live in a way that respects and enhances the freedoms of others. The true test of our devotion to freedom is just beginning."

Those words stayed with me for the next four weeks.

—

AFTER I LANDED IN Durban, South Africa, I was driven to a bed and breakfast called the D'Urban Elephant. The neighborhood was green and lush and affluent, but tall cement walls with barbed wire on top surrounded nearly every home. It looked as if people were living in an upscale prison complex. Which shouldn't have been surprising. Although South Africa was celebrating twenty years of democracy in 2014, the country was still dealing with entrenched poverty and high unemployment caused by decades of discrimination, and that fueled crime. South Africa, for example, had the worst rape rate in the world, which had turned into a public health crisis—too many girls and women were brutally exposed to HIV. AHF was already tackling the rape epidemic with a campaign spearheaded by advocacy manager Larissa Klazinga in Umlazi.

Before I went to bed, I watched a TV news report from West Africa. It showed medical personnel, dressed in bulky biohazard suits, treating people at an outdoor clinic. Health officials in Guinea and Liberia were battling a rare and deadly virus known as Ebola.

I figured authorities would soon have the situation under control, but that would turn out to be the wrong assumption. Over the next several months, nearly 11,300 people in Guinea, Sierra Leone, and Liberia would die.

—

The next day, Alec "Boy" Mdlalose, an AHF driver, picked me up in a red Toyota Highlander. He drove us away from downtown Durban on a highway to Umlazi. The natural beauty of the country was unmistakable—elegant green hills and a blue sky dotted with puffy, white clouds. At the same time, my mind played a grainy newsreel of violent, apartheid-era images I had seen on TV as a teenager—from white soldiers in riot helmets shooting tear gas into a large crowd of Black protesters to angry-faced white soldiers swinging metal batons at old Black men and children.

After we got off the highway, we arrived in Umlazi, where shanties blanketed the hillsides. Mdlalose drove deeper into the township, then took a right toward a strip mall. We had arrived at Ithembalabantu Clinic. It was no longer located in a storefront between two funeral homes, and it was no longer a pilot program for one hundred people. To handle an ever-expanding patient roster, it had moved into a former bank, which was three stories tall with long, wide hallways and numerous treatment rooms and offices. Starting at 7:00 a.m., up to five hundred patients visited the clinic each weekday to pick up medications, to be diagnosed, or to be treated for one illness or another, not just HIV.

As of April 2014, Ithembalabantu Clinic served 12,383 clients; 10,803 were receiving free antiretroviral therapy. Five hundred and twenty-one of the patients were children. Almost everyone was poor. I couldn't help but think that if AHF had succumbed to political pressure and left South Africa in 2001, many of those clients would now be dead.

After working in South Africa for twelve years, AHF now supported thirty-four clinics and served a total of 44,328 clients;

39,451 were taking antiretroviral therapy. As official policy in South Africa, only people living with HIV who had a CD4 count of 350 or lower received free antiretroviral therapy, although pregnant women and children under the age of five immediately received HIV drugs. (In January 2015, due to the advocacy of AHF and other HIV/AIDS organizations, South Africa changed the CD4 requirement to 500 or lower, allowing more people to start antiretroviral therapy.) As a result, one of the most important pieces of medical equipment at an AHF clinic in South Africa and other countries was a CD4 testing machine—as soon as a person met the CD4 threshold, AHF moved them into free drug treatment.

In South Africa, the government paid for the medications. AHF picked up the tab for everything else—from advocacy campaigns to building clinics to mobile testing to staff salaries. The organization also stocked clinics with extra medications—sometimes government inefficiencies created delivery problems—so patients would never stop treatment. This arrangement was the norm at many AHF global clinics.

According to UNAIDS, in 2014, an estimated 6.8 million people lived with HIV in South Africa, with a prevalence rate (among ages fifteen to forty-nine) of 18.9 percent—the largest AIDS epidemic in the world. Heterosexual sex was the primary mode of HIV transmission, and 3.9 million females aged fifteen or older were living with HIV. An estimated 140,000 South Africans died from AIDS in 2014, but whites were far less likely to be infected than Blacks. Despite the tragic policies of President Thabo Mbeki, who left office in 2008, South Africa had created the largest treatment program in the world, which was initially supported by The Global Fund to Fight AIDS, Tuberculosis and Malaria and PEPFAR money from the United States.

Countless lives throughout Africa had been saved through PEPFAR, and every year it prevented huge numbers of HIV infections. So it made sense that AHF and South African Archbishop

Desmond Tutu felt a moral obligation to criticize President Barack Obama for allowing PEPFAR funding to drop by 12 percent since 2010. It was a sign that Obama wasn't fully committed to controlling the global spread of AIDS and avoiding more suffering, despite his rhetoric of wanting to achieve an "AIDS-free generation."

In June 2013, Obama spent two days in South Africa. Hilary Thulare, AHF's South Africa program director, didn't pull any punches when a *Washington Post* reporter asked what she thought of the American president.

"Knowing that Africa has many challenges," Thulare said, "we were really expecting President Obama to continue where President Bush had left off. But it's been a disappointment. Obama is retreating on AIDS and, by this, retreating on Africa."

I met Thulare, who was forty-three and had a dry sense of humor, in her office at Ithembalabantu Clinic. She appeared to be handling twenty tasks at once—like all of AHF's country program directors around the world, she supervised staff, oversaw clinic and advocacy operations, and worked with government officials and nongovernmental partner organizations. One of her tasks was to organize a groundbreaking ceremony for a state-of-the-art clinic in Umlazi, which Weinstein would attend in May. The construction of the facility was part of AHF's scale-up for the 20×20 campaign, which challenged the global AIDS movement to bring twenty million people into HIV treatment by the year 2020. AHF promised to do its part by bringing in one million.

Thulare started working for AHF in 2011. On a bookshelf across from her desk, there was a plaque that displayed AHF's management philosophy; it included the values of "mission driven," "fairness," and "tenacity."

"We know from our principles that we have to do things right and perfect them as we move on," Thulare said. "So it is a tough environment, and you have to be tough. You can't waste time when people are dying."

With so much on her plate, Thulare suggested that I first talk with Cynthia Luthuli, also known as Sister Cynthia. She was a person of no small standing.

—

I FOUND LUTHULI IN her office. She was a warm woman who exuded a kind of battle-tested grace. In 2002, Luthuli started working as the nurse for AHF's first treatment program outside the United States. It was an uneasy, crucial time. The government was still antagonistic toward AHF, and there were people in South Africa's medical community who distrusted antiretroviral therapy. In addition, if AHF's pilot program failed in Umlazi, that would have harmed the organization's reputation and, therefore, its ability to provide more treatment in other countries.

With so much on the line, Luthuli was determined to keep things simple. She stayed clear of the naysayers and insider politics, and focused solely on saving lives.

"I had seen people die with no treatment," Luthuli told me, recalling her work at a hospital before AHF arrived in South Africa. "People would be sent home to go and die."

But with AHF, she could finally provide antiretroviral therapy, and her patients quickly realized that they had found an organization that cared about them.

"The word of mouth got around that there was treatment," Luthuli said, "because we were the only ones giving treatment and giving it free of charge."

After a year, people from all over South Africa traveled to the clinic. "It was like a marketplace," she said. Amid all the hustle and bustle, Luthuli witnessed what she called daily "miracles."

"People are going back to work," she explained. "Somebody was dying, and now they are getting up and doing all sorts of things. You feel good, you know? You can actually see a child who is starting to crawl and is now an adult. You can see the person dying, and, in a

few weeks' time, you are now talking to someone who is not going to die. This person is now well."

As I sat with Luthuli, I felt I was in the presence of a hero—but the kind who didn't get media attention and probably didn't want it. She simply worked hard and saved lives and did it all anonymously. When I said she was a hero, Luthuli seemed slightly irritated and went silent, then switched the topic. Her response only proved what I already believed.

—

THE NEXT DAY, I met Hilary Thulare at her office. I was leaving for Zambia in less than twenty-four hours, and I was curious about HIV stigma in South Africa and how AHF dealt with it. Her explanation sounded remarkably similar to what had been happening in the United States.

South African religious leaders, for example, held major sway in communities. "If you go to the same church," Thulare said, "and most do, the minister has people think that HIV is associated with promiscuity."

That kind of stigma caused a significant problem for women. South Africans endured high unemployment—in 2014, the jobless rate hovered around 24 percent—and women often relied on men for financial support.

Thulare explained further: "So they think, 'If I test positive, I'm not going to get married.' Or 'If I test positive and tell my partner, then my partner would ask, "How did you get infected?"' and think you've been sleeping around. So then they won't test themselves."

Those women also wouldn't receive HIV treatment.

In addition, she said, HIV-positive men and women faced total community rejection in some parts of South Africa.

"Then that works on their psyches and works on their emotional well-being," Thulare explained.

AHF, though, aimed to diminish religious and cultural stigmas through billboard campaigns in South Africa, which brought HIV

issues out into the open, normalized them, and made them less of a dirty secret. AHF also set up support groups so clients could meet others living with HIV and talk openly about their disease, including the fears and discrimination they battled in their everyday lives.

"It is a work in progress," said Thulare, "and it isn't easy. When they come to this clinic, there is no discrimination, and they're treated equally. We don't stigmatize anybody or talk negatively about anyone who is infected."

She added, "No government facility can provide services to so many people. You saw yesterday, our numbers were over five hundred patients. So we play a critical role and complement what the government is doing, and complement it on a very large scale."

AHF, for example, dramatically beefed-up HIV testing in South Africa and provided a vigorous patient retention program at its thirty-four clinics.

Having addressed every point at which human failure, fear, or prejudice could fuel the spread of HIV, AHF now rarely saw one of its South African patients die from AIDS-related causes—a major achievement in a country with the world's largest AIDS epidemic.

The next morning, Alec Mdlalose drove me to the airport. On the way, he explained that Ithembalabantu Clinic was cutting into the business of traditional healers, who pushed a regimen of healthy foods and homemade medicines to combat HIV. Also, funeral homes were losing business since fewer HIV patients were dying. As a result, Mdlalose said, many healers and funeral home directors blamed AHF for lost profits. Whether it was gay-bar owners in West Hollywood or local businessmen in Umlazi, it was the same old gripe.

—

IN LUSAKA, ZAMBIA, INSIDE a shopping center, AHF's Chifundo Clinic was packed, wall-to-wall, with patients. I walked up to the second floor, and found Victoria Kalota, the Zambia program director, staring intently at her computer screen. In a few weeks'

time, AHF was moving to a larger, more modern facility that the organization had spent millions to build, and Kalota needed to tie up numerous loose ends before Weinstein arrived for the ribbon-cutting ceremony. Kalota was so busy, in fact, that I spent most of my visit with an AHF driver named Henry Musariri. He was soft-spoken and street-smart and knew much about the organization's work in Lusaka.

Around the same time that AHF started working in South Africa and Uganda, the organization opened shop in Zambia. It had been, and still was, difficult work. In 2014, according to UNAIDS, 1.2 million Zambians were living with HIV—and 540,000 of them, or 45 percent, were women. (In the US, women make up 23 percent of all HIV cases.) The adult HIV prevalence rate in Zambia was 12.4 percent, and 100,000 children under the age of fifteen lived with HIV, another shocking reality. The center of Zambia's HIV/AIDS crisis was Lusaka, the nation's capital and largest city. It had a worse HIV prevalence rate—20.8 percent—than any other region in the country.

AHF operated in six districts throughout Zambia and had 19,588 registered clients—14,838 were receiving antiretroviral therapy. For an HIV-positive person to receive free antiretroviral therapy, he or she needed to have a CD4 count of 350 or lower, according to official Zambian policy.

Like many other countries around the world, Zambia wasn't urgently, and wisely, attacking the spread of HIV/AIDS. From what I was told, patients at government-run clinics often waited weeks to start antiretroviral therapy—even after they met the CD4 threshold. And people regularly spent an entire day at a government-run clinic, waiting to be seen. For AHF, this was no way to handle a crisis.

AHF learned years ago, by surveying its patients, that even though a client's health was in danger, he or she would willingly fall out of treatment if inconvenienced. Good customer service, in other words, directly impacted the larger mission of controlling the global spread of HIV. As a result, AHF placed a premium on getting people

in and out of clinics quickly and providing HIV treatment as soon as possible. These were two more reasons AHF kept growing around the globe.

On my second day in Lusaka, I asked Henry Musariri to drive me to a mobile testing site. Within moments, we were heading to a popular open-air market called Chawama, about three miles away from the Chifundo Clinic, where people could buy clothing and fresh food or meet up with friends.

Traffic moved slowly on the way, and I asked Musariri about his work. He explained that he used to be a mechanic and taxi driver but yearned for something more fulfilling. He then saw an advertisement for an opening at AHF. After a few days on the job, driving patients from the Chifundo Clinic to their homes, Musariri realized he'd found exactly what he was looking for.

"I was upgrading myself by working at AHF," Musariri said. "AHF is a growing operation that's there for people. Other organizations wouldn't provide a ride home."

In time, Musariri became protective of the patients he was helping, some of whom had mental health issues and couldn't take good care of themselves.

"You need to have love and concern for the people," he said. "You need to have a heart for them."

Musariri was particularly excited about the grand opening of the Chifundo Clinic.

"The new place will give us a lot of exposure," he said with a smile. "We'll be able to give better care for people."

Musariri was a good man, but he wasn't uncommon at AHF. In Los Angeles and Florida, staffers regularly told me that they were desperate to leave unfulfilling jobs and found their calling by serving people—in this case, AHF clients. Many were not only surprised that this calling was within them, but they were also grateful that they could make a living by serving people. For them, it was a way of life they never wanted to leave.

Musariri turned onto a main street that passed through a red-light district and led to the open market. He pointed at rows upon rows of shanties. "This is where you find the most vulnerable people," he told me. "They may be sick but can't make it to the hospital." He then spotted a group of young women, whom he thought were sex workers. Musariri said most of them insisted that a man wear a condom, but that changed if he offered more money.

Musariri made another turn, and we came upon an entrance to the market, where one of the AHF mobile testing teams had pitched a tent. A second team was at another entrance. AHF's mobile testing began in Zambia in 2009 and played a key role in expanding the organization's patient roster. AHF testers also walked neighborhoods, going from household to household to offer free HIV testing and counseling.

Inside one of the AHF tents, three young boys, who looked no older than eighteen, were giving their personal information to a tester—anyone below the age of fifteen needed parental consent to take an HIV test. They looked calm and relaxed, and they held out their hands as one of their fingers was pricked. When the results came back, all three were free of infection. None of the boys smiled when receiving the news, and they casually walked back to the market. I was possibly more relieved than them because I knew something they did not. Out of the hundred people who had been tested by AHF at the market, three were reactive for HIV.

—

THE NEXT MORNING, I took a flight to Uganda. As I waited in the airport, I checked my email and read devastating news: Dr. Charles Farthing, the man who was largely responsible for upgrading AHF's system of medical care, had died from a sudden heart attack. He was sixty years old. Peter Reis first got the news, and he called Weinstein, who was sitting in a cab in New York City.

"I was shocked," Weinstein later told me. "I just felt it was such a terrible loss; that someone like him was cut down relatively young."

It was particularly tragic for AHF. Farthing had left the organization years earlier but agreed to return as the global chief of medicine. With AHF adding more clinics, Farthing would have played an indispensable role as an onsite inspector and HIV treatment educator. He also would have been a tireless advocate for more universal access to HIV drug therapy. AHF, and the AIDS movement, lost a warrior.

—

IN UGANDA, I WAS shuttled around the country by Jacob Wabyoda, a driver who started with AHF in 2005. Together, we visited a sprawling public market in Kampala called St. Balikuddembe, where an AHF clinic served 5,414 registered clients; ventured out to Masaka, where AHF's first Ugandan clinic worked with 10,717 registered clients; and inspected a new AHF clinic in Lukaya that served 1,378 registered clients and was funded in part by rents collected at a nearby AHF-owned shopping center. Wabyoda was smart and savvy and held a deep understanding of AHF.

"People know what we do," Wabyoda told me about AHF's reputation. "Even soldiers and police officers, who have benefited from our services. They'll see us in the car, and they'll know who we are."

Which was true. Wherever Wabyoda and I went, we were treated with a kind of deference by the police and military. It may have helped that AHF had a strong relationship with First Lady Janet Museveni and President Yoweri Museveni, the longtime leader of Uganda. But around the time of my visit, people within AHF were wondering if that relationship would suddenly go sideways.

In February 2014, Museveni had signed an anti-gay law that sent people to prison for engaging in or promoting homosexual activity. Only a few days before I arrived in Uganda, for example, a worker for an HIV/AIDS research center was arrested for allegedly recruiting gays and conducting unethical research. The employee was eventually released without charges, but AHF staff were on edge.

(In August 2014, the Ugandan Constitutional Court overturned the law on a technicality, although homosexuality remained illegal.)

Another controversy that routinely popped up was the bribing of HIV testers. Wabyoda mentioned that people planning to get married would pay off a tester in exchange for an official document that deemed them HIV negative. Engaged men and women didn't want their partners to know that they were, in fact, HIV positive.

"It happens all the time," Wabyoda said. "You see it in the newspapers. At Uganda Cares, they'll never do that."

In Uganda, AHF goes by Uganda Cares, led by country program director Henry Magala. It had been twelve years since Weinstein had come up with that name, and AHF had expanded from a hundred-person pilot program in Masaka to thirty treatment sites across the country, including partnerships with government-run clinics in rural towns far from any city. I went to one such clinic at Gombe, which served 2,569 registered clients and could only be reached by driving miles on a dirt road.

According to UNAIDS, 1.5 million Ugandans lived with HIV in 2014, with an adult prevalence rate of 7.3 percent. Women were extraordinarily impacted—770,000 adult females lived with HIV. So were children—150,000 kids under the age of fifteen were HIV positive and there were 650,000 orphans due to AIDS. But people were not dying in huge numbers like before AHF arrived in Uganda.

"AHF brought a lot of hope," Vincent Ssempijja, the Ugandan politician who approached Weinstein in 2000, told me one evening in Kampala. "You know when people are hopeless, they thought they were going to die. People could not plant perennial crops. These are crops that take time to mature and give you products. So that was the way people were living. They didn't know if they would live the next five years, so why should I do this? The first thing we got from AHF's support was bringing back hope in the people's minds. That, 'Oh, I'm going to live after all! I'm not going to die!'"

In 2014, AHF served 47,490 registered clients in Uganda—38,795 were receiving antiretroviral therapy. The CD4 requirement was 350. Due to AHF's rigorous retention program, 98 percent of all Ugandan clients stayed in treatment. One reason for AHF's incredible success was addressing the socio-economic problems that sometimes caused people to fall out of treatment, such as not making enough money to afford a ride to a clinic.

For one program, AHF had bought a tractor, a crucial piece of equipment in Uganda, where many people made a living by farming. AHF patients could borrow the tractor, get their work done, and only needed to pay for gas. Another project was SEEP, or Socio-Economic Empower Program. AHF gave modest loans to patients to create businesses such as a hair salon or grocery store. The loans, which came with a small interest payment, were paid back 95 percent of the time. The program was self-sustaining and extraordinarily popular. If patients' businesses were successful, and they always made their payments, they could receive additional loans.

—

AFTER DAYS OF TRAVELING, I finally sat down with Dr. Penninah Iutung Amor, a witty, personable woman affectionately known as Dr. Penny. We met in her office in Kampala, the official headquarters of AHF's Africa Bureau. She was born and raised in Uganda and started working for AHF in 2004 when she was twenty-nine—she was the only full-time doctor at the organization's Masaka clinic. Ten years later, as the Africa Bureau chief, she supervised country program directors in ten African countries. It was a massive and important job: in April 2014, 151,622 of AHF's 303,834 registered clients were living in Africa. Weinstein trusted her absolutely, much in the same way he trusted Mike Kahane in South Florida.

I asked Dr. Penny about her days as a young doctor, working with AIDS patients, before AHF came to Uganda. It was a period that still haunted her.

"It was very depressing," she said. "I am a person who doesn't like to fail, and at that point, as a doctor, I felt like I was failing these patients because there was nothing more for me that I could do. So the most we could offer at the hospital was hospice care. But you knew that one week you're treating this patient, and a week later, another one is going to come. Some of them had very severe end-stage of the disease. You just had to counsel them, and make sure that they continue to have pain medications, and continue to treat their opportunistic infections, just to make sure they can be okay."

Dr. Penny sounded like Dr. Patricia Campos in Mexico or Dr. Esther Schumann in Florida when recalling her work at AHF's Masaka clinic.

"Unlike general patients where they may come in once," she told me. "With HIV care, you can actually build a bond. At the end of the day, the success of the patients really depends on the patient, more than just the doctor. So for me, with HIV care, you are building a bond and going on a journey with the patient."

Dr. Penny added, "A lot of doctors don't want to do that. Some doctors do find that it is a burden, and they back out. I know sometimes doctors take the patient's burden and then make it theirs, instead of empowering the patient. In HIV, you have to empower the patient. You can't just give them something and do nothing for them."

During the trip, I had repeatedly heard that one of the major problems around the world was that international AIDS programs were only funded for a number of years and would leave a country once the money ran out. AHF, on the other hand, stayed for the long haul. I asked if that was a key to its expansion and success in Africa.

"At the community implementation district level," Dr. Penny said, "we have a lot of community support. They know we are not going to go anywhere, and that they can always go to their provider and always find us there. So we are always popular at that level."

She continued, "But the government sometimes wants you to fund some of their programs. You'll find some AIDS organizations

do agree to fund government jobs, but we have never done that. We always felt that it wasn't the right thing to do. Our model of operation is to reach the patient directly as much as possible, and we wanted the money to go directly to the patient."

As a result, Dr. Penny said, government officials weren't always happy with AHF.

"The government will want you to fund training activities, and that goes directly into the pockets of the government folks. We haven't done that. Sometimes it's been unpopular, and they'll favor other organizations over us. But we've stayed fine by doing what is right."

Dr. Penny was now trying to figure out ways to do "social enterprise" in Africa, rather than rely so heavily on revenue generated by AHF Pharmacy.

"We need to make the programs sustainable," she said. "If you don't have money, what can you do? We're still looking at avenues regarding what is going to be the right investment for AHF. The reality is that the markets in Africa are still going to be very risky. We are continually evaluating that."

Dr. Penny had another appointment, but I'd see her in a few weeks in Nairobi, Kenya, for the biannual Africa Bureau meeting, which would include the grand opening of another AHF clinic. Before committing millions of dollars to purchase or construct a facility, Weinstein almost always inspected a site in person, even if that meant traveling halfway around the world. For the new clinic in Nairobi, Weinstein never made a trip. Dr. Penny's judgment was gold.

—

AT ENTEBBE INTERNATIONAL AIRPORT, as I waited for my flight to India, I read a bizarre news item coming out of Los Angeles. A young man named Eric Paul Leue, who had gained minor fame in LA's gay community as winner of a "Mr. Leather" contest, had started a petition that called for the resignation of Michael Weinstein. After

spending nearly two weeks in Africa and seeing AHF's lifesaving work firsthand, it was the oddest thing I had read in years. But now the PrEP controversy had broken wide open.

Several days earlier, the Associated Press ran a story about a "rancorous debate" in the gay community over PrEP, the HIV-prevention regimen that utilizes the drug Truvada. With his continued concerns about patient adherence and a possible spike in unprotected sex among people who took the pill, Weinstein said in the article, "If something comes along that's better than condoms, I'm all for it, but Truvada is not that. Let's be honest: it's a party drug."

Gay news outlets and AHF's critics jumped on the "party drug" remark, saying Weinstein was stigmatizing PrEP by associating it with hedonistic, reckless behavior. When the gay media then reported about Leue's petition, things only snowballed.

Weinstein, however, was speaking a truth that many gay men knew—that people were taking PrEP a day or two before and after a spree of partying and sex but didn't take the drug daily as prescribed.

With the "party drug" quote, PrEP supporters seemed to believe they had a political weapon to bash Weinstein and AHF—and win a months-long public relations battle. Some AIDS organizations, who had long despised AHF's lone-wolf style of operating within the AIDS movement, also seemed to consider the PrEP controversy as an opportunity to damage AHF's overall reputation. It didn't matter that the organization was bringing free antiretroviral therapy to hundreds of thousands of impoverished people in Africa and Asia and the American South.

I wondered if critics ever thought of how damaging AHF could also impact its hundreds of thousands of patients around the world. In fact, what would the global fight against AIDS look like without AHF and Michael Weinstein? Did AHF's critics think about these things? Did they even care?

—

WHEN I ARRIVED AT the hotel in Delhi, India, our car was checked for bombs. This also happened in Uganda. Terrorism was a constant threat in many of the countries that AHF operated in, but it never seemed to faze the organization. It kept doing the work of serving the vulnerable.

On the second day of my visit, Dr. Nochiketa Mohanty, AHF's India program director, who's known as Dr. Nochi, took me to a government-run hospital. Dr. V. Samuel Prasad, AHF India's clinical affairs manager, or "Dr. Sam," and Shyam Gupta, the national prevention program manager, joined us. They wanted to show me one of the numerous problems that plagued India's approach to controlling HIV in the world's second-most populous country.

The hospital, one of the largest in India, was clearly overwhelmed. As we walked into the reception area, the facility was jammed with people, many of whom sat on the floor as they waited their turn to check in. As we walked by offices and treatment rooms, there were still more long lines. Things didn't get better at the HIV/AIDS clinic, which was also overcrowded.

Squeezing through a hallway filled with patients, Dr. Sam, an outgoing man, led me to the office of a young doctor. He was far behind schedule, and one of his colleagues was late for work. The doctor told us that he was treating 2,500 people. The other doctor worked with the same number.

"How is it possible for doctors to treat 2,500 each per year?" Dr. Sam said rhetorically.

The doctor just shrugged. As we left, Dr. Sam told me over his shoulder, "You can only imagine the quality of care going on there."

Dr. Sam, who was forty-two, and Dr. Nochi, who was thirty-six and more soft-spoken than Dr. Sam, were deeply involved in AHF advocacy campaigns in India—and they had the kind of oddly effective partnership that could make for an entertaining buddy movie. Their work was difficult. Over the course of a few days, I learned that the government didn't approve of mobile testing in

public, thinking it was ineffective because people wanted their anonymity—a mindset that was similar to officials in Mexico. But as with Mexico, AHF conducted mobile testing anyway. In 2013, in India, AHF had conducted 75,153 rapid tests and handed out 186,920 free condoms. Another problem was that in rural parts of India, people didn't know that antiretroviral therapy existed, which caused them to not take HIV tests, thinking AIDS was a death sentence that they'd rather not burden themselves with. And cultural, religious, and community stigmas were serious problems in India.

In addition, many doctors were either hesitant to treat HIV patients or were insensitive to the emotional turmoil that came with living with HIV. Treatment clinics were also overcrowded and understaffed. At the same time, Indian government regulations made it very difficult for AHF to import free condoms and lubrication. And India's politicians had a low tolerance for strong advocacy, especially AHF's brand. That led to constant struggles with government agencies, which wasn't all that different from the battles AHF sometimes faced when dealing with local governments in the US. In fact, wherever I traveled, I routinely heard about bureaucrats who were power hungry and resistant to change.

AHF started working in India in 2004, opening its free antiretroviral therapy clinic in Delhi in 2006. But due to the skirmishes with the Indian government, AHF had only 722 registered clients in India by April 2014—513 received antiretroviral therapy. (By September 2015, AHF India worked with 1,388 registered clients, and 1,090 were taking drug treatment.) The organization paid for all patient medications in India and started giving patients antiretroviral therapy once their CD4 count was 500 or lower, which was the official threshold in the country.

In a nation of 1.2 billion people, the Indian government estimated that 2.4 million were living with HIV, but Dr. Nochi and Dr. Sam thought that figure was low. In addition, according to UNAIDS, only 424,800 people out of the 2.4 million were receiving antiretroviral

therapy in 2010—a meager 17.7 percent of the HIV population were taking lifesaving drugs.

Dr. Sam, who joined AHF in 2012, told me, "AHF doesn't get dictated to by the government. We go and tell them that this is what you should do, and you should implement community HIV testing and help increase those numbers. That is actually what is exciting, and that is the big difference that AHF has always had. Also, it is why AHF doesn't have a 'good reputation' in India. But that doesn't matter. As long as we are doing our things right, it is okay."

—

ONE AFTERNOON, AT AHF's clinic in Delhi, where Dr. Sam worked as a clinician and Dr. Nochi and his small staff were headquartered, I talked with a couple of AHF clients. Dr. Nochi was my interpreter. At times, the clients became emotional when discussing their disease and what AHF's work meant to them, which was everything.

The first person I met was Vinod Mehra. He was twenty-nine years old and had the smile and look of a young movie star. He was diagnosed with HIV in 2007, when he was twenty-two, and came to AHF in 2009 after receiving poor care at a government-run clinic. Mehra, a self-described AIDS activist, loved that AHF took strong public stands on behalf of people like him—and he was deeply grateful that the organization provided quality care.

"I was part of support group meetings," Mehra said about his first months at the AHF clinic, "and I realized there were other people who were positive and people listened to me. They counseled me. So I felt comfortable."

In 2012, Mehra devoted himself entirely to AIDS work, hoping to land a job with AHF. There were no openings, but he found work as an HIV counselor with another AIDS organization.

"Those who get infected shouldn't have to go through a down phase emotionally," said Mehra, who went through a dark period when he first learned he was HIV positive. "So I want to help with

that. I talk with people who learn that they are positive, and they are devastated. But I give them my story, and then try to motivate them."

Mehra started to choke up and paused for a moment to gather himself, then nodded and smiled. I asked what he liked about AHF's services.

"The best part is that I get to talk to people," he said, "and people listen. At other centers, the doctor wouldn't give me that much time since there are so many other patients waiting, so I can't talk to the doctor about all the issues."

I also met "Rohan," another AHF client. He asked us not to publish his real name. Rohan was HIV positive for years before he knew, and when he finally learned that he was living with HIV in 2007, Rohan realized his wife and children needed to get tested. Everyone came back HIV positive.

"It was completely devastating," Rohan told me. "I thought my family was going to be wiped out."

To make matters worse, he lost his job, didn't know where to find HIV treatment, and was extremely depressed. He thought that there was no hope. Then an AHF outreach worker found him. He was told that he and his family could receive free antiretroviral therapy through the organization.

"AHF is like God to my family," he said. "In those days, I thought there was no way out. I came to the support groups and meetings and talked with the doctors and counselors and found a reason to live."

As he thought back, Rohan started crying.

"He gets a bit emotional talking about those days," Dr. Nochi told me.

One of the things Rohan most liked about AHF was that he didn't have to wait in long lines.

"If I need anything," he said, "I can get it immediately."

It was a remark that shot through me. Whether it was Fort Lauderdale or South Africa or India, clients were constantly saying that good customer service mattered. AHF took note, but

governments were another story. In fact, AHF wasn't only fighting a lethal disease but also a global epidemic of mediocrity and indifference. It was another reason why more than one million people around the world died from AIDS complications every year.

—

In Phnom Penh, Cambodia, soon after I landed at the airport, I was driven to the headquarters of AHF's Asia Bureau. It was located in a former private residence that looked like a small mansion. But there was nothing showy about Dr. Chhim Sarath, the Asia Bureau chief who grew AHF's extensive operations in Cambodia from nothing.

Approximately 75,000 people live with HIV in Cambodia, with an adult prevalence rate of 0.6 percent, according to UNAIDS. The country is not facing a catastrophic crisis like Africa, but out of the total number of HIV cases in Cambodia, 36,000 of them, or 48 percent, are women. Six thousand children under the age of fifteen also live with HIV. The CD4 threshold was 350, although tuberculosis patients, late-stage AIDS patients, and pregnant or breastfeeding women immediately received antiretroviral therapy.

AHF arrived in 2005. Over the next decade, under the leadership of Sarath, the organization forged a strong partnership with the Cambodian government, providing treatment and care at thirty-one clinics. In 2014, AHF worked with 26,747 registered clients, 23,744 of whom were receiving free antiretroviral therapy. AHF had a larger presence in Cambodia than any other AIDS organization.

I met Sarath in his office. He sat behind a desk in a bright room with floor-to-ceiling windows. Sarath was fifty years old, amiable, and unassuming—but shrewd. It was a trait he had to cultivate when he was child, living through the Khmer Rouge regime, which committed mass exterminations that took the lives of up to two million people. His aunts were killed by the Khmer Rouge, and he had been forced to work in a forest without his family, without shoes, and without a blanket to keep him warm at night.

"Every day I learned about people dying and being injured," he told me.

When Sarath first approached Cambodian officials, they were leery of AHF.

"The government didn't really trust us," he explained. "They wanted to try us out."

So the officials offered a program site far away from Phnom Penh that no other organization wanted. Sarath wasn't insulted. Instead, he saw an opportunity.

"I agreed with that because it was an entry point with the government," he explained.

Rather quickly, AHF brought large numbers of people into HIV treatment, which the government couldn't ignore. Officials also liked AHF's cost-effective model. In fact, Sarath said, the minister of health told other nongovernmental organizations that they needed to be cost-effective like AHF.

"One person who worked for an NGO complained to me for running such an effective model," Sarath said with a chuckle.

What lured Sarath to AHF was the simple fact that the organization wanted to bring free antiretroviral therapy to Cambodia.

"Not many people were on treatment yet," he said. "It would save people's lives."

What also grabbed Sarath's interest was that AHF was self-sustaining and did not leave a country once the international funding ran out.

"That's why people in government are very careful about an NGO coming into their country," he said.

Sarath added, "We have changed a lot of thinking in this country."

—

THE NEXT DAY, I visited a low-income, industrial neighborhood in Phnom Penh, where the organization had established a drop-in center for HIV testing and counseling. It was also a former

residence and served as a kind of casual gathering spot—much less formal and forbidding compared to a hospital. Ung Kim Heang, AHF's Cambodia program director, was particularly proud of the center, which held a "Friday Club" for the LGBTQ+ community and entertainment—or sex—workers.

"It's a safe place for them to come and share," Heang told me. "It can be difficult for them to talk freely."

A small group of young people, composed mostly of female entertainment workers, was setting up a circle of chairs for a chat. A young female AHF employee was on hand to talk about condoms and how HIV was transmitted.

"They have many partners," said Heang, referring to the women, "and they don't use condoms with their boyfriends."

If the women tested positive for HIV, they didn't always disclose that to their clients, fearing they would lose income.

"Once they start the life of an entertainment worker," Heang said, "they don't want to go back."

A few hours later, Heang and I sat in the back room of a Phnom Penh nightclub where some twenty young women, all entertainment workers, waited to be tested for HIV. The AHF team had arrived before the place would be swarmed with men looking to party. Everyone was quiet, perhaps because I was in the room, but no one tested reactive for HIV.

Then the women walked outside to the front of the nightclub, looking to draw in business. As cars zipped by, the women, wearing tight dresses, looked straight into the darkening night. AHF served them without judgment.

—

THE DAY AFTER LANDING in Beijing, China, Bao Yugang wanted to show me the gay cruising spots. Like other countries around the world, homosexuality made government officials squeamish, and gays were largely marginalized in Chinese society. But

Yugang, AHF's China program director, understood that new HIV infections among men who have sex with men were increasing, and that MSM and injection drug users were the two most impacted groups in China—recently, there had been a rise in heterosexual HIV transmissions.

"At the beginning," said Yugang, who once worked for China's Ministry of Health and the Bill & Melinda Gates Foundation, "HIV spread among the injection drug users. Then it spread to the sex workers, and then it went to the MSMs. And it is the most difficult work—how to stop the spread of HIV among MSM."

We first went to Dongdan Park, which, according to Yugang, was the most famous gay cruising spot in China.

"It's like the Great Wall," said Yugang, who's not gay. "If you have not visited Dongdan Park, you are not a true gay."

We walked up a trail, and a local AIDS activist joined us. He didn't want to use his real name and asked to be called Zhang Wei. He ran his own organization and acted as AHF's liaison to the gay community, handing out condoms, providing information, and doing anything else that was needed. When we arrived at the cruising spot, Zhang Wei immediately got to work, chatting up a group of young men. Yugang told me that he noticed a couple of "money boys," or male sex workers.

Yugang explained that less affluent gay men met each other at places like Dongdan Park, while gay men with money went to nightclubs and bars, where there were back rooms for sex. Getting any of them to wear condoms was difficult. So Yugang decided to bring in a person with deeper connections to the gay community than him. He hired Zhang Wei after a long search for the right partner.

"Some organizations just want the money," Yugang told me. "Some of them, it is from their heart, and they want to do work for the MSM community."

Zhang Wei, Yugang believed, worked from the heart.

—

We then took a drive across Beijing to Mudanyuan Park, another gay cruising spot. During the ride, Yugang explained that government officials were becoming more concerned about AIDS. For years, China had maintained a low HIV prevalence rate, and, in 2014, it was still less than 0.1 percent, with an estimated 780,000 people living with HIV. But HIV infections had been rising, and the government didn't want HIV/AIDS to spiral out of control.

The Chinese government had taken one important step, changing the country's CD4 threshold from 350 to 500, which improved accessibility to antiretroviral therapy. But from AHF's point of view, the government also needed to adopt the one-minute rapid test—more people could be tested and placed into treatment. According to Yugang, more than 60 percent of Chinese living with HIV didn't know their status, and China still used laboratory testing to confirm an HIV diagnosis, which caused a waiting period as long as six months for people living in remote areas.

But it wasn't easy to change minds. AHF started in China in 2006 and now served 31,210 registered clients, with 25,412 taking free antiretroviral therapy. The organization also worked with one of the country's most prominent AIDS experts, Dr. Wu Hao, the director of a top-notch AIDS program at a government-run hospital in Beijing. AHF's success in China, and its government connections, helped the organization earn some political clout, but Chinese officials still wanted more research on the reliability of the rapid test, despite the fact that it had been widely accepted in the Western world.

"If AHF can do that," said Yugang, "it would be great."

Always ready to go the extra mile, AHF and Wu were preparing a pilot program to demonstrate the effectiveness of rapid testing.

—

At Mudanyuan Park, Yugang, Zhang Wei, and I walked up a dirt trail that ran along a ridge covered with trees and bushes. Used condoms and home HIV tests littered the trail, which, in a way, was a

good thing. But this cruising spot was more hidden than Dongdang Park—a disturbing, real-life example of the marginalization that gay men endured in China.

As we kept walking, I saw two large mounds of dirt on the side of the trail with flowers laid on the top. I asked Yugang and Zhang Wei what they were, and the answer shocked me: the mounds, according to Zhang Wei, were gravesites for two gay men.

The men, I was told, were probably disowned by their families. They had no home, and they wanted to be close to their friends. So, they probably asked their friends to bury them near the trail. I stared at the mounds and would never forget them. They were outrageous monuments to the consequences of stigma and discrimination. If the Chinese government didn't address those things, I thought, the spread of HIV, and more human suffering, would only get worse.

—

DURING THE FLIGHT BACK to Los Angeles, I leafed through my notebooks, thinking about all the people I had met and Nelson Mandela's take on freedom. To me, AHF as a "global movement" wasn't just a concept. It was a real, palpable thing. How else would you describe the collective work of Hilary Thulare and Cynthia Luthuli and Henry Musariri and Jacob Wabyoda and Dr. Penny and Dr. Sam and Dr. Sarath and Bao Yugang and all the other AHF employees all over the world? It was a movement.

Just as special, AHF, now an international force, was still operating with the same activist mindset that drove Weinstein and his friends to start up Los Angeles AIDS Hospice Committee.

And this global movement wasn't only about providing HIV drug treatment. Things went deeper than that. AHF was also breaking the chains of sickness and stigma and discrimination—helping people reclaim their personal freedom. Perhaps that was why Mandela's words stayed stuck in my mind.

What also became apparent was that every country, in its response to AIDS, went through a standard set of stages that were similar to the stages of loss and grief—and AHF was constantly dealing with a country that was going through each particular stage.

First, people got mysteriously sick and died. Second, the government went into denial and failed to act. Third, as a result of government inaction, people needlessly suffered and died and more people got infected. Fourth, when the government finally took action, the epidemic was well underway. Fifth, cultural and religious hang-ups created stigmas and a backlash against the sick, which fueled more illness and death. Sixth, once a country became more effective in battling HIV, apathy eventually settled in, which threatened the long-term goal of controlling the disease. Seventh, stigma continued to harm progress. Eighth, the lack of proper funding to fight HIV/AIDS was a constant threat. Lastly, only people or groups outside of government, such as AHF, initiated true change—and if they didn't stand up and fight, the politicians would roll right over them.

As I thought more about the trip, one thing stood out: at AHF, wherever I went, the patients always came first. And since that was true, I could only reach one conclusion: AHF was the real deal. As a veteran journalist who's covered powerful people and institutions, I was impressed, even excited. AHF showed that we didn't have to go along with the status quo or lose our values in order to succeed. We could stay true and fight and win.

Chapter 14

May 2014—Los Angeles, Kenya, & Las Vegas

AHF parade in Nairobi, Kenya

A FEW DAYS AFTER my return to Los Angeles, I met with Michael Weinstein. He was preparing for a trip to Africa and working on the final draft of a manifesto, titled "AHF Statement of Principles on Prevention." It included such thoughts as "telling the truth no matter how unpopular is the right thing to do" and "advocacy must be forceful enough to overcome all the prejudices that work against it." The statement appeared to be a response to AHF's critics who were still slamming Weinstein for his "party drug" quote. It would run as an advertisement in newspapers across the country.

Weinstein was also monitoring Las Vegas, where public health officials had still not taken action against AHF for continuing its mobile testing program. And AHF announced that one hundred AIDS organizations, community churches, and local politicians supported AHF's push to shift more federal HIV/AIDS funding to the hard-hit but neglected American South. AHF's legislation, however, wasn't getting traction in Congress.

Weinstein and I talked about my trip, and I mentioned Uganda. He said that the AHF board of directors had discussed pulling out after the AIDS researcher was arrested under that country's anti-gay law, but he was opposed to leaving.

"I said X-thousands of people would die because of that decision," he explained. "We would tell patients to go somewhere else, but either they wouldn't get there, or if they got there, they'd be turned away. So while it may come to pass that someday we may need to leave, we have to be very thoughtful about that decision. A board member was arguing that we had to protect our staff. I said, 'Yes, we do have that responsibility. But on the other hand, the people who work for us in these countries, it is their own country, and they made the decision to do this work.' You can't take that decision away from them if they've already considered taking some amount of risk in the work."

I brought up the problems in Ukraine, where AHF still maintained an office in Kiev. Pro-Russian militants were starting up what amounted to a civil war, and, in the Crimea territory of Ukraine, voters had passed a referendum in March to join the Russian Federation. Things were so tense and unsteady in Crimea that AHF was forced to abandon operations there.

"The situation right now in Ukraine is getting very extreme," Weinstein said. "But it is not our place to get involved in politics. It is a dangerous world. We are in harm's way to a certain degree, and that falls on the people in these countries more than it falls on us. But the other side of the coin is if we shut down in the United States,

patients would be harmed, but very few would die. If we shut down over there, where would all those people go? It is unlikely all those people would survive."

Weinstein and his senior management team regularly dealt with geopolitical strife, and they didn't have much time for the insider politics and gamesmanship that sometimes ran through the American AIDS movement. But with the PrEP controversy, AHF was now caught up in exactly that. I asked Weinstein if he regretted the "party drug" quote.

"No, not at all," he said. "In fact, the reaction to it is proof positive that I hit the nail on the head. It put all the worst elements in the community out into the open. I just got a call this morning from a gay reporter at *Al Jazeera*, and we were talking about the loss of HIV providers. Then he was talking about his own situation in going to a doctor and asking about PrEP, and his doctor didn't really know anything. He said the reason why he went to his doctor was because there were these guys on [the gay dating and sex app] Grindr who were advertising for bareback [unprotected] sex because they were on PrEP. So doesn't that make my point?"

Weinstein added, "I've done dozens of interviews on PrEP, and I've said a lot of different things. This particular statement was seized upon. It caused a discussion that I think is a good discussion to be having. I've always felt with doing work in the gay community that it is very Stalinistic: everyone has to agree. And, if you want to club somebody over the head with stigma, it isn't going to shut them up. It isn't going to shut me up. You know, if I think about it, all the things that I've done over the years, prevention has been the one that has gotten the most vehement opposition."

I asked why that was.

"I think, to a large degree, men don't want people telling them what they can and can't do [when it comes to sex]," Weinstein said. "There is also a lot of money being made on promoting unhealthy lifestyles involving drugs and sex."

I brought up AHF's biannual Africa Bureau meeting, also known as the ABM, which was taking place in nine days in Nairobi, Kenya. All of AHF's African program directors would be attending. I asked what he hoped to accomplish.

"It gives me an opportunity to have contact with a lot of people that I don't have otherwise. The subject matter at these meetings is less important than the sentiment when you leave, which is unity. You hope for inspiration, but you'll settle for motivation. I think that it's an opportunity for mentoring and sharing communication. But there are practical goals. We want to treat 500,000 people in Africa, so we have to plan how we are expected to do that. This meeting won't happen again for two years. We have to have a firm foundation for how we are going to get there."

In mid-May, I flew to Nairobi.

—

THE NEWS IN AFRICA wasn't good. In West Africa, the Ebola outbreak was only worsening. In Kenya, terrorist bombs had recently killed several people in Nairobi and Mombasa, prompting AHF global advocacy chief Terri Ford to cancel our visit to a clinic in Mombasa. Nairobi was bracing for more violence—when I arrived at the hotel, my driver's car was searched for bombs and weapons.

Before the ABM, Weinstein had traveled to South Africa for the groundbreaking of a new AHF clinic in Umlazi and then went to Lusaka, Zambia, for the ribbon-cutting ceremony for another new clinic. In Umlazi, Weinstein led a spirited procession through the streets, taking his customary position behind an AHF banner. Dr. Penny walked next to him, and some hundred AHF employees and clients followed behind. The contingent then arrived at a white tent for the speeches from various dignitaries, which included Dr. Sibongiseni Dhlomo, the health minister for the KwaZulu-Natal provincial government and a longtime member of the African National Congress.

Dhlomo stood behind a podium only a few feet away from where Weinstein sat. A newspaper reporter was present, and AHF was filming the ceremony. Speaking into a microphone, Dhlomo was about to shock Weinstein, who had stared down the South African government nearly thirteen years ago.

"We are humbled that South Africans are such a forgiving community—extremely forgiving," Dhlomo said. "Because there was a time when AHF was putting together programs to get our people into programs to use antiretroviral therapy. There were those of us in the country who did not believe that this program was a priority, and many other people died before they could get treatment, and we're extremely sorry for those issues that took place, and we're very happy that South Africa continues to be a forgiving community."

Dhlomo continued, "I don't know how many of us are aware, working together with AHF and many others, that we have made strides in this country and government, and we can now say that people are no longer dying like they were dying before. AHF, not me, helped us during those hard times through 2013."

After running through various statistics, including a huge drop in deaths and babies being born with HIV, Dhlomo exclaimed, "Viva AHF! Viva!"

Weinstein was floored. It was the first time any South African official had publicly apologized to AHF. He later told me that it was perhaps his most memorable moment of 2014.

So going into the Africa Bureau meeting, Weinstein was in good spirits. He was joined by all the Africa country program directors, along with Peter Reis; Terri Ford; Loretta Wong, AHF's director of global partnerships and advocacy; and Arin Babakhani, senior director of grants and contracts. In total, thirty-two people attended the three-day retreat.

On the first day of the ABM, everyone met in a sunlit conference room on the main grounds of the Fairview Hotel. Each person was given a packet, containing, among other things, a single page

of inspirational sayings. Several of them were from prominent management consultant Margaret Wheatley. One read, "I believe that the capacity that any organization needs is for leadership to appear anywhere it is needed, when it is needed." Another read, "I think a major act of leadership right now, call it a radical act, is to create the places and processes so people can actually learn together, using our experiences."

Toward the front of the room, near a large projection screen, Weinstein sat next to Dr. Penny. They looked as if they thoroughly enjoyed each other's company—always chatting and laughing and smiling. Dr. Penny started the meeting with another inspirational statement. "You have to be burning with an idea or a problem or a wrong that you want to right," she said, quoting Apple cofounder Steve Jobs.

With that, Dr. Penny explained that she wanted to "ignite" a passion among the country program directors and right a wrong that was the AIDS crisis in Africa.

Weinstein, who's not religious, followed up by quoting the Bible.

"Where there is no vision," he said, "the people perish."

Weinstein then ran through a quick history of AHF's work in Africa, including the South African government's initial resistance to it. "But," he added, "we are absolutely committed to partnership with government."

And he praised Dr. Penny for her "outstanding leadership."

"Personally," Weinstein said, "it allows me to sleep better at night."

He wrapped up by saying, "Keep your eyes on the prize. The prize is toward global AIDS control, and we're on a march in attaining that goal. We cannot be defeated."

After additional comments from Reis, the program directors gave PowerPoint presentations about what was happening in their countries. Several themes about AIDS and AHF in Africa emerged.

First, AHF had strong credibility in Africa because it worked with so many governments to provide free antiretroviral therapy, it did not leave a country due to funding problems, and it went

into places that other organizations would not go. Additionally, government leaders appreciated that the people who operated and staffed AHF's programs were born and raised in that particular nation. It was the way AHF operated all its global sites.

Second, HIV stigma was a persistent problem in Africa, and one that prevented people from getting tested and into treatment.

Third, AHF clinics often provided healthcare beyond HIV, picking up the slack of government clinics, which was becoming a mounting concern of both time and money.

Fourth, AHF needed to improve keeping young people in care.

"If we're going to focus on bringing them in," said Dr. Penny, "then we need to be prepared to keep them!"

Weinstein proposed hiring youth counselors for each country in the Africa Bureau.

Fifth, AIDS continued to decimate Africa—in Swaziland and Lesotho, for example, one out of every four people between the ages of fifteen and forty-nine were infected with HIV. But political leaders were still not acting swiftly to turn things around.

Lastly, AHF's Love condoms were wildly popular all over Africa. In fact, Dr. Stephen Karau, the program director of Kenya, said that the demand was so strong that AHF had briefly run out of condoms in his country.

At the end of nine hours of reports and discussion, Weinstein told the group, "I just want to thank you for bringing your very best selves to your work." People got up stiffly and slowly walked back to their rooms. The next day they would take a special field trip.

—

IN THE MORNING, FORD, Reis, and Weinstein hopped into a small van and rode four miles through traffic-clogged streets to City Park, the gathering spot for the AHF team. Weinstein, Ford, Reis, and the country program directors would form a procession, with a marching band behind them, and walk a few blocks to the organization's newest

clinic, AHF Plaza. It would house Dr. Karau and his staff and provide free clinical services to thousands of clients.

At the park, under a big, leafy tree, Dr. Nduduzo Dube, AHF's program director of Swaziland, was full of ideas about what AHF needed to do in Africa. Among other things, he wanted AHF to decide on a "minimal" treatment package, which would guide doctors and medical staff about what kind of healthcare services they could and could not provide.

"They need to finalize what we need to do," he told me.

Dube, who had been working for AHF since 2008, also thought the organization needed to keep a strong focus on antiretroviral adherence monitoring, hire more doctors in Africa, better empower patients, and come up with new strategies to increase AHF's patient roster in Africa. He had even more ideas, but then the marching band started to sound a few practice notes. The parade was about to take off.

The band was loud, as if it were signaling that the cavalry was coming to save the day, which in a way it was—in the form of AHF. Police officers with machine guns protected the procession, and bystanders on either side of the road looked confused and then happy, if only for the music. At the end of the walk, everyone made a left onto the grounds of AHF Plaza, where white tents and foldout chairs were set up. Weinstein took a seat at a dais with Ford, Karau, Reis, Dr. Penny, AHF board member Diana Hoorzuk from South Africa, and Angelina "Mama" Wapakabulo, an AHF board member, who was also Uganda's ambassador to Kenya. After a minister blessed AHF and the building, the speeches started.

Karau, an elegant, sixty-two-year-old man, who once headed up the Kenyan Air Force Medical Department as a colonel, kicked things off with a humorous story about his first encounter with AHF in 2006.

"Two ladies and a gentleman walked into my office," he said, "and they informed me that they worked for an organization called

AHF. They wanted to start an HIV program jointly with the army. I told them I was interested, but as the discussion went further, it became clear that they were looking for the Salvation Army and not the Kenyan army."

The crowd chuckled.

"However, I asked them to tell me more, and they were kind enough to do so. So I asked, 'Although you want to work with the Salvation Army, can you work with the Kenyan army?' I thought that they would be scared, but they accepted. As fate would have it, within a year, AHF started its operations, and we were able to open our first clinic in collaboration with the Salvation Army."

He continued, "Since then, eight more clinics and five satellites have been opened, giving a total of fifteen in four counties. Through these facilities, we currently have 13,848 [patients] enrolled, and 80 percent of them are on ART. Cumulatively, we have also tested over two million people in the country for HIV."

Karau expected that by 2020, AHF would be working in 50 percent of Kenya's forty-seven counties and have at least 50,000 registered clients. He smiled and looked proud and thanked Dr. Penny and Weinstein.

"I'm always calling him 'Sir Michael Weinstein,'" said Karau, who was educated in the United Kingdom. "If we were British, I'm sure you'd have been knighted. This man has done a lot for the world, not just for the US."

Karau ended the talk by telling his staff that he loved them.

Dr. Penny spoke, and Weinstein followed her. He said, "When you're not quite sure where you want to live and permanently be somewhere, you rent. But when you're there for a long haul, and you know where you want to be, you're home. What you see here behind you is the AHF estate here in Nairobi. It is twice as large as our main office in Los Angeles, and this building is a sign of the commitment of AHF. We will be here as long as we are needed."

He continued, "When you look across the world and you see where the battle against AIDS has advanced the most, it is where

the commitment comes at the highest level and all the way down the chain of command. So when I think about the slogans that AHF has and the different ways in which we promote what we do, I have to say that really it comes down to such a simple elemental idea. We are a heart of hearts that lead and believe that every human life is of value, that every human life is precious, and that everything that can be done, must be done to preserve it."

Weinstein paused for a moment.

"I stand in front of two of my bosses, as we all know, whether people realize it or not, we all have a boss. I'm standing in front of two of my bosses—two members of our board of directors. I probably shouldn't say this, but I really have the best job in the world. Sometimes I'll feel a little guilty that I get paid for doing it. What better job could there be but being in the business of saving lives? So I just want to leave you with this idea—because when we have a vision, and when we have a dream, that is the beginning of it being realized. My dream is to have a ceremony one hundred times this large, and we come together because we conquered AIDS. Thank you."

Soon after, Weinstein and his team cut a red ribbon at the front entrance of AHF Plaza. Big smiles were everywhere.

Later in the afternoon, another session of the ABM began, which went into the early evening. During one presentation, Karau interrupted to share tragic news: a terrorist bomb had gone off at Gikomba Market. It was a popular shopping area four miles southwest from AHF Plaza and two and a half miles from the Fairview Hotel. Karau was unsure about the number of fatalities. The room went silent. The next day, newspapers reported that two bombs had killed at least ten people and wounded seventy. In photographs, it looked as if a hurricane had hit the area. There were no discussions about AHF pulling out of Kenya.

—

ON THE FINAL DAY of the ABM, Weinstein asked for a panel debate about the appropriate degree of advocacy when trying to force a government to change. Sierra Leone program director Miata Jambawai, Rwanda program director Dr. Horatius Munyampundu, and Hilary Thulare were chosen to talk about using diplomacy. Uganda program director Henry Magala, Dr. Nduduzo Dube, and Nigeria program director Dr. Adetayo Towolawi considered a more hard-charging approach. It was a debate that stirred up the most passionate discussion during the three days of the ABM, and one that made some country program directors feel the most uncomfortable.

Jambawai said she wasn't afraid to press hard, but like several of her colleagues, she was concerned that if pushed too much, government officials would tell AHF to pack up and leave, and that would be disastrous for clients. Hilary Thulare said it was important to have strategic alliances within government, which could lead to implementing a program quickly.

On the flip side, Magala argued that government had a "moral obligation" to help citizens, and AHF needed to make sure politicians and bureaucrats followed through on that. Dube said one needed to be armed with plenty of facts before entering into a fight with government, and that one shouldn't waste time battling with lower-level bureaucrats. Towolawi, who appeared as if he would have been more comfortable with Jambawai's group, said that although media is a good tool to get the word out about a particular outrage, sometimes one needed to compromise. Towolawi's contribution seemed to arouse something inside of Jambawai, who appeared to be in the wrong group as well.

"For me," she said, "I'm very mission driven."

Then Jambawai explained that she would do almost anything to fulfill that mission, including carrying out AHF's core value of fighting for what is right, which prompted her to ask why AHF's mode of operation in Uganda seemed to be "fight and retreat."

Magala looked surprised by the remark and said there had been "leadership issues" within the Uganda government that his team had to navigate. That got Thulare's back up. She insisted it was crucial to push people in power who were complacent or wrong. She and Magala probably should have switched teams, too.

"You must analyze your key allies in a system," she said, "but it doesn't mean you have to sleep with them."

Dube agreed.

"At the end of the day," he said, "it's important to know when to be patient and when to attack."

Terri Ford then added a thought that most of the country program directors had not mentioned. She said that as the world's largest AIDS healthcare provider, AHF had tremendous international clout and therefore could be more aggressive than smaller AIDS organizations.

"We're too big now," Ford said. "They won't arrest us, and if they did, we'd make it an international incident."

Ford urged the country program directors to think and act in ways that utilized AHF's global power. Some country program directors appeared delighted by the thought. Others looked as if they weren't so sure.

A couple of hours later, Weinstein declared the ABM to be "one of the very best global meetings" he had ever attended, and Dr. Penny reminded everyone that one "can't grow if you don't change." With that, she said with a smile, "The meeting is closed. See you in two years' time."

—

In the United States, AHF was certainly leveraging its power and resources. Only days after returning to Los Angeles, Weinstein received news that Las Vegas health officials had finally taken the bait, and the state of Nevada was suing AHF for "illegally" operating a mobile testing unit. Ged Kenslea, AHF's communications director,

immediately sent out a press release. Laura Boudreau, AHF's chief counsel for operations, said in a statement:

"AHF's mobile van is certified by the federal government through what is known as a CLIA waiver to administer HIV rapid tests, which are a fast, easy, reliable way to help people know whether they are HIV positive....Nevada law makes it clear that the state cannot impose regulations on HIV rapid tests that are more stringent than CLIA, yet the Nevada Department of Health and Human Services, Division of Public and Behavioral Health, insists that AHF comply with unnecessary licensing and registration processes that pose barriers to community organizations wishing to conduct rapid tests."

She added: "We will challenge the legal action to halt our HIV-testing program and will also press Nevada to update its outdated licensing practices to conform to state and federal law."

In the meantime, AHF kept sending a mobile testing unit to Las Vegas every other weekend. No one was arrested, and Whitney Engeran-Cordova was feeling confident.

"I thought that they were full of crap and that they were going to lose," he told me. "More than that, I talked to Laura Boudreau to make sure they knew how bad this was going to look. Here comes this agency, and all we want to do is help people. We are trying to make more testing available, and they want to sue to stop us? What the hell? They aren't even paying us to do it. We were doing this for free. The Southern Nevada Health District is charging people!"

The Nevada Attorney General's Office then approached AHF with a settlement, but it would only benefit AHF. It was turned down.

"We wanted it to be applicable to everybody," Engeran-Cordova explained. "We said that this needs to be applicable to all testing organizations in Las Vegas."

Boudreau kept talking with the state attorney general's office.

"The health department had a bee in their bonnet," she told me, "they didn't like what we were doing. But the attorney general's office got it."

So much so that, in early June, the Nevada Attorney General's Office and AHF agreed to a more wide-reaching settlement.

"I was surprised they folded so quickly," Weinstein told me. "I think they assumed that we'd fold quickly. The legal might that we have has become a big factor in our success—the quality and quantity."

AHF could keep testing, and the state agreed to come up with new regulations that didn't conflict with federal law and allowed other AIDS organizations to more easily perform mobile testing.

In Las Vegas, Engeran-Cordova said, "We have totally changed the way that people do HIV testing and the direction of their AIDS programs."

The Las Vegas showdown was a remarkable case study. If AHF had continued a safe, plodding approach, it would have taken months, possibly years, to finally get Nevada politicians and the Southern Nevada Health District to change mobile testing regulations. Instead, the organization moved boldly and, within a matter of weeks, brought mobile HIV testing to Las Vegas, which would move more people into treatment. Hard-charging tactics couldn't always be done, but under the right circumstances and with just the right moves, it was undeniably effective. In fact, it saved lives.

Chapter 15

*June, July, & August—California, Louisiana,
Las Vegas, & Ebola in Africa*

AHF participates in San Diego LGBTQ+ Pride Parade

CONDOMS IN PORN. AHF continued to lobby and advocate and
strategize to pass legislation that required condom use in all adult
films produced in California. State lawmakers had been uneasy
about the push, but progress had been made: the State Assembly
approved the bill in May, and the California State Senate Labor and
Industrial Relations Committee, in late June, also signed off.

Throughout the process, AHF had sent former adult film per-
formers who had been infected with HIV while working to lobby state
legislators. One of them was Cameron Adams, a tenacious twenty-
nine-year-old who was born and raised in Southern California.

After a breakup with her boyfriend, Adams quickly needed money—a situation that pushed many women around the world into sex work. She went into adult films in 2013. Three months into her job, after shooting a sex scene in which her condom-free partner was bleeding from his penis, Adams tested reactive for HIV. It was the first time she tested positive for any kind of sexually transmitted disease.

"I felt like I was on *Candid Camera*," Adams told me, recalling the day she got the news. "I was in shock. I was like, okay, bring out the cameras, you guys are joking. Then it was like, okay, no, this is real."

Word about Adams's HIV status went public within hours, and AHF, which kept close tabs on the adult film industry, reached out to her, asking if she needed medical treatment. Adams had never heard of the organization, but her friends in the industry vouched for AHF, despite the fact that they loathed its longtime Condoms in Porn push. Within days, Adams met with an AHF doctor and started taking antiretroviral therapy. She was impressed and had a yearning to team up with the organization.

"I kept telling them that I wanted to work with them," she said. "I forced the issue maybe a little bit, but I wanted to help. I couldn't let up."

AHF then asked if Adams wanted to lobby for the Condoms in Porn bill. She loved the idea.

"If everyone else in the world needs to be protected from blood-borne pathogens and sicknesses," she explained, "then I don't see why people in pornography are any different—because they are people, too. They need to realize that they have the rights that everyone else does, that a nurse has, that a firefighter has, that a construction worker has. They need to realize that. And if they aren't going to realize that, then it needs to be shoved in their faces to a certain extent. It's about being safe in a workplace and knowing that you are allowed that choice."

Adams's work appeared to be paying off, but AHF's Whitney Engeran-Cordova still wasn't brimming with confidence as the bill waited for a vote in the state senate.

"Every time we talk to an elected official and say, 'How do you vote?' we're winning," he told me. "Every time politicians go behind closed doors, we lose."

—

THINGS COULD GET CRAZY at AHF.

"The biggest challenge is the complexity," Weinstein told me at one point. "I've felt that more strongly than ever before. We run so many different operations, and we have advocacy, testing, prevention, managed care, pharmacies, global, research, etc. And all these different funding sources. So things can come at you from left field, and it happens almost daily: some audit that doesn't go well or some legislative change that we weren't anticipating or there is a war in Ukraine. It is just endless."

But by the middle of the year, AHF businesses were performing quite well, particularly the pharmacy division, the breadwinner for the organization. Without the pharmacy, AHF wouldn't be a global powerhouse.

"AHF Pharmacy has freed up and empowered AHF to do everything that we're doing," Terri Ford explained. "That was absolutely critical, because if that didn't happen, we wouldn't be in thirty-three countries. People would be dead—a lot of people would be dead—if that didn't happen. Prior to that, we did have managed care that funded some stuff but not in a big way. Managed care was what gave us the revenue to be able to start in South Africa because we needed millions. The pharmacy changed the whole thing; it changed the whole channel. We could create such a large amount of revenue in the US, and we could advocate in any way we want and say what needs to be said; that is super important. It enabled us to expand and go where we needed to go before other funding even came. That has always been important."

As soon as the AIDS cocktail was introduced in 1996, Weinstein thought about launching a pharmacy division, but AHF needed millions to purchase the drugs to stock its pharmacies.

"A lot of organizations don't want to go into the pharmacy business," Jonathan Petrus, the chief financial officer of performance and investments, told me. "Michael and the senior managers realized that there was a substantial upside in doing that, but it required a massive amount of capital up front. Drugs are very, very expensive."

Peter Reis explained, "There were specialty pharmacy outfits that were cropping up to do AIDS pharmacy, and we also knew that if we could grab that pharmacy business, then we'd be in a better position to do specialty pharmacies because we'd have access to [the federal government program] 340B."

To get the capital, AHF partnered with a pharmaceutical distributor in the early 2000s, but the business relationship became problematic and the organization wasn't happy with the revenue split. AHF broke away from that distributor and got a better deal with another one—and it decided to build, operate, and staff its own pharmacies. In 2007, when AHF placed pharmacies inside its clinics, revenues took off.

"That was the real jet fuel," Weinstein said.

Another key move was building a sales team that could talk with patients at AHF clinics. Sales staff took them directly to the pharmacy and walked them through the paperwork. Patients gained quick access to HIV medications while AHF generated a steady flow of new clients by conducting HIV testing at thrift stores, mobile units, and clinics.

"The testing numbers have been phenomenal," Petrus said. "They drive our growth."

The heart of AHF's work, though, was not merely making money. The focus was providing a public health service by testing and treating people living with HIV. It was then rewarded for that lifesaving work with huge revenue, and that money was invested back into serving an ever-expanding clientele in the United States, Africa, Asia, South America, and Europe. It's a point that's often missed by critics who think AHF simply wants to generate big revenues with

no larger purpose. AHF, in fact, shares its revenue with other AIDS organizations through grants and financial partnerships.

Over the years, Peter Reis had been a key figure in the success of AHF Pharmacy, handling deals and overseeing operation standards. Scott Carruthers, a seventy-six-year-old native of San Diego and former pharmacist, was also integral in the expansion and smooth operation of AHF pharmacies.

"We had this kind of debacle with the first distributor," said Weinstein, "and client satisfaction was poor, and we needed to have a high-functioning pharmacy program. Scott was the one who really gave us that. He knows how to outfit a site, hire the people, and make it hum. And he likes purchasing pharmacies and starting them up."

Carruthers was a surfer years before surfing was popular, practically living at the beach and riding the waves as often as he could. After college, he operated his own pharmacy in San Diego, which he sold to a large company that moved him to Los Angeles. For years, Carruthers was a top executive in the pharmacy world, but his career had taken a dramatic shift by the late 1990s—he decided he wanted to spend more time with his daughter, who was a standout soccer player. Carruthers took a job as a pharmacist at a Rite Aid, working the graveyard shift.

"I didn't miss a single game her senior year in high school or in her four years at the University of Texas," Carruthers told me, "and I'm sorry that I didn't do that sooner."

In 2004, after his daughter finished school, Carruthers got a call from a recruiter asking if he wanted to work for AHF. He was interested, thinking AHF's mission was unique and important and that he could use his experience to help the organization expand.

"When I came," said Carruthers, "there were six pharmacy locations, and we have more than thirty-five now, so growth became a huge part of the responsibility. We find the locations, make sure we get licensed, build them out properly, get the staffing, and train the

staff. And we make sure that we're doing the kinds of things that our mission dictates, and that we take care of our patients."

Carruthers, who became part of AHF's senior management team, was the opposite of a bean counter. He believed that the organization needed to focus first and foremost on clients' needs, and revenue would naturally follow.

"The pharmacy plays a huge role in keeping patients in care," Carruthers explained. "They see their doctor only every four to six months, so in our pharmacy program, we contact the patient monthly. We keep in close contact with them and build a rapport with them. We take interest in them as human beings. So if the dog was sick last month, we record that. When we call and talk, we ask, 'How is your dog?' That kind of stuff. We build a trust."

He added, "It has to be a trusting relationship, so when we give them advice or ask them why they aren't taking their meds or what is going on, they will confide in us so that we can help and keep them in care. If they aren't going to the doctor, we can encourage them to do that and track their medicine. We use different kinds of dispensing systems to remind them to take their medicine. Obviously, the other part of the mission is generating revenue, which is so important for AHF to be able to do the things that we do."

2012 was a game-changing year for the pharmacy operation: AHF bought a pharmacy chain known as MOMS, which had locations in Seattle, San Diego, New York, and San Francisco. "That doubled our revenue," said Carruthers, "and certainly put us in a lot of new locations."

With an increasing emphasis on profits in the pharmacy industry as a whole, AHF's patient-centered model was difficult for some new pharmacists to grasp.

Carruthers explained, "It's surprising to me that pharmacists who've been working at CVS or Walgreens often have a hard time with our policies. We talk about our mission—and the important thing is that the patient has their medicine, and they don't miss

doses. Yes, we try to collect every penny because that is an important part of what we do, but, on the other hand, it is more important that the patient doesn't skip doses."

He continued, "The new pharmacists think that's great, but they get on the job, and when the first patient comes in who doesn't have the copay, they won't give them their medicine. So we need to turn that switch with some people, and that has been a real challenge sometimes. It amazes me. If you don't have the money for your prescription, then we find every possible way to get the coverage, so we'll give patients whatever is necessary for whatever length of time is necessary until we can get some sort of coverage."

Recently, AHF Pharmacy's expansion into different cities has received pushback from local AIDS organizations. Despite the fact that the HIV Care Continuum showed that only 444,000 people out of 1.2 million HIV patients in America are receiving antiretroviral therapy, they see AHF as a financial threat.

"New geographies are becoming a bigger challenge for us," said Carruthers.

Regardless, AHF Pharmacy generated $241.8 million in revenue in 2011, $411.5 million in 2012, $619.9 million in 2013, and $698.5 million in 2014. Hand in hand with that revenue growth, AHF clinics around the world expanded from 108 in 2011 to 268 in 2014—223 of those clinics were outside the United States. Its patient roster increased from 134,003 in 2011 to 320,749 by July 2014. As Terri Ford pointed out, none of it could have happened without AHF Pharmacy.

—

DURING THE SUMMER, CONDOM Nation, AHF's free condom distribution program, toured the Southern states. I spent a few days in New Orleans with Nadira Rahman, a young African American woman who was the new program manager for Condom Nation, and Wilson Cruz, a mobile tester based in South Florida who was helping out. We also went to Baton Rouge, a city with the second-

highest rate of AIDS diagnoses among all American cities—27.5 cases per 100,000 people.

In Baton Rouge, John Reed, an AHF mobilizer, had organized a Condom Nation stop at a battle of the bands contest held at Memorial Stadium, where high school marching bands from Louisiana and Texas competed against one another. The teenage musicians, as well as the crowd, were nearly all African American.

African American youth are startlingly impacted by HIV. According to the CDC, the greatest numbers of new HIV infections among men who have sex with men in the United States were young African Americans between the ages of thirteen and twenty-four. They also accounted for 45 percent of new HIV infections among Black MSM, and 55 percent of all young MSM. Young Black women were also getting infected with HIV.

At Memorial Stadium, Rahman stood underneath a white Condom Nation canopy and behind a table filled with Love and Icon condoms. Reed and I sat a few feet away. We sipped on cold drinks in the shade as we talked about his work—he held double duty as a mobilizer for both Texas and Louisiana.

Reed, an engaging, fifty-year-old African American, was born in Louisiana, but raised in Fort Worth, where he currently lived. Reed served five and a half years in prison for a drug-related crime in the early 1990s. When he was released, a woman from his church asked him to join her on a trip to the home of low-income people living with HIV.

"I went there that day," Reed said, "and I knew what I was supposed to do. Seeing the people, talking with the people—they told me how stigmatized they were."

Reed became an ordained minister in 1997 and started his journey. In 2010, AHF's Earvin "Magic" Johnson Testing America Tour, which provided free HIV testing in forty-eight states, stopped in Texas. Reed made a connection with the organization and became an AHF mobilizer in 2012. A politically savvy man, he worked closely

with local organizations and politicians. Reed was also determined to convince Black pastors that they needed to address HIV and AIDS in the African American community—to get them to see, as he put it, "the bigger picture."

"I'm trying to get them to realize that only by the grace of God do we stand behind the pulpit and not have HIV and AIDS," Reed told me. "It doesn't matter what color you are and what is your sexual orientation. We can't choose and pick who we help. HIV is a people's disease."

Over the past few months, I'd been asking AHF employees, particularly African Americans, what they thought about the AIDS Is a Civil Rights Issue campaign. Sometimes I heard Black employees question the fundamental idea of the campaign—that AIDS was, in fact, a civil rights issue. When I asked Reed, his face lit up.

"It brought a lot of light to people who were in the dark," he said. "It was fantastic that AHF did that."

In the field, Reed sometimes ran up against the same kind of resistance from local AIDS organizations that Scott Carruthers encountered. That happened in Baton Rouge to some extent, despite the city's serious HIV/AIDS crisis, which needed an all-hands-on-deck approach. In most cases, Reed thought, hostile groups merely saw AHF, with its free clinics, large operating budget, and global reach, as a threat to their fiscal bottom lines.

"We have to stop worrying about the numbers," he said, "and start worrying about people. We have plenty of people living with HIV to go around. We can do more together. So I tell them, 'Get to know AHF before you pass judgment.'"

In fact, AHF had recently teamed up with two AIDS groups that were struggling financially: Women Organized to Respond to Life-threatening Disease (WORLD) in Oakland, led by Cynthia Carey-Grant, an African American woman, and the AIDS Taskforce of Greater Cleveland, run by another African American woman named Tracy Jones. AHF bolstered both organizations with much-needed funding when no other AIDS group was coming to the rescue, and

they both largely continued with the same work they had always done. WORLD worked with women with HIV while the Taskforce had a strong HIV housing division—different from AHF's longtime mission to provide medical care.

The partnerships were successful and would eventually be replicated in other cities where community-based groups faced the possibility of closing. In time, AHF would team up with organizations in Chicago, New York City, and Atlanta, which make up what was officially deemed the "AHF Federation."

As we finished our drinks, Reed and I could hear the bands starting up. Before our chat ended, I asked about AHF's chances to reprioritize the Ryan White CARE Act. Reed smiled again and said, "It may not happen this session, but it will happen. I'm going to go to every congressman until they get tired of me." I had no doubt he would do that.

—

BACK IN LOS ANGELES, in mid-July, AHF got news of a new UNAIDS study, which reported that HIV infection rates in the United States were double those of Western European and other wealthy nations. A headline for a *Miami Herald* article blared "US Losing Battle Against HIV."

Ged Kenslea immediately sent out a press release. In it, Weinstein said, "We simply cannot achieve global AIDS control and halt the spread of the virus without a radical overhaul of how we approach HIV testing, linkage, and treatment access—and nowhere is this more apparent and more needed than in the US, which is falling woefully short in its handling of its portion of the global AIDS epidemic."

Weinstein said nothing critical about President Obama or other major AIDS organizations.

Around the same time, a commercial airplane was shot down by a missile launched in eastern Ukraine, where heavy fighting was

taking place between pro-Russian insurgents and the Ukrainian military. Within a day or two, it was reported that numerous AIDS experts were passengers on the doomed flight—they were heading to Australia for the 2014 International AIDS Conference. No one from AHF died, but the fatalities included world-renowned AIDS researcher Joep Lange, who famously said, "If we can get a cold can of Coke to any part of Africa, we can certainly deliver AIDS treatment." It was a devastating loss of talent for the global AIDS fight.

In West Africa, the spread of Ebola was still expanding, and the slow international response was increasingly becoming both irresponsible and morally reprehensible—one thousand people had died between December and early August. The French-based organization Médecins Sans Frontières, or "Doctors Without Borders," was handling huge numbers of Ebola patients on the ground, but the World Health Organization was virtually nowhere to be found. Dr. Penny was livid, writing to me, "WHO has not provided the requisite support needed for such dangerous epidemics; there has hardly been anything in the media to highlight the extent of the problem."

Hours later, on July 29, I received emails from Terri Ford and Dr. Penny: one of AHF's doctors, Sheik Umar Khan, had died from Ebola. At thirty-nine years old, Khan was a top virologist in Sierra Leone, and he'd been leading that country's response to the Ebola epidemic. Khan was overwhelmed by the patient load, but he never quit. When he got sick and AHF tried to fly him to Europe for treatment, no country allowed him to enter.

Dr. Penny wrote to me, "For a country that has less than two hundred doctors in the public health sector, the loss of one doctor is too much for the country."

Khan was special, and his death eerily fulfilled a kind of tragic prophecy. When he was fifteen years old, he'd read an article about a German doctor who'd come to Sierra Leone to treat people with Lassa fever and subsequently died from the fatal virus himself. Khan was profoundly impacted, deciding he wanted to become a

virologist. Twenty-four years later, he, too, passed away while trying to help the sick.

His brother, Sahid, who lived in the United States, talked to Khan when the Ebola epidemic started to take hold in Sierra Leone.

"I told him, 'Maybe you should leave?'" Sahid later explained to me. "But he said, 'Who would treat them?'"

Sahid added, "We miss him every day. He was there fighting on the front lines."

AHF and Weinstein sounded off.

While "commending" MSF for its work in West Africa and for taking care of Khan during his final days, Weinstein said in a press statement, "I must also chastise world leaders for the lax global response to this deadly outbreak that has been growing in Africa since February."

The WHO finally declared Ebola an "international emergency" a few days later, but the organization's lagging response gave rise to something that Weinstein had been thinking about for years—maybe it was time for AHF to expand its mission beyond AIDS and jump squarely into the global public health arena.

"There's no question that there's a need," Weinstein told me, "and there's no question that the WHO is a disaster."

He added, "What is the global response? Why isn't there a Navy SEALs for disease? It would be so inexpensive."

But Weinstein wasn't sure exactly what AHF would do, and he was hesitant to have AHF handle outbreaks like Ebola without support from other organizations and governments.

In the meantime, Khan's death turned into an international news story, and AHF continued to come down hard on the WHO, trying to get it to move more quickly and efficiently. By September, President Obama said the epidemic was "spiraling out of control."

—

Before AHF's Condoms in Porn bill went to the full California State Senate for a vote, the legislation suddenly died in committee in mid-August. While AHF expected resistance from Governor Jerry Brown, it was surprised when State Senator Kevin de León, the chair of the appropriations committee, refused to take action on the bill.

"We were optimistic that we had enough votes in the committee," Ged Kenslea told me, "but de León didn't move it, and the clock ran out."

Weinstein suspected that de León got word from the Brown administration that the legislation should be killed.

From his office at the Public Health Division building, Whitney Engeran-Cordova was watching a live video feed of the appropriations committee meeting and realized that the Condoms in Porn bill wasn't on the list.

"We were all stunned," Engeran-Cordova told me. "Kevin de León had given us no indication that he was going to hold it."

State Assemblyman Isadore Hall III, the sponsor of the bill, was furious.

"People had invested a lot of time and energy in this," said Engeran-Cordova, "and it went by—there was no process."

A few weeks later, AHF was thinking of other ways to institute mandatory condom use in the adult film industry. First, AHF could apply pressure on the California Division of Occupational Safety and Health, also known as Cal/OSHA, to come up with regulations that would apply the state's Bloodborne Pathogens Standard to the porn industry. The other move was to place a Condoms in Porn initiative on the state ballot, asking California voters to decide the matter once and for all.

"It is the natural conclusion and the pinnacle of our efforts," said Engeran-Cordova. "If you can pass a ballot measure in this state, then we amplify our political abilities all over the country and probably all over the world. But within the country, we'd be a force to be reckoned with—to mount and do a ballot measure in a state that is, in effect,

its own country. It is one of the largest economies in the world, with thirty-eight million people, right? So that is a big deal."

But the multibillion-dollar adult film industry would spend tens of millions to defeat the ballot measure, which would force AHF to spend big as well.

"The idea of dropping even five million dollars on something like this gives everyone the heebie-jeebies," Engeran-Cordova told me.

The AHF team needed to mull things over.

Chapter 16

September & October 2014—London, Amsterdam, Switzerland, Ukraine, Estonia, Russia, & Texas

AHF honors World AIDS Day in Estonia

IN SEPTEMBER, I TOOK another trip overseas, visiting London and Amsterdam and Switzerland and Ukraine and Estonia and Russia. By the end of it, I had talked, in total, with dozens of AHF staffers and other AIDS activists and service providers on four continents: Africa, Asia, Europe, and North America. I could see that the most effective people had a number of common traits that drove their difficult work.

The best and brightest AHF employees and AIDS activists were deeply committed to their cause. They were also smart and resourceful, figuring out different ways to get things done. And they

were somewhat obsessive about changing the world. Many of them worked in circumstances in which the system was mightily stacked against them, but they refused to back down. No matter what happened, they clung to the belief that they could make a difference.

At the same time, many politicians in different countries also had similarities, but those were far less honorable than those of the AIDS activists. Beyond the politicians' lack of urgency to control the HIV/AIDS crisis, they often wrapped their agendas in patriotism and morality and so-called progress and usually pitted one group of people against another. It was the age-old tactic of divide and conquer. Once the public took the bait, the politicians went about getting what they really wanted: more power for themselves, more power for their political allies, and more money for their benefactors.

What was frustrating to see was that the public, time and again, allowed themselves to be manipulated by the politicians. It happened in South Africa, Uganda, India, Russia, and the United States. AHF, though, never allowed itself to be played for a sucker.

—

In London, AHF was a cosponsor of the 2014 International Association of Providers of AIDS Care Conference at the Royal Garden Hotel in Kensington, a posh neighborhood not far from Buckingham Palace. It took place in mid-September, and the theme was "Controlling the HIV Epidemic with Antiretrovirals: Avoiding the Cost of Inaction." AHF's participation was a way to influence global AIDS policy, and the event drew respected doctors and researchers and activists from around the world. They included Terri Ford, AHF Global Ambassador Dr. Jorge Saavedra, and AHF Europe Deputy Bureau Chief Anna Żakowicz.

The conference was a time for sharing ideas and making speeches about the state of the AIDS crisis and holding plenary sessions that tackled such topics as "Controlling the HIV Epidemic—Perspectives on Turning Aspiration into Reality" and "Placing PrEP

in Perspective—Ethical, Sociological, and Community Views." The speeches, at times, were politically motivated, which was apparent when US Global AIDS Coordinator Deborah Birx, an Obama appointee, spoke.

Birx oversaw the implementation of PEPFAR. To explain the Obama administration's philosophy on how to fight AIDS, she used the slogan: "Right thing, right place, right time." By that, she meant that the global AIDS movement needed to be more strategic in using money, antiretroviral drugs, and other tools to eradicate AIDS. Compared to AHF's motto of "cutting-edge medicine and advocacy, regardless of ability to pay," Birx's catchphrase signaled a less charitable approach to the HIV/AIDS crisis. In fact, it could be interpreted as an argument for the Obama administration's constant squeeze on PEPFAR funding. She was essentially saying that as far as the US government was concerned, the global AIDS movement needed to do more with less.

In that context, Birx threw out another catchphrase: "Delivering an AIDS-free generation with sustainable results." Birx, a skilled public speaker, said it as if this was a fresh concept. But sustainable results and controlling the spread of global AIDS were goals AHF had been pursuing, with remarkable success, since 2002.

In fact, one of the great oddities within the global AIDS movement is that prominent experts have rarely talked with Weinstein and AHF about best practices in delivering HIV treatment. And Weinstein has never been asked to deliver a speech of any kind at the International AIDS Conference, although AHF is possibly the most experienced AIDS medical provider in the world.

Sitting in that ballroom made me realize why Weinstein detested such conferences. There was little vigorous debate; it was very polite; and too often leaders seemed unaware of what was actually happening in communities. Undoubtedly, the people in the room had come to the global AIDS movement with good intentions, and many had done important, lifesaving work. But thirty years into the

epidemic, things had become too insular. In fact, Dr. Julio Montaner, a noted AIDS researcher, decried the cliquish "small circles" within the global AIDS movement and told the conference, "We've been talking to ourselves for too long."

As I leafed through my notebook after each day of the conference, a few things kept popping out. First, on more than one occasion, a speaker pleaded with the audience to put more focus on serving people, which begged two questions. Why did they have to urge something so obvious? And what was the prevailing focus in the global AIDS movement if not to serve people?

Second, many conference attendees were concerned that AIDS activism had greatly diminished or was nonexistent. If that was the case, then one could argue that AHF's aggressive brand of advocacy was not only rare but also needed.

Third, many spoke of the need for more innovation—from testing to linking patients to treatment to retaining patients—but many established people in the global AIDS movement had largely ignored AHF's cutting-edge work for the past twelve years. Just how serious were these experts about bringing innovation to the global fight against AIDS?

PrEP, the HIV-prevention drug regimen that proved so hard for gay men to take regularly, also came up. Terri Ford told me that several attendees walked up to her and said they admired AHF's stand on PrEP. The problem was that no one wanted to say that in public. In fact, during one panel, Jim Pickett of AIDS Foundation of Chicago singled out AHF for "scare-mongering" and "paternalism." No one said a peep in response.

In addition, Sheldon Fields, a dean and professor at the Charles R. Drew University of Medicine and Science in Los Angeles, said there was no time to consider all the ethical issues surrounding PrEP—a stunning comment from an academic. Fields and Pickett sat on the same panel, which took a far different line from that of a group of doctors and researchers in a previous discussion. The

earlier panel said they were concerned about patient adherence, problems of resistance to antiretroviral therapy if a patient didn't take PrEP properly, and people not using condoms and therefore making themselves vulnerable to other sexually transmitted diseases. Remarkably, PrEP supporters on the second panel mentioned virtually none of those things.

Soon after Pickett had demonized AHF, two UNAIDS officials met with Ford and Saavedra in the hotel lobby. Throughout the conference, UNAIDS was pushing its newest global AIDS control strategy, "90/90/90." By 2020, the organization wanted 90 percent of all people in the world living with HIV to know their status, wanted 90 percent of all people diagnosed with HIV to receive antiretroviral therapy, and wanted 90 percent of people receiving ART to have undetectable levels of the virus.

It was very ambitious, and AHF was skeptical. AHF believed that UNAIDS needed top-notch logistics for such a complex plan; billions of dollars to pay for HIV testers, doctors, clinics, and HIV drugs; and widespread cooperation from government officials in numerous countries who were still dragging their feet on addressing AIDS. Only then, and with a lot of luck, could 90/90/90 happen. But Weinstein and his team did not publicly criticize the plan.

The UNAIDS officials were wary of AHF, the so-called lone wolf of the global AIDS movement. But they needed a well-established, global HIV testing program for 90/90/90 to be successful. That was why they wanted to talk with Ford and Saavedra.

"We're implementers," Ford told me after the meeting. "They know that."

By the end of the sit-down, which was cordial, there were no promises, but AHF was open to a partnership. More talks needed to take place.

—

AFTER LONDON, I FOLLOWED the AHF contingent to Amsterdam—Ford was holding a global advocacy summit for key AHF managers. There were nineteen of us, including several people from the United States, such as Ged Kenslea, creative manager Stacy Fong, and associate director of community outreach Jessica Reinhart. Most of Ford's team from LA were attending: global marketing associate director Salvador Guillen, associate director of global policy Denys Nazarov, director of global marketing Adela Ramirez, and Herb Fisher. Miller Everette, Ford's administrative coordinator, stayed in LA to hold down the fort.

Others came from Africa, Europe, and Mexico, including Oluwakemi Gbadamosi, the advocacy manager in Nigeria; Alice Kayongo, the regional policy and advocacy manager for East and West Africa; Mary Nyaguthii, the prevention and advocacy manager in Kenya; Nina Schat, the Europe programs coordinator; Denis Godlevskiy, the Eastern Europe advocacy manager; and Zoya Shabarova, the Europe Bureau chief.

Everyone was excited and enthusiastic, especially since many of them had never met each other in person.

On the first day of the summit, we gathered in a nineteenth-century courthouse that had been turned into a space for theater and community activism. Ford wanted to streamline AHF's global advocacy efforts, which would be crucial for the success of the organization's 20×20 campaign—any government policy that stood in the way of moving people quickly into treatment needed to be addressed and changed.

For global advocacy, Ford and her crew first tried to meet with government officials and talk things out. If diplomacy didn't work, Ford and her team shifted into a more aggressive gear. There was constant internal debate over how forcefully AHF could advocate in certain countries.

There was no question, however, that AHF was going to apply full pressure on the WHO over the Ebola crisis in West Africa. A

few days before the summit, AHF had publicly blasted the WHO for refusing to evacuate another doctor in Sierra Leone who had fallen ill while treating Ebola patients. That physician, Dr. Olivet Buck, had died on September 14.

In addition, South African advocacy manager Larissa Klazinga helped Sierra Leone program director Miata Jambawai write a first-person account of the public health disaster. The op-ed was titled "We Are Dying; Where Is the World?"

"On Friday," Jambawai wrote, "Sierra Leone started a three-day national shutdown for a house-to-house Ebola sensitization campaign, deploying thousands of government staff, NGO workers, and volunteers in an attempt to identify infections and educate a frightened public.

"As the country program manager for the AIDS Healthcare Foundation, I am a member of the rapid response team during the three-day shutdown.

"There is no hospital or clinic that is untouched by this disease, and we are losing healthcare workers every day. AHF lost Dr. Khan, our medical director, to Ebola in August, and his passing has left a vacuum in our organization that cannot easily be described, let alone filled. He was a leading expert in his field, and our country is in dire need of medical professionals if we are to halt the spread of this disease."

The op-ed was picked up by a South African newspaper and, soon after, other publications.

Inside a large theater space, in the basement of the converted courthouse, Ford emphasized to her team that relentless advocacy drove AHF's work. Weinstein then showed up via Skype from his office in Los Angeles. He acknowledged that regularly taking bold stands made AHF "vulnerable."

"We know that advocacy is tough," he told everyone, "and that's why a lot of people avoid it. But we also don't want to be paralyzed by that."

The managers nodded as they stared at a large projection screen. When it was their turn to talk, one of them told Weinstein that AHF's public stances on issues sometimes caused problems when dealing with other AIDS organizations. This was especially true, the manager said, with AHF's nuanced position on PrEP.

Weinstein listened quietly and gathered himself for a moment.

"Our concern is public health," he replied, "and it really can't be swayed by public opinion."

Weinstein added, "Over the years, we've had so many issues like this. These things are never easy, but that's what has made us grow and succeed. I am very confident we will be vindicated."

A few hours later, Weinstein called me after talking with Kenslea and Ford. He wasn't happy with the manager, but it had nothing to do with being challenged in front of the others. He had hoped that employees could understand that AHF was taking a principled stand for a larger good, and that they would back him up, particularly since PrEP supporters were increasingly lashing out with harsh, personal attacks directed at Weinstein.

While the organization's critics were busy disagreeing with AHF's position on PrEP, discussions during the summit provided ample proof that AHF was doing a lot of things right:

- In Uganda, Alice Kayongo said that government-made condoms were widely criticized for being too small and, as a result, men weren't using them. AHF got involved and provided larger-sized condoms for free.

- In South Africa, Klazinga and her colleagues brought public attention to the country's rape epidemic by organizing a silent protest march and "die-in" in Durban. More than seven hundred women, empowered and strong, took part in the action.

- In Russia, where many international AIDS organizations were leaving or were forced out, Denis Godlevskiy

reported that AHF was working with government officials to develop a national HIV/AIDS strategy.

- In the Netherlands, Anna Żakowicz said that only the government conducted more HIV tests than AHF.

- In Myanmar, AHF manager Loretta Wong noted that the organization had successfully lobbied government officials to provide free antiretroviral therapy for the first time. "People were just dying," Ford added. "There were no antiretroviral drugs. It's a huge win."

Those were only a few of AHF's most recent accomplishments. And by the end of the summit, Ford, Saavedra, and Kayongo would fly to Geneva, Switzerland: AHF's persistent advocacy resulted in a sudden, top-level meeting at World Health Organization headquarters.

—

IN GENEVA, A FEW hours before the WHO meeting, Ford, Saavedra, and Kayongo met at a Starbucks to discuss strategy. Saavedra, a doctor with keen diplomatic skills who once ran Mexico's national AIDS program, thought it would be good to come up with a list of requests. The team agreed upon several key items: provide lifesaving evacuation and treatment for any doctors infected by Ebola; move more well-trained healthcare workers into West Africa; ship and properly distribute more protective equipment to local communities; introduce home care and train people to do that properly; improve the WHO's media and public communications efforts so the world better understood what was happening on the ground; rethink and reshape the international community's response to a sudden public health crisis, which would include an emergency action team; and include nongovernmental organizations that have extensive field experience in that response.

Ford, Saavedra, Kayongo, and I then took a taxi to WHO headquarters, a nine-story structure that was wide and squat and

without much personality. The building looked weirdly appropriate for a cautious, risk-averse bureaucracy.

The World Health Organization, led by Director-General Margaret Chan, a sixty-seven-year-old doctor from Hong Kong, was established through the United Nations with a focus on public health education, eradicating various diseases, and monitoring international health trends, among other duties. Nearly all the member states of the United Nations belonged to the WHO, but it operated with a relatively small annual budget of approximately $4 billion. If one believes that the amount a government spends on one thing compared to another is a sign of its priorities, global public health doesn't rank highly in the United States—in 2013, the country contributed $180 million to the WHO but spent $98.7 billion on military operations in Iraq and Afghanistan.

Once inside the headquarters, we were led to a conference room where two high-level staffers waited for us. We all sat down at one end of a long, wooden table. Miata Jambawai and Dr. Penny joined us by phone. It was a delicate situation, and I was asked to not take notes and to not name the officials. Setting the tone for the meeting, Dr. Penny said she wasn't interested in rehashing past mistakes. Instead, she wanted to know what were the WHO's immediate plans for dealing with Ebola. The staffers appeared to appreciate the opening remark.

The bulk of the talk focused on how to get medical personnel and supplies to places that needed them and the obstacles the WHO faced when trying to provide an emergency response on the ground. The WHO, for example, could not enter a country without a government's approval. Alice Kayongo, a soft-spoken young woman from Uganda, then ran through the list of AHF's requests, which met no resistance from the WHO people. They were especially quiet when Kayongo and Ford mentioned the need for better communication. Afterward, Ford, a veteran of such meetings, was neither optimistic nor pessimistic.

"We'll see what happens," she told me. "It was a good first meeting, but we have to see what they'll do."

Ford and I then hopped on a plane for Kiev, the capital of Ukraine, where a bloody revolution had taken place in February. And in the eastern part of the country, where the commercial airplane was shot down in July, a war was still raging. Ford wanted to see how AHF staff were holding up.

—

IN UKRAINE, I TRAILED Ford and Europe Bureau chief Zoya Shabarova to an AHF-supported tuberculosis and HIV clinic, then to a clandestine lunch with a prominent health official in the back room of a restaurant, and then to AHF's Kiev headquarters for a series of presentations. One thing was obvious: Ukraine was in serious trouble.

The new government that was formed after the revolution was very unstable; various medical supplies were running out or not getting to clinics; and the ongoing war with pro-Russian separatists was only exacerbating an existing public health crisis—with an HIV prevalence rate of 1.2 percent among adults between the ages of fifteen and forty-nine, Ukraine was one of the worst AIDS hotspots in Eastern Europe. According to UNAIDS, approximately fifteen thousand people died from AIDS in 2014. Of the estimated 290,000 people living with HIV, 120,000 were women aged fifteen or older. Tuberculosis was another major problem.

Even with those statistics, Ford and I were told that it was difficult to drum up political support for the people most impacted by HIV and AIDS—injection drug users and their sexual partners, female sex workers who inject drugs, and prison inmates—when so many other Ukrainians were struggling. The situation in Ukraine was an example of the kind of obstacles that UNAIDS needed to overcome for 90/90/90 to be successful.

Despite the difficult circumstances, AHF management in Ukraine got results: the organization served 8,124 registered clients,

6,086 of whom received antiretroviral therapy. AHF got things done by partnering with smaller AIDS organizations and working government contacts.

"It takes a very big person—someone who's respected—to change an old, broken system," Ford explained to me, "and we search for them."

AHF worked with such a person in the Ukrainian government, and I was asked to keep that individual's identity a secret—the political scene was especially dangerous and vindictive. AHF won that person's admiration because the organization didn't pack up and flee during or after the revolution.

During dinner, at an old Kiev restaurant, Ford told the Ukrainian team, "We know it's been a tough year for you. Thank you for sticking with us."

Everyone raised their glasses and drank up, and one of the AHF team members, Grigory Tyapkin, wanted to add something. "We all feel a part of the AHF family," he said. "Being a part of AHF is not a company but a lifestyle." Ford laughed knowingly.

—

AFTER UKRAINE, I WENT alone to Estonia, a country of 1.3 million people on the western border of Russia and next to the Baltic Sea. Estonia was more politically stable than Ukraine, but it was also facing a grave AIDS crisis, especially in Narva, located on the Narva River directly across from Russia. It was the third-largest city in Estonia, with a heavy Russian-speaking population—the country was part of the Soviet Union between 1940 and 1991.

In Narva, the Soviet Union had manufactured weapons, which provided plenty of work. But when the Soviet Union collapsed, jobs were lost, stubborn unemployment followed, and heroin and alcohol abuse spread. Fueled by needle sharing and sex, an AIDS epidemic exploded, which contributed to Estonia having the highest HIV prevalence rate—1.3 percent—in the European Union by

2010. Injection drug users and their sexual partners and female sex workers were most impacted by HIV.

If one doesn't see a pattern by now, it's safe to say that the global AIDS epidemic disproportionately strikes the impoverished and underserved, which may be why there's been little urgency among the world's political leaders to eradicate the disease. In fact, in numerous countries, AHF staffers told me that government officials considered people living with HIV to be disposable. Beyond the inhumanity of such a belief, what the officials failed to see, or purposefully ignored, was that public health issues don't only impact the individual. Since we're all a part of the same community, what affects the individual will eventually, one way or another, impact the community as a whole.

In Estonia, AHF's Denys Nazarov had told me earlier, the national government held little interest in helping Narva and its large Russian-speaking population—old grudges against anyone associated with the Soviet Union had still not faded away. But in 2009, the Estonian Network of People Living with HIV (EHPV) reached out to AHF and started a partnership in which AHF provided free HIV rapid tests, condoms, and advocacy support. EHPV was led by Igor Sobolev, who would later become AHF's Europe prevention, testing, and linkage manager. A few years into their work together, both organizations decided that Narva needed a free HIV treatment clinic.

AHF wanted the Estonian government to pay for antiretroviral drugs, and the organization would pick up the tab for everything else, including medical staff. An agreement with the government was struck, but when AHF opened Linda Clinic in Narva in 2013, the HIV drugs never arrived—the government went back on its word.

By the time I arrived in Estonia, with Sobolev and current EHPV director Latsin Alijev showing me around, AHF was seriously considering shutting down the clinic and leaving—staying in Ukraine during wartime was one thing, but dealing with a government that didn't keep its promises was quite another. AHF gave Alijev a deadline to secure a deal with the Estonian government by the end of 2014.

One afternoon, Alijev and Sobolev proudly showed off the Linda Clinic. It was bright and clean and essentially perfect. Patients received medical care, but they had to make an additional trip to a local hospital for antiretroviral drugs. The clinic, however, ran support groups for clients and their families, and a doctor, nurse, social worker, peer counselor, and psychologist all worked in the facility.

"Only because of AHF do we have the opportunity to work in this environment," Tamara Dmitrijeva, a nurse, told me.

Sobolev later added, "AHF gave us the ability to be independent and to speak to problems in Estonia. A lot of groups can't do that." He was referring to the fact other AIDS groups rely heavily on government funding.

AHF was also paying for rapid HIV testing in a Soviet-era housing project not far from Linda Clinic. With Alijev leading the way into a rundown building, we walked through a corridor lined with men and women waiting to be tested—three fresh-faced teenagers were among them. We then entered a small, faded room where we talked with an HIV tester. Alijev, a warm and generous man, spoke to her in Russian, and then he turned to me. He wasn't smiling.

"Forty-three people got tests and two of them are positive," he said with frustration. "No one is getting treatment. And people are infecting each other. Our government can't understand that the rapid test and treatment can stop the epidemic!"

Alijev looked away and shook his head.

A few months later, however, the Estonian government finally came around. With the international community concerned about Russia's possible intention to grab land in Ukraine and other Eastern European countries, the United States government didn't want to give Russian President Vladimir Putin any reason for moving into Estonia, such as claiming that Russian-speaking citizens were not receiving once-guaranteed antiretroviral therapy in Narva. From their discussions with American officials, Weinstein and Terri Ford realized that AHF was in the middle of a geopolitical chess game,

and the Estonian government was coming under pressure from the international community to follow through on its promise to AHF. In December, the Estonian government agreed to supply AHF's Linda Clinic with antiretroviral drugs.

—

AFTER A FEW DAYS in Estonia, I flew to St. Petersburg, Russia. My guide and translator was Denis Godlevskiy, an affable thirty-one-year-old who was the AHF Eastern Europe advocacy manager. Due to numerous political and bureaucratic issues, it appeared as if Russia would be a tough nut for AHF to crack. But the organization refused to abandon one of the countries hardest hit by the HIV/AIDS crisis in Eastern Europe.

"During the past four years," Godlevskiy told me, "most of the international donors have left Russia. But Michael has said he's committed. He will stay here, support advocacy, and fight for treatment. So this counts for something."

Only a few months earlier, UNAIDS had published a global AIDS study called the "Gap Report." There was little, if any, good news about Russia. An estimated 1.1 million people lived with HIV in Eastern Europe and Central Asia, but 88 percent of those cases were located in Russia (69 percent) and Ukraine (19 percent). And, according to UNAIDS, the epidemic was only growing in Russia.

Just like Estonia and Ukraine, Russia's HIV demographic was primarily made up of sex workers and injection drug users and their sexual partners. Men who have sex with men were also impacted. UNAIDS stated it was critical for Russia to move more people into antiretroviral therapy and to utilize opioid substitution therapy for recovering drug addicts.

The Russian government, however, banned methadone use for recovering addicts and didn't robustly promote condoms and safer sex. In fact, in August 2015, Russia banned foreign-made condoms in response to economic sanctions placed on the country by the US and

other nations, which came about due to Russia's involvement in the ongoing war in Ukraine. A Russian government official rationalized that a condom ban, which did not impact AHF's distribution of free condoms in Russia, could turn around the country's poor birth rate.

Russian activists were constantly running into such odd logic, which wasn't all that different from what American politicians cooked up—take, for example, the Congress member whose primary strategy to fight AIDS was to strengthen the family.

In Russia, I was told, many government officials held the belief that injection drug users were of weak moral fiber, and, therefore, were not good Russians who contributed to the homeland. As a result, the government felt they deserved little sympathy or help. If a drug user came down with HIV, he or she was completely written off. With this mindset, Russian officials largely ignored a growing AIDS epidemic for years, which, of course, only worsened the crisis. It wasn't until a group of recovering drug addicts and gay men turned into hard-charging AIDS activists that the government, in the early 2000s, was forced to rethink things.

"We knew there were HIV drugs," Sergey Golovin, the thirty-two-year-old advocacy officer at International Treatment Prepared-ness Coalition (ITPC), a global AIDS advocacy organization, told me in St. Petersburg, "and we didn't have the treatment and didn't have any friends that had the treatment. So that mobilized us."

The Russian government started expanding antiretroviral therapy in 2006, but Golovin and his fellow activists continued to run into problems such as high drug prices and poor HIV treatment services.

AHF's Denis Godlevskiy explained further: "What we are facing now, as more and more people are coming to the clinics, is that doctors are overloaded with patients, and there are lines. When government officials try to decentralize and involve other clinics to link them to other AIDS centers, the doctors don't know the basics of HIV, they stigmatize the patients, and they don't know how to provide treatment."

He added, "Right now, we treat 140,000 people [living with HIV] for half a billion dollars. The need by 2020 will be at least 600,000 people—so four times more. If we multiply half a billion dollars by four, that is $2 billion. The budget for healthcare, and the projected budget for healthcare for 2017, which was recently published by the Ministry of Finance, will be around $10 billion. Nobody in their clear mind would pay one-fifth of the healthcare budget to buy the medications for one disease only. It is impossible."

Russia also had problems with providing steady, easy access to antiretroviral therapy, which was something ITPC focused on. The organization had started its own database from which the activists monitored the procurement of HIV drugs throughout the Russian Federation, looking for clinics that had run out of HIV medications. If a problem was found, ITPC brought that information to the government's attention—and the public's.

Russia's worsening economy and strained relationships with Western nations were also impacting HIV prevention efforts.

"Now it's a crisis in Russia," Gregory Vergus, the thirty-four-year-old ITPC regional coordinator, told me in St. Petersburg. "It's very hard for government to find the funding because there is an economical crisis, plus a donor crisis, plus a political crisis. The political situation in Russia is not very good for reducing the spread of HIV."

Vergus and Golovin were two of the most prominent advocates in Russia, and Godlevskiy once worked with them at ITPC. Anastasia Solovyeva, AHF's thirty-six-year-old country program manager in Russia, was also a former ITPC staffer. So Godlevskiy and Solovyeva plugged AHF directly into a vibrant Russian AIDS movement. But in addition to having good connections, AHF won over many activists by bringing HIV prevention, testing, and lifesaving treatment services to Russia—the same thing that impressed activists and public officials in South Africa, Ukraine, and other countries. In Russia, at the time of my visit, AHF served 10,203 registered clients, and 4,458 received antiretroviral therapy.

"I like the ideals of AHF and most of their projects," Golovin said. "We don't have any resources to open new clinics. We aren't very interested in terms of the administration of these clinics, but for us it is very interesting to see how we can work together. Plus, rapid testing—it shows so many interesting things about AHF. So now we see AHF as our partner. We try to help them in projects, and we're very happy when they involve us."

AHF's global model of hiring locals to operate a country's program was particularly important in Russia, where one needs to be exceptionally savvy and knowledgeable when dealing with a complex, highly politicized bureaucracy. "We understand the specifics of the country and how everything should be done here," Anastasia Solovyeva told me in Moscow.

While other nongovernmental organizations were fleeing Russia or had been kicked out, AHF was working to increase its patient roster as part of the 20×20 campaign, which meant opening more clinics. That couldn't be done without government support. One idea was to showcase an AHF clinic in Kazan rather than Moscow—government officials were not thrilled about an American organization operating a clinic in the capital city. Godlevskiy and Solovyeva knew Weinstein wanted to make a bigger splash and favored Moscow, but they believed Kazan, a major metropolis that's known as Russia's third capital, was a better way to move forward.

"I understand that every big foundation or donor organization dreams about making things better immediately," Dr. Larissa Badrieva, AHF's medical coordinator in Russia, explained to me, "but that isn't how it works here. It is step-by-step. Russia is a completely different country."

Additionally, Solovyeva, Godlevskiy, and Europe Bureau chief Zoya Shabarova looked to strengthen prevention programs and distribute more free condoms in partnership with the Russian government. All of this work—from new clinics to more condoms— brought forth a need for effective advocacy.

But advocacy was hazardous in Russia, and AHF needed to move cautiously. In Kazan, I asked Dr. Badrieva, who had a comprehensive understanding of Russia's AIDS epidemic, what would happen if AHF was forced out of the country.

"AHF is the last foundation that remains in Russia from abroad," Dr. Badrieva said. "AHF is the last piece of serenity; it's surrounded with wisdom, has the newest scientific technology, knowledge, and information. Nobody would provide this information here if it wasn't for AHF. Nobody else remains."

Weinstein, Terri Ford, and AHF's global team understood that quite well.

—

WHEN I RETURNED TO Los Angeles, American newspapers and the TV news were obsessing over Ebola. A man named Thomas Duncan had flown to Dallas, Texas, from West Africa, and subsequently tested positive for the virus. On October 8, he died from the virus. In addition, two nurses who treated Duncan were infected, but they survived. The mainstream media went into a panic, wondering if hospitals were ready for an Ebola outbreak.

Around the same time, Miata Jambawai's op-ed was making the rounds in American newspapers, and Dr. John Taban Dada, who was consulting with AHF, had died from Ebola in Liberia after working with patients. The death toll in West Africa was now more than four thousand people.

Dr. Penny was still calling on the WHO to do more, and AHF sent out a press release on October 24, stating that political leaders needed to "rethink" the role of the WHO.

Weinstein said in a statement, "The world needs a different kind of international public health body, probably one that can be created via a UN Security Council resolution, and one without the bureaucracy that involves the current international health system, that is capable of directly intervening to bring effective and rapid

control to situations involving emerging or transmitted diseases that can metastasize and grow to become a global threat as Ebola has become."

Coincidentally, in late October, AHF's annual board of directors' retreat was going to take place in Dallas. Weinstein had no plans to cancel it.

—

GOING BACK TO THE days of Proposition 64, Weinstein had talked about protecting the public's health. Then he watched Chris Brownlie die, visited young men and women in South Africa who faced certain death, and attended countless funerals of friends who had passed away from AIDS. All of it reinforced his belief that much of the devastation could have been avoided if only the proper public health systems had been in place. And then Ebola showed up in Dallas.

The board of directors' retreat was a prime opportunity for Weinstein to talk about expanding the organization's role as a protector of global public health. He firmly believed that was AHF's future—and so was operating in Texas.

Within the AIDS movement in the United States, Texas was somewhat off the grid. It was a predominantly conservative state that many gay men had fled for Los Angeles or San Francisco or New York City. When AIDS first hit the US and activists were pressing Washington, DC, for resources and money, Texas wasn't a huge part of the conversation. Bret Camp, AHF's Texas regional manager, told me this went on for decades.

"There was a lot of denial," Camp explained. "People thought it was a New York or Los Angeles problem."

Texas, in other words, was a place that still needed help, and AHF decided to provide it.

In Dallas on October 24, the day before the official start of the retreat, a group of AHF board members gathered in the grand lobby of the Warwick Melrose Hotel. A chartered bus waited outside.

It would take them on a thirty-two-mile trip to an AHF clinic in Fort Worth.

Bret Camp was the tour guide and sat at the front of the bus. He was fifty-three years old and one of the most connected and well-respected AIDS activists in Texas. For nearly thirteen years, he worked at AIDS Resource Center (later known as the Resource Center) in Dallas. In 2012, he started working for AHF. Perhaps tellingly, Camp believed that joining the organization was a way to get back to his activist roots.

"My priorities shifted," he told me on the bus. "I wanted to focus on something meaningful, and that was community based rather than taking the corporate track."

There was much work to do.

By 2013, according to the CDC, Texas ranked third in the nation with the most new HIV infections, 4,854. Only California (5,334) and Florida (5,377) were ahead of Texas, which also ranked sixth in the country for syphilis cases and second for tuberculosis. In 2012, 1,394 Texans died from AIDS, yet that never triggered the mass alarm that exploded after one Ebola death in Dallas.

Men who have sex with men were overwhelmingly impacted by HIV and AIDS in Texas. That group was followed by injection drug users. Forty percent of people newly infected with HIV were African American, 32 percent were Latino, and 24 percent were white. The African American population in Texas, however, was only 12 percent.

With Camp at the helm, AHF's patient roster rapidly increased, especially in 2014. In January, there were 652 registered clients in Texas. By November, there were 1,041 clients and over 90 percent of them were taking antiretroviral therapy. The AHF clinic in Fort Worth served 444 patients while Dallas worked with 597. The organization was going to expand into Houston and was considering other places such as San Antonio and El Paso.

—

THE BUS ARRIVED AT the AHF clinic in Fort Worth, located across the street from a giant mill, in the early afternoon. The delegation included AHF board members from across the US and around the world.

"The stigma in rural Texas is incredible," Camp told them, adding that the Fort Worth clinic had been very successful in building up its patient numbers. The reason was simple. "This is their only option," Camp explained. "There aren't a lot of HIV doctors in Fort Worth."

In addition, he said, clients hated going to hospitals for treatment—they feared that their neighbors or coworkers or friends would see them and figure out that they were HIV positive. I'd heard the same thing in Florida and Louisiana.

Camp then showed off the spotless offices and treatment rooms and pharmacy. AHF shared the building with an organization called AIDS Outreach Center, and the board members met its executive director, Shannon Hilgart. The center, which offered such services as mental healthcare, dental treatment, support groups, and HIV testing, referred HIV-positive clients to the AHF clinic next door for antiretroviral therapy.

The board of directors then returned to Dallas to visit another AHF clinic. Weinstein and Peter Reis were waiting for them in the lobby. In a hard-hit state where too many politicians had ignored people living with HIV for decades, Weinstein was particularly proud of AHF's work in Texas.

"This is one of the fastest-growing clinics," Weinstein told the board with a big smile. "Texas is becoming a huge success story."

Everyone walked through the clinic and checked out more spotless offices and treatment rooms. Soon, the board members were smiling as big as Weinstein. AHF's entry into Texas didn't come without some resistance from local AIDS groups and their political backers, but not everyone was against AHF. A few days later, Jamie Schield, a prominent AIDS activist in Texas, told me that the organization was an important addition to the fight against AIDS in his home state.

"They made some changes," he said, referring to AHF, "and they made us open up our eyes and see that the way the system had always been done wasn't always the best. They've shown that it can be done differently."

Change, though, wasn't always welcome when people had figured out how to make the status quo work for them.

On October 25, inside a small conference room, Weinstein and the board officially got down to business. They would receive numerous reports from AHF staffers, and they'd talk about ways to better serve high-risk groups, such as African Americans and young gay men. But Weinstein wanted to kick things off with a discussion about placing AHF at the "cutting edge" of global public health. Days earlier, he had sent the board members a four-page white paper on the topic.

"Specific circumstances exist today that make the [spread of infectious diseases] more urgent," Weinstein wrote. "Never in the history of civilization has it been possible for people to travel so easily from one side of the planet to another in the course of a single day. Like-wise, mass migration is commonplace. Many of the most dangerous diseases cross over from the animal world to humans. Diseases that would most commonly have been restricted to rural regions are now coming into direct contact with highly populated areas."

He continued: "AHF is uniquely positioned to advocate for new structures that protect global public health. We are innovative thinkers; we have credibility based on the size and scale of our global operations. We are well positioned on various advisory bodies. The questions are: How much of a priority should AHF make the overall issue of global public health versus the narrower goal of controlling AIDS? Do these priorities support or distract from one another?...

"Now that we have seen the consequence of our neglect, we will have only ourselves to blame if we leave the world undefended against the incredibly serious threat that infectious disease represents to civilization."

With the board assembled before him, Weinstein explained further.

"When the first organization of AHF, called Stop the AIDS Quarantine Committee, was formed," he said, "its banner was to protect the public health, but also I would say that throughout all of these years, we have said that the public health system—locally, nationally, and internationally—is broken and that diseases would not stay localized without an international response mechanism. Bad things would happen.

"I was watching a promo the other day for a show called *The Newsroom*. It said something that really struck me as very apropos of what we are discussing. It said, 'Don't just search for common ground, search for higher ground.' I think that when you're dealing with all of the bureaucracies that exist in the world in every field, and then specifically in this field, the pressure to go along and get along and to be a part of the consensus is very, very strong.

"The idea that the largest presence that AHF has anywhere in the world is in South Africa is truly amazing. We've gone from fighting the government to being invited to many different places in South Africa. South Africa is now becoming one of the leaders in the world in the control of HIV. Given the fact that it has the most cases, that is absolutely vital.

"Thinking about the history of the organization, and even going back to that very first committee that we had, there was a big argument because people would say that we cannot talk about AIDS concentration camps—it will turn people off. And we shouldn't be out demonstrating against this initiative, and we should put people in lab coats on TV commercials and that will lead the way. We didn't go along with that consensus.

"Now, it is almost impossible to imagine or believe that when we were championing hospice care, there was controversy, and that people would actually say that by championing hospice care that we were consigning people to death.

"And I'm sure that when we go through the next couple of days that we will be talking about other things like that. It seemed so outrageous that we called for the head of the Global Fund to step down, which interestingly enough he did shortly after. They also said, 'Don't talk about what is wrong with the Global Fund because the donors won't give money, and we will destroy it.' Then we said, 'No, it is the only way to save it and clean it up,' and I think that has shown to be true.

"So I talk about these things as an introduction because I feel like when we're talking about global public health, we're talking about a specific purpose, but we're also speaking about human nature and how we deal with things. I'm always humbled by the ability of human beings, individually and collectively, to be in total denial. While denial is very necessary, psychologically, I think that it is safe to say that we overdo it. I think that what you see throughout our history is that AHF means what it says and says what it means.

"I hope we come out of this discussion today with a commitment to doing everything that we possibly can to change the way that global public health is conducted. I really, in my heart of hearts, believe that we are really on a collision course with catastrophe if we continue to operate the way that we are now."

Weinstein then said that the United Nations should hold a special meeting to discuss ways to improve the response to a sudden public health epidemic, that AHF should continue to work on infectious disease, and that it should play a significant role in addressing global public health issues beyond HIV/AIDS.

Weinstein went on to say that in recent meetings with top AHF managers, people believed that the organization was already tackling public health issues outside of AIDS, and that work could be slightly increased without losing focus on AHF's central mission of serving people with HIV. He laid out five basic principles to guide AHF on public health policy:

1. All nations needed to appropriately invest in public health.
2. No drug patent or trade restrictions should prevent stopping the spread of infectious diseases.
3. A rapid response mechanism was needed.
4. A minimal level of public health infrastructure was needed.
5. The public should be kept informed about public health epidemics.

By the end of Weinstein's presentation, the board looked down at his white paper. There were only a few comments. Dr. William Arroyo, a regional medical director for the Los Angeles County Department of Mental Health, was concerned about the complex, international politics of taking on global public health work. Jose Ramos, who was a leader of Impulse Group, was uneasy about deviating from AHF's core mission to serve people with HIV and AIDS and somehow letting them down.

The board then broke up into groups for more discussion. When they returned, what Weinstein heard wasn't all that different from what Ramos and Arroyo first brought up—the politics could be too problematic, and AHF shouldn't stray from providing top-notch HIV/AIDS medical care.

"I don't think any of us want a radical shift," Weinstein told them. "I envision a 10 to 20 percent shift from where we are now."

When I later talked with Weinstein about the board's response, he was disappointed.

"That didn't really go anywhere," he said.

Regardless, Weinstein wasn't going to back off.

"I still have this itch about the way that public health is conducted," he said, "and I still feel that there is so much to be done."

Past AHF board members had been concerned about such things as buying the AIDS cocktail and providing medical care in Africa, but that didn't stop Weinstein from pursuing his vision. It seemed inevitable that he would start AHF's transformation into a major player in global public health.

Chapter 17
November & December 2014—California & South Florida

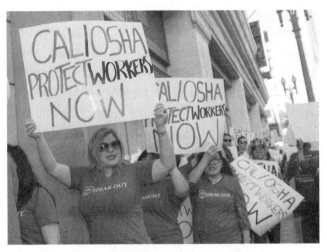

AHF protesting at Cal/OSHA headquarters in Los Angeles

UNSURPRISINGLY, THE SUDDEN SQUASHING of the Condoms in Porn bill in the California legislature didn't demoralize AHF. In November, the organization sent two charter buses filled with AHF employees, clients, and adult film performers to Cal/OSHA's office in downtown Los Angeles. They held a peaceful, yet loud protest and delivered a letter, written by Whitney Engeran-Cordova, to Cal/OSHA officials.

"December 17, 2014," the letter read, "will mark the fifth year since AIDS Healthcare Foundation's petition to amend California Code of Regulations Title 8 5193 was accepted unanimously by the Standards Board. The petition seeks to provide specific protections

for workers in the adult film industry as these workers have been shown to carry a disproportionate disease burden. The regularity of on-set exposure to infectious disease is alarming given that the adult film industry is a legal California industry. Negating any ambiguity in the regulations will have a real effect on the health of this group of workers.

"We demand that our rights as petitioners be honored and that the petition process move forward immediately. A further delay until 2015 is unacceptable, and we do not have any faith that the newest in a long string of timelines will be honored. On behalf of AIDS Healthcare Foundation and the thousands of workers who are needlessly exposed to infectious disease during the production of adult films in California, we are angry and disappointed that this amendment has been delayed year after year."

For nearly an hour, AHF protesters marched up and down the sidewalk in front of Cal/OSHA headquarters. They wore red T-shirts and chanted and pumped their fists in the air and carried placards that read "Safety over Bureaucracy" and "Cal/OSHA Protect Workers Now." It was colorful and raucous and earned a few honks from people driving by. It was only the first in a series of well-coordinated whacks against the state of California.

The next day, AHF sent a bus to Oakland and held a protest at a Cal/OSHA office there. That event made the local TV news. The day after that, AHF struck a final blow, and a serious one at that. On November 7, Weinstein announced that AHF would move forward with a statewide ballot measure to require adult film performers to use condoms in productions shot anywhere in California. AHF expected to place the initiative on the November 2016 ballot. Since that would be a presidential election year, California voters would probably turn out in force.

AHF's three-day barrage appeared to spook Cal/OSHA and possibly other state officials. On November 14, for the first time in five years, Cal/OSHA officially corresponded with AHF and stated

in a letter that it "has committed resources to the development of regulatory language" and a "final rulemaking document will be sent to the [OSHA] Standard Board by the end of 2014." The organization's hard press against Cal/OSHA was getting movement.

—

By mid-November, AHF had finalized the theme for its annual Rose Parade float: Ebola first responders. Several members of Dr. Sheik Umar Khan's family would ride on the float. "We're keeping the issue alive because the crisis isn't over yet," Weinstein explained at a marketing meeting. At the time, more than five thousand people around the world had died from Ebola and fourteen thousand had been infected.

It was an interesting thing to watch. Only weeks after AHF board members had tepidly received his pitch in Texas, Weinstein was already steering the organization in the direction he wanted to go—the float was a public health advocacy campaign that would be seen by millions of TV viewers across the nation. In Los Angeles, AHF would also run a billboard campaign that featured a ticker of the number of people who had died from Ebola with the phrase "Lest We Forget: Ebola Deaths in Africa…"

Weinstein also wasn't letting up on PrEP, the HIV prevention drug regimen. In mid-November, AHF bought newspaper ads in New York, Los Angeles, San Francisco, Oakland, Dallas, Washington, DC, and South Florida that featured an "open letter" to the CDC that asked, "What if you're wrong about PrEP?"

"Both the community and the government must be accountable for the guidance they give to vulnerable populations," the ad read. "The debate about safer sex goes back to the beginning of the [AIDS] epidemic. Every time we didn't heed advice to protect ourselves, we paid a terrible price. AHF will do everything that we can to make sure that doesn't happen again. However, if we are wrong, we will take responsibility for our decisions. We hope that everyone else will do the same."

Once again, AHF was carrying out its cutting-edge advocacy. In fact, November was full of righteous aggression: the protest on Cal/OSHA, the Condoms in Porn ballot measure, the constant advocacy involving Ebola, and now the nationwide PrEP ads. It was a huge amount of work, but AHF had been conducting business that way—day in and day out—for more than twenty-seven years.

People outside the organization often told me that they didn't know how Weinstein could battle so hard for so long. When I asked Weinstein, he said, "The main question to me is, 'How could I leave this work unfinished?' I won't have a choice at some point, and who is better qualified than me? I don't have to be here until the last day of the AIDS crisis, but I need to be here until we get over that last hump, and I don't think we're over that hump yet."

In addition to the Rose Parade, AHF was preparing for World AIDS Day, held annually on December 1. In the United States, the organization came up with the theme "The War on AIDS in the US is Being Lost." That was backed up by the fact that HIV infection rates were far worse in the US than other wealthy nations. Worldwide, AHF was emphasizing its global campaign to get twenty million people on antiretroviral therapy by 2020.

"To us," Terri Ford told me, "every day is a World AIDS Day, but it's one day the media focuses on, so it's a day to sound the alarm."

AHF held 150 World AIDS Day events around the world, including free HIV testing events in twenty-eight countries such as Argentina, Cambodia, China, Estonia, Haiti, India, Kenya, Mexico, Netherlands, Russia, Sierra Leone, South Africa, Uganda, Ukraine, Vietnam, and Zambia. There were also fifty-two events in fifteen states. It was AHF's largest ever World AIDS Day effort.

—

BEFORE THE YEAR ENDED, I checked up on Dr. Esther Schumann in Fort Lauderdale, one of AHF's best doctors. We talked one afternoon in her office. Schumann said that since my last visit, she'd

seen a female African American patient in her early forties who was sick with full-blown AIDS. The woman, who was near death, was wheeled into the doctor's office by her mother.

"She looked like a skeleton," Schumann said, "wrapped up in several blankets and big sweaters."

I asked the doctor what she thought when she first saw the patient.

"Catastrophe," she replied. "The mother was very nice, and she was very excited about the visit—and nervous also. She knew something was grossly wrong. They thought it was a kidney issue—because in the past she had a kidney problem. She must have known that she had AIDS. But the mother looked us up, and that's how they found us."

Schumann continued, "I was told she hadn't been out of bed since February. Then I wanted to examine her, and I asked the mother to help me. She couldn't stand. There was no muscle at all. So I asked the mother whether she could help me to put her on the table, and we hoisted her at the knees. She was so light that she nearly flew in the air. It was awful, and we were both shocked.

"We examined her, and she couldn't really participate. I laid her down in the position there, and it was terrible. She was probably going to die. If someone like that is wheeled into the ER, they don't really do anything about it. She would have maybe gotten an IV, but nothing drastic, and she probably would've been put in hospice, and people would say that's it.

"The mother refused that day to go to the hospital, and I said that perhaps we could turn it around, and we could give her medicine. But she had a mouth full of rashes and wasn't swallowing well enough—she wasn't really talking. She was making gestures that her mouth hurt."

Schumann started the woman on small pills and liquid drugs, in very small doses and hoped to take blood for lab tests. But the doctor couldn't find a vein.

"She was about five-foot-eight and forty-nine pounds," Schumann recalled. "That is nothing. She was a heap of bones. She was barely living."

Schumann told the mother and patient that they should come back in a week. They still refused to go to the hospital, despite the warning from Schumann that the daughter might die. The woman immediately started taking the medicine, but when she returned to Schumann, the patient had lost more weight, her kidney functions had shut down, and she was about three days from death.

Schumann contacted another HIV specialist, and they worked together to figure out the best way to help the patient. The woman finally agreed to go to a local hospital, where she got nutrition and fluid intravenously—her front teeth had fallen out by this point. The patient also continued to take her antiretroviral therapy.

In the end, the woman didn't die—Schumann's persistence saved her. She lived at a nursing home for some time, and a month after first visiting Schumann, the woman's viral load was undetectable. She was also gaining weight and starting physical therapy. She received dental treatment from Dr. Debbie Davis, a well-respected AHF dentist in Fort Lauderdale.

Schumann was relieved that the woman lived, but she was perplexed that the patient hadn't sought treatment sooner.

"She said she didn't want anybody to know," the doctor told me. "The phrase that these types of people say is that they don't want anybody to know their business. There's still a great deal of stigma."

Stigma could be as lethal as AIDS itself.

—

BACK IN LOS ANGELES, Jonathan Petrus, AHF's chief financial officer for performance and investments, was finalizing the organization's operating budget for 2015, which was expected to be $1.1 billion. Weinstein was already talking about ways to increase that figure to $2 billion, and for a pragmatic reason: AHF had to pay for more resources—more medical staff, more clinics, more testing kits, more mobile testing vans—to reach the goal of serving one million clients by 2020.

I met Petrus at his office at Sunset Media Center in Hollywood. He was hired by AHF in 2012 and played an important role in helping to grow AHF's business lines.

"It was an interesting opportunity to essentially use the dark arts of capitalism," joked Petrus, explaining why he joined the organization, "and to leverage my legal and financial skills toward something that is so needed—to run a public service as a business. What that means is to essentially make it sustainable, scalable, and accessible. At the end of the day, our dividend is lives saved instead of dollars in the bank or shares of stock traded."

Petrus was born and raised in Los Angeles and married with newborn twins. He had a law degree in taxation and worked in the corporate world. But like many other AHF employees, he wanted to do something more meaningful. The transition from big business to AHF wasn't a problem for Petrus.

"We already take care of nearly 400,000 people," he said, explaining his business approach, "and we can't jeopardize their continuity of care when we expand. We serve two populations—the population that we already serve and the population we're trying to reach. You've got to maintain what you're doing and you have to expand it. Not just grow, but reach an unmet need."

In 2015, Petrus was expecting AHF to open new clinics in Chicago, Seattle, Houston, Dallas, Atlanta, Washington, DC, New York City, and East Los Angeles. At locations where there was a market for secondhand clothes, the organization would also open Out of the Closet thrift stores. With the additional revenue generated by new clinics, thrift stores, and pharmacies, Petrus told me, AHF could then pour more money into growing the global program.

From everything I'd seen over the course of 2014, AHF was living up to its global mission as a patient-centered organization. But the final proof, in my mind, would be in the pages of the 2015 proposed budget—I wanted to see what AHF was spending its money on. I asked Petrus for a copy, and the document was enlightening.

The numbers showed a heavy investment in patient care, advocacy, and helping other AIDS organizations. AHF subsidized Public Health Division with $14.5 million and the operation of its domestic healthcare centers with $30 million. It spent $12 million for domestic advocacy and directed $2 million to the AHF Fund, which gave grants to nonprofits around the world.

AHF also subsidized $8 million for the operation of Positive Healthcare, which provides specialized managed care for certain patients. It shelled out $45 million for its global program, including advocacy, HIV testing, condom distribution, and the operation of clinics. AHF had $94 million available to invest in future operations around the globe, such as buying land and paying for the construction of new clinics.

The organization spent $50 million on salaries and benefits for the people who carry out the everyday work of keeping AHF up and running. And it budgeted another $30 million to pay for pharmacists, drivers, and technicians, among others, in the pharmacy division—people who ensure that AHF clients receive their lifesaving HIV medications.

AHF used another $43 million on such things as insurance, operating costs, leasing payments, and office supplies for its vast network of pharmacies around the US. The organization expected to spend $940 million and have net revenues of $60 million. That money would go back into its operations. In addition, the budget revealed that AHF was trying to do more with less—it was not looking to hire huge numbers of new employees as it continued to expand around the globe.

A few days after my talk with Petrus, Weinstein met with Engeran-Cordova and his management team for a budget meeting. After the managers gave their presentations, Weinstein signed off on budget increases totaling $3 million, which would pay for more testing, more condom distribution, and more clinic services. He was given good reason to approve those hikes. In 2014, the Public

Health Division, which operated only in the US, had found 1,740 people who tested positive for HIV; conducted 157,333 HIV tests (22 percent more than in 2013); and opened and operated nine new clinics.

Weinstein later remarked, "In business, if you don't grow, you die. So you always need to have some seeds planted so you can harvest down the road. That is just a given. The idea for planning for a second billion—all high-growth companies think that way, and they have to. This is a nonprofit, so that seems like an anomaly, but that's how we got here. If we stop doing that, we're going to fail."

On December 30, two days before the Rose Parade in Pasadena, I met with Weinstein in his office. The holiday season was still upon us, and he was feeling antsy—employees took vacations, the world tended to slow, and he had no choice but to dial things down for a bit, which made him uncomfortable.

By now, AIDS Is a Civil Rights Issue had wrapped up. It generated so much interest that AHF was planning more town halls for 2015, and a spin-off project, called the Black AIDS Task Force, which would shine even more light on the AIDS epidemic in the African American community. More than thirty years into the crisis, there had been few nationwide campaigns that so thoroughly addressed HIV/AIDS among African Americans.

The reprioritization of the Ryan White CARE Act to funnel more money to southern states, however, remained stalled in Washington, DC, and critics still dinged AHF now and then for its position on PrEP. Regardless, AHF kept moving full steam ahead with the statewide Condoms in Porn ballot measure, and, in 2015, it would secure more than 557,000 signatures for the initiative. No backroom deals in Sacramento could stop AHF now—Condoms in Porn was guaranteed a spot on the November 2016 ballot.

On the global front, AHF's upcoming Rose Parade float was receiving wide attention from national media outlets in the United States, and AHF would soon call for the resignation of World Health

Organization chief Dr. Margaret Chen, noting that the WHO needed to carry out serious reforms so it could better respond to deadly outbreaks such as Ebola. The WHO had implemented some of what AHF had asked for in Geneva—it had shipped more protective equipment directly to nongovernmental organizations, promoted safe home care, improved its communications regarding Ebola, and created a panel of experts to examine better ways to respond to public health crises. But the WHO could not ensure evacuation for doctors infected by Ebola, and it was noncommittal for utilizing nongovernmental organizations to help with sudden emergencies.

Elsewhere in the world, AHF clients in Estonia would receive free antiretrovirals at the Linda Clinic in August 2015. The testing partnership with UNAIDS, however, had fallen through—the two parties couldn't agree on the scope of AHF's contribution. Most importantly, the organization continued plugging away to control the global spread of HIV/AIDS through its "test and treat" model—a massive undertaking that received little fanfare.

In fact, for 2015, AHF had set a major goal—to serve 500,000 registered clients by the end of the year. The organization then wanted to add at least 100,000 patients annually through 2020 to achieve one million people being served. On November 24, 2015, it made good on the first part of its 20×20 promise: 506,101 registered clients were in AHF's system of care around the world, with 397,270 receiving antiretroviral therapy. It was an eye-popping accomplishment by anyone's standard.

The year 2014 was an impressive period of nonstop, thoughtful action—it was hard to believe that such a far-reaching, deep-pocketed global outfit had started in 1987 with only $50,000 and one full-time employee. How could something like that happen? Could other people do the same thing? At his office at Sunset Media Center, Weinstein explained the early dynamics to me.

"Sometimes you're trying to create a wave," he said, "and sometimes you're riding it. We created this wave with Stop the AIDS

Quarantine Committee, but once it started, it took on a life of its own. We were still stoking it, but it didn't take that much."

From that point on, AHF kept creating, riding, and stoking waves, constantly agitating against the status quo. The organization grew into a billion-dollar nonprofit by continually, and fearlessly, rocking the boat.

It's a counterintuitive operating style that many people think can't work. But during a year in which AHF was fighting drawn-out battles over PrEP, Condoms in Porn, and the reprioritization of the Ryan White CARE Act, it finished 2014 with 380,119 registered clients, up from 276,000 patients in 2013. The operating budget had grown from $903 million in 2014 to $1.1 billion, and AHF was working in thirty-six countries compared with thirty-two at the start of the year.

There were additional gains. One million more HIV tests were conducted around the globe than in 2013. Nearly nine million more free condoms distributed. And 23,241 more people were identified as HIV positive—72,584 people in 2013 compared to 95,825 in 2014. That meant that AHF had helped more people to know about their HIV status, which could prompt them to get into lifesaving treatment and prevent them from spreading the virus.

These were mind-boggling numbers that meant, in turn, huge reductions in human suffering, which no AIDS organization in the world had come close to achieving.

In 1987, Weinstein, Chris Brownlie, Paul Coleman, Albert Ruiz, Mina Meyer, Sharon Raphael, Mary Adair, and John Brown never expected AHF to be a global force. They were a small group of friends who vigorously exercised their rights and freedoms, fought back against bigots and slow-moving politicians, and changed things for a cause bigger than themselves.

Then when AHF expanded internationally, men and women in faraway countries embraced the fighting, can-do spirit of Weinstein, Brownlie, and the other LA activists from the 1980s—and AHF

shared its money, knowledge, and experience with them. Around the world, people banded together to create a lifesaving movement, and AHF became a real-life, global example of "people power" in action. Yet Weinstein didn't think AHF had pulled off something that was impossible.

"People act like it's magic," he said. "It's weird. Because it's 90 percent bricklaying."

The foundation for that bricklaying was an unwavering commitment to a principled mission: to provide cutting-edge, patient-centered medicine and advocacy, regardless of ability to pay. Looking at AHF's track record from 1987 through 2014, it was obvious that the organization never strayed from that focus.

With such a mission in hand, AHF then moved relentlessly each day to do the bricklaying—from opening more outposts around the world to conducting millions of HIV tests to treating hundreds of thousands of people to pushing forward countless advocacy campaigns.

"Our strength is that we're really practical," Weinstein explained.

He added, "It's really the interrelationship between the practical and the policy—when those two things intersect, that's the golden thing. The best policy is sort of meaningless if it isn't implemented properly, and you can have wonderful model programs all over the world, but if they don't change the policy, then they just become isolated examples of a better practice. That doesn't do you any good either. So the interplay between those two things is what makes the big difference."

After our talk, I drove west on Sunset Boulevard. Cars zipped by, and my heart was racing—I felt as if I'd been given a life-altering secret.

Weinstein often said that he didn't think what AHF had accomplished was all that complicated. It was just a matter of coming up with a goal, asking the right questions to achieve that goal, and then implementing whatever needed to be done to make that goal a reality. He and the AHF team have done just that time and again,

even when politicians, bureaucrats, and naysayers set up obstacles. And the AHF team, always tenacious, never takes their eyes off their goals.

It's something anyone can do, I thought. It's a blueprint to change the world for the better.

Afterword

Righteous Rebels was published in 2016. Since then, AIDS Healthcare Foundation has continued to expand and battle and help millions of people around the globe. For this anniversary edition, I thought it would be good to give an update about AHF's work, which may be more important, and more relevant, than ever. One afternoon, in July 2021, I sat down with Michael Weinstein, and we talked about what AHF had accomplished since 2014 and what it planned to do in the future.

Weinstein and I met inside a sunlit office on the second floor of 6500 Sunset Boulevard, a building that once housed a TV and film sound editing company and is a five-minute walk from AHF headquarters at Sunset Media Center. AHF bought the property a few years ago. Outfitted with a small movie theater by the previous owner, it has been used to hold retreats, special events, and large meetings. It's also the headquarters of Housing Is A Human Right, AHF's new housing advocacy division.

AHF recently returned to its roots. In the late 1980s and into the 1990s, the organization provided housing for terminally ill AIDS patients through its three hospices. Decades later, AHF saw that its clients, in Los Angeles and San Francisco, struggled with housing instability because of gentrification and sky-high rents. Without stable, affordable housing, that threatened their ability to adhere to HIV drug treatment and maintain good health. So, in 2017, AHF established the Healthy Housing Foundation.

AHF wanted to produce affordable housing quickly. It came up with an adaptive reuse model in which AHF buys hotels and motels, renovates them, and turns them into housing for low-income and homeless tenants. Healthy Housing Foundation manages the properties and has a goal to expand to 10,000 units around the country.

Sticking with its model of providing services *and* advocacy, AHF also created Housing Is A Human Right. It fights harmful policies, pushed by the real estate industry, YIMBY groups, and politicians, that fuel gentrification, excessive rents, and homelessness. At the same time, it advocates for solutions based on the "3 Ps": *protect* tenants through rent control and other protections, *preserve* affordable housing and communities through land-use policies that keep middle- and working-class residents in their longtime neighborhoods, and *produce* truly affordable housing for moderate- and lower-income residents.

AHF and Housing Is A Human Right, for example, battled the real estate industry by attempting to pass California ballot measures (Prop 10, in 2018, and Prop 21, in 2020) that sought to end statewide restrictions on rent control. Both times, several of the nation's largest corporate landlords shelled out tens of millions in campaign cash to successfully defeat the initiatives. But there were victories of another kind for AHF and Housing Is A Human Right.

In 2019, as AHF collected signatures for what would become Prop 21, California politicians passed a "rent cap" law. It was a crafty move to undercut AHF's work on a second rent control ballot measure. But, the law still provided new tenant protections that hadn't existed before. It wouldn't have happened without AHF and Housing Is A Human Right pushing the envelope.

And Prop 10 and Prop 21 created a broad, statewide coalition of hundreds of social justice groups, housing justice organizations, racial justice groups, and labor unions that stood up to the real estate industry and backed the measures, which could be deployed for future battles.

"This is not the end," Weinstein said after Prop 21 failed. "Our fight for housing will continue. Martin Luther King Jr. famously said, 'The arc of the moral universe is long, but it bends toward justice.' Together with our growing coalition, we will carry on in the fight for housing justice."

AHF has been hugely successful in many other areas since 2014. One of the top achievements was making good on its promise to bring one million people into HIV drug treatment by 2020. In fact, AHF pulled off that feat two years ahead of schedule—and now operates in forty-five countries and serves 1.6 million patients. I asked Weinstein what went through his head the day he learned about reaching the one-million milestone.

"It was one of those things where you know you're headed to the goal," Weinstein told me, "but it still takes your breath away that something that momentous was accomplished. And it served as a tremendous confidence builder for AHF."

He added, "It also contributed to the feeling that this was a collective accomplishment because it took us across all of these countries and all of these departments. And, again, we had made some very important, fateful decisions about how this was going to be set up through a bureau structure. We kept investing in it and growing it. So now we have a very strong management infrastructure in all these different regions in the world. And I don't think we could have gotten to the million, and then to a million and a half, without that."

Weinstein further said, "I've always felt that AHF was a kind of field of dreams: if we could imagine it, we could do it. I looked at getting to one million as an extension of what we had been doing. But also I thought it's hard to imagine what we can't do if we can do this."

What boosted AHF's ability to bring one million into HIV care was a historic change in global policy that the organization had long advocated for. In 2015, the World Health Organization instituted

"Treat All," which recommended antiretroviral therapy for anyone infected by HIV, regardless of one's CD4 count. In addition, AHF's "test and treat" model had become universally embraced, which focused on actively finding people who are HIV positive and then swiftly moving them into treatment.

"We always brought urgency to these issues," said Weinstein. "We were always trying to light a fire under bureaucracy and under different entities to get things to move faster. We were always thinking about, for all these issues, the degree of human suffering, and that the sooner you acted, the more you could prevent in terms of suffering and death. So when I look at our list of accomplishments, the single most important thing to my mind is getting global institutions, and the world in general, to accept 'test and treat.'"

When Weinstein and I talked, the world was at the height of the COVID-19 pandemic. By July 2021, it had killed at least four million people around the globe and more than 600,000 in the US, but some experts thought those numbers were higher. From the very start, AHF was consistently one of the most vocal watchdogs. It urged the World Health Organization to act more quickly; advocated for the timely, widespread distribution of COVID-19 vaccines in the developing world; and denounced pharmaceutical companies that sought to make sizable profits by charging exorbitant prices for its vaccines, which reduced access to treatment and harmed the global effort to control the spread of the virus. AHF also provided vaccination shots, donated emergency funding to nonprofits, and gave protective gear and food parcels to numerous countries. I asked Weinstein if there were similarities between the HIV/AIDS and COVID-19 pandemics.

"It's basically every country for themselves," he said, "which not only has deprived the poorer countries from access to vaccines and medications, but it's been very, very confusing. One important part about dealing with a pandemic is communications. And this has just been a Tower of Babel all the way: there's no central authority

to look to for authoritative information. And, of course, the chaos has contributed to the politicization [of COVID-19], which is what happened with AIDS as well."

Weinstein added, "So this is a textbook case of what the lack of a global public health system does. What you see in this case, too, is that an ounce of prevention is worth a pound of cure. In money terms, this is destroying tens of trillions of dollars in wealth, and yet the cost of investing in preventing pandemics, or responding to them quickly and limiting them, is so cheap by comparison. Public health just begs for a few billions of dollars. Just nothing in the scheme of things."

With the devastation caused by COVID-19, Weinstein was even more determined for AHF to handle not only HIV/AIDS but also other public health crises. In addition to its work on Ebola, AHF tackled a Zika outbreak in America and continued increases of chlamydia, gonorrhea, and syphilis cases across the US.

"Our philosophy has always been not just to tell politicians and bureaucrats," Weinstein said, "but to show them. And when you have the reach that we now have, in forty-five countries, when you have the resources that we have, it allows us to do that on a much different scale. Also as the largest AIDS organization in the world, and as an organization that has so strongly promoted global public health, we came into this crisis with credibility."

He added, "We are also the proverbial person who says the emperor has no clothes, and that's so desperately needed because the whole public health world is like one big country club. It's all people flying around in first class and arriving in Geneva and going to fancy dinners and detached from what's going on. Also there are these kinds of gentlemen's agreements that you're not going to call out China for covering up COVID-19, and also you have to please the donors. And then you're running for reelection to these institutions. Almost everybody is controlled by that. So it becomes very important to have independent voices."

Since its founding, AHF had addressed racism as a public health issue, such as establishing a hospice for Black and Latino AIDS patients in South Los Angeles, whom had been grossly underserved by Los Angeles County government. AHF has only ramped up that work in the past several years. That includes playing a major role in removing the Confederate emblem from the Mississippi flag; working on gentrification and homelessness issues, which dramatically impact communities of color; urging local and state governments to declare that racism is a public health issue; and unveiling Stand Against Hate advocacy campaigns in 2017 and 2020. I asked Weinstein to explain the connection between racism and public health.

"I look at it from two different lenses," he said. "One is the lens of stigma and self-worth, meaning that the clients we serve feel extremely stigmatized in terms of having HIV. There's also a lot of distrust in the healthcare system—they feel they've been discriminated against greatly there. And just the lack of healthcare resources to communities of color flows out of systemic racism. So that's one: the stigma and discrimination, and the impact that has on healthcare."

Weinstein explained further: "And the other is the culture of healthcare really has to change if it's going to be successful in this day and age. AHF has worked hard to do that. We have, for example, our affiliates and affinity groups. Affiliates are smaller social services agencies that have become part of AHF, and those have community connections. They're trusted in the community, and we're seeing that relationship is very important, especially with [COVID-19] vaccination now. All the talking heads and experts are trying to get hard-core people to get vaccinated, but the only thing that's going to work with them are people and groups they trust."

He added, "So when you're caring for patients, they're not just their biology. They are their personality and sociology. And we're failing patients because of our prejudices. We're failing them because we're not relatable to them."

Weinstein believed AHF Media, the in-house marketing team, continued to be vitally important.

"Over the past six years," he said, "we've dramatically expanded our marketing and media efforts in a way that it's not just promoting AHF, but it's a service in itself....It's been a whopping success both in terms of infiltrating the culture and building AHF as a brand and improving people's access to care and helping them see the value of [health] prevention."

And AHF kept plugging away at lowering drug prices so people had better access to HIV treatment and other medications, such as the COVID-19 vaccine. The organization, in fact, placed initiatives on the California and Ohio ballots in 2016 and 2017, respectively, in an effort to reduce skyrocketing drug prices in those states. The pharmaceutical industry spent tens of millions to kill the measures, but the campaigns ignited a nationwide dialogue about Big Pharma greed.

"Every one of these things we're all talking about these days," said Weinstein, "whether it's problems with poverty or climate change or public health, comes back to the fact that the profit motive and the greed are so out of control. It's really destroying our way of life."

To that point, Big Pharma had been aggressively pushing to weaken the federal 340B program, which helped AHF fund its lifesaving work in the US and around the globe.

"They're just insanely greedy," Weinstein said about the pharmaceutical industry. "When the Affordable Care Act, or Obamacare, was being debated, Big Pharma was being given a huge bonanza. Forty million more people were going to have health insurance, and they would have to be prescribed drugs and be paid for it. The Obama administration said to Pharma, 'You're getting all these goodies. So you need to give something back.' One of the things that was negotiated was the expansion of the 340B program, which is basically extending government pricing to nonprofits."

He added, "The Obama administration opened 340B up to hospitals in other ways. It's still like five percent of the whole market,

but suddenly it became a thing that was showing up on their balance sheets, and it was costing them money. Not nearly as much as they gained, but they don't want to give a penny."

In the next ten years, Weinstein expected AHF to continue to be a global leader in making the world more fair, more just, and more healthy—whether it's finally controlling the spread of HIV/AIDS or creating new approaches to solve homelessness or changing the global public health infrastructure to better respond to, and prevent, outbreaks and pandemics.

Weinstein explained, "If the world is going to make progress about the biggest issues we face—climate change, democracy, poverty, public health, women's rights—then the nonprofit sector has to be a big part of that. Because what you have now is private capital, which is motivated by profit and efficient to a certain degree, but generates inequality. And you have government whose mission and job is to provide service, but is so plodding and inefficient."

He added, "Potentially, you can marry that in the middle with nonprofits that are businesses but have social purpose. That's really been at the heart of what AHF has done."

Acknowledgments

THIS BOOK WAS INFORMED and helped along by many people who were extremely generous with their time, skills, and knowledge. I want to sincerely thank them now: Miki Jackson, Corina Pop, Kevin Kurator, Miller Everette, Jacquie Burbank, Mary Ann Cherry, Shirley Oliver, Sarah Ogola, Harry Watters, Loretta Pelham, Mimi Mihaylov, Jill Stewart, and my assistant, Reilly T. Bates. I'm also grateful for the hard work of Colleen Dunn Bates, Amy Inouye, Maya Myers, and Anna Russell at Prospect Park Books and Tyson Cornell, Hailie Johnson, and Jennifer Psujek at Rare Bird Books.

And: Whitney Engeran-Cordova, Jonathan Petrus, Mike Kahane, Peter Reis, Terri Ford, Samantha Granberry, Tom Myers, Scott Carruthers, Anita Castille, Donna Stidham, Ged Kenslea, Lyle Honig, Dr. Esther Schumann, Dr. Penninah Iutung Amor, Albert Ruiz, Cynthia Davis, Mina Meyer and Sharon Raphael, Paul Coleman, John Brown, Gene La Pietra, Jonathan Kreuyer, Dr. Jorge Saavedra, Dr. Chhim Sarath, Dr. Patricia Campos, Jess Dector, Hilary Thulare, Larissa Klazinga, Diana Hoorzuk, Dr. Nochiketa Mohanty, Dr. V. Samuel Prasad, Denys Nazarov, Herb Fisher, Igor Sobolev, Latsin Alijev, Denis Godlevskiy, Bao Yugang, Loretta Wong, Lori Mizuno, Phil Reh, Ses Soltani, Alex Goncalvez, Mike McKany, Michelle Morgan, Jamie Rudd, Gregory Jacques, Eric Boyd, Ed Jones, John Reed, David Poole, Joey Terrill, Tim Boyd, Garith Fulham, Tracy Jones, Cynthia Carey-Grant, Dale Gluth, Bret Camp, Richard Conard, Stacy Fong, Bill Guss, Gabriel Rotello, Joseph Mitchell, John

McPhee, Lillian Ross, Hunter S. Thompson, Frederick Wiseman, AHF clients, AHF mobile testers, AHF Out of the Closet employees, AHF mobilizers, AHF Pharmacy employees, AHF Worldwide and Public Health Division employees, AHF country program directors, many other AHF employees, and the AHF board of directors.

Lastly, I want to thank Michael Weinstein for his time, patience, and support. He gave me incredible resources and insider access, permitted me to delve deep into his thinking process and motivations, and followed through on his word to allow me to write an honest book.

Index

CLIA waiver 240
Clinica Condesa 71
Clinton, Bill 45
Coleman, Paul 111, 117, 119, 120, 122, 127, 128, 129, 130, 132, 138,
 292, 303
Collins, Chris 40
Condom Nation tour 11, 81, 82, 83, 248, 249
"condom Nazi" 16, 18
"Condoms in Porn" bill 46, 83, 242, 243, 254, 282, 285, 290, 292
Congressional Quarterly 190
core values 30, 31, 74, 75
Cornell University 102
COVID-19 12, 298, 299, 300, 301
Cruz, Wilson 248
CVS 247

D

Dada, John Taban 274
Dana, Deane 137
Danziger, Mort 101
Davis, Cynthia 150, 152, 160, 164, 170, 174, 198, 303
Davis, Debbie 287
DeConcini, Dennis 191
Dector, Jess 72, 74, 75, 76, 78, 303
Democratic National Convention 101
Democratic Party 40, 120
Deukmejian, George 137
Deutch, Ted 193, 194
Dhlomo, Sibongiseni 231
Dillon, Stephen 186
Disney 41
Dmitrijeva, Tamara 269
Doctors Without Borders 29, 252
Dodger Stadium 9, 26, 138
Dongdan Park 224
Dube, Nduduzo 235, 238
Dubin, Mel 100
Duke, Patty 123
Duncan, Thomas 274
D'Urban Elephant 201
Durex 80

Medicaid 55, 189
Mehra, Vinod 219
methadone 270
Meyer, Mina 42, 107, 113, 119, 127, 128, 138, 292, 303
Miami Herald 251
Minority AIDS Project 129, 151, 152
minority stress model 19, 20
Mississippi 43, 188, 300
Mizuno, Lori 83, 303
Mlaba, Nomaswazi 168, 173
mobile testing 62, 64, 65, 74, 187, 203, 209, 210, 217, 218, 229, 239,
 240, 241, 287
Mohanty, Nochiketa 217, 303
MOMS pharmacy 247
Montaner, Julio 259
Montefiore Medical Center 66
Moral Majority 16
Moratay, Alejandra 197
Morgan, Michelle 67, 303
MSM ("men who have sex with men") 60, 70, 224, 249, 270, 276, 318
Mudanyuan Park 225
Municipal Elections Committee of Los Angeles (MECLA) 106
Munyampundu, Horatius 238
Murray, Cecil "Chip" 84
Musariri, Henry 208, 209, 226
Muscle & Fitness 58
Museveni, Janet 176, 211
Museveni, Yoweri 171, 211
Myers, Tom 22, 32, 46, 179, 188, 189, 303

N

National Enquirer 57, 58
Nazarov, Denys 261, 268, 303
Neighbor, Marc 148
Nevada 41, 83, 84, 196, 239, 240, 241
 Las Vegas 7, 8, 79, 81, 83, 84, 185, 187, 196, 197, 228, 229, 239, 240,
 241, 242
 Nevada Division of Public and Behavioral Health 83, 240
 Southern Nevada Health District 196, 240, 241
Nevada Attorney General's Office 240, 241
News 145

W